Henry Stupart Foote

War of the rebellion; or, Scylla and Charybdis

Consisting of observations upon the causes, course, and consequences of the late

Civil War in the United States

Henry Stupart Foote

War of the rebellion; or, Scylla and Charybdis
Consisting of observations upon the causes, course, and consequences of the late Civil War in the United States

ISBN/EAN: 9783337114749

Printed in Europe, USA, Canada, Australia, Japan

Cover: Foto ©ninafisch / pixelio.de

More available books at **www.hansebooks.com**

WAR OF THE REBELLION;

OR,

SCYLLA AND CHARYBDIS.

CONSISTING OF

OBSERVATIONS UPON THE CAUSES, COURSE, AND CONSEQUENCES

OF

The Late Civil War in the United States.

By H. S. FOOTE.

Et pater Anchises: Nimirum hæc illa Charybdis;
Hos Helenus scopulos, hæc saxa horrenda canebat.
Eripite, o socii; pariterque insurgite remis.

NEW YORK:

HARPER & BROTHERS, PUBLISHERS,

FRANKLIN SQUARE.

1866.

EPISTLE DEDICATORY.

To the Honorable NOAH H. SWAYNE, *one of the Justices of the Supreme Court of the United States.*

MORE than forty years ago, my dear sir, you and I were youthful fellow-students of the legal science in the bosom of our loved native state, and in the sweet village of Warrenton, so memorable in its connection with the ever-shifting current of the recent most deplorable civil war. We were examined for license by the same judges, and at the same time, in the year 1823; after which, in a few months, you migrated to the State of Ohio, where you have since attained such eminence as a jurist and forensic advocate as few of your fellow-countrymen have been able to reach; while the graces which distinguish you in social and in domestic life have been such as to surround you with almost innumerable friends, and apparently, too, without the customary *drawback* of those enmities which are unfortunately sometimes awakened in ungenerous bosoms even by the exhibition of superior merit. The friendly relations which existed between us in the days of opening manhood have been maintained up to the present moment, undisturbed even by the occurrences of a deplorable civil war, the *territorial* character of which necessarily located us, during its sanguinary continuance,

A

on *opposite sides;* a circumstance which, though it would have been necessarily fatal to *ordinary friendship,* has, in our case, only served to draw more tightly the cords of sympathy, and to afford *you* an opportunity of proving in a thousand ways, as you have done, how possible it is for a truly magnanimous spirit to do justice, and to exercise the most generous kindness, too, toward those around whose character and motives of action untoward circumstances may have for a time cast clouds of un- merited suspicion, and which the undimmed eye of a true and resolute friendship could alone have been able to penetrate.

Allow me the honor of giving you some additional assurance of my esteem, as well as of my *gratitude* for past kindnesses, by dedicating to you the following vol- ume; which, though the imperfect product of a few weeks' labor, and written under circumstances not very propitious to the display of mere literary ability, yet will, as I hope, serve to yield you more or less of en- tertainment in such moments of relaxation as may be occasionally allowed you when temporarily withdrawn from the arduous duties of the very responsible official position which you now so deservedly occupy and so signally adorn.

H. S. FOOTE.

NEW YORK, December, 1865.

CONTENTS.

CHAPTER IV.

CHAPTER V.

CHAPTER VI.

CHAPTER VII.

CHAPTER VIII.

CHAPTER IX.

CHAPTER X. ·

CHAPTER XI.

CHAPTER XII.

A 2

CHAPTER XIII.

CHAPTER XIV.

CHAPTER XVIII.

SCYLLA AND CHARYBDIS.

CHAPTER I.

Introductory Remarks.—Allusion to the "Irrepressible Conflict" Theory.
—Direct Issue made therewith.—Sectionalism.—Its dangerous Tend-
encies.—Geographical Parties.—Washington's Warning against them.
—Mr. Webster's Remarks upon Sectionalism.—Author's first Acquaintance with Mr. Webster in 1825.—Renewal of that Acquaintance twenty Years thereafter.—Allusions to Mr. Webster's Life and Character.—
Remarks upon his great Ability as a Statesman and Orator.—His amiable Qualities in private Life.—Mr. Webster's funeral Notice of his great
Rival, Mr. Calhoun.

IN no community of Christendom can the public mind
be reasonably supposed, at the present moment, to be
prepared to receive with a fitting respect an honest and
impartial account of all the exciting and lamentable occurrences which have had their progress on this continent, and in the bosom of our own country, during the
last four years.   Various and conflicting interests, existing to some extent wheresoever commerce is known or
free intercourse by mail has been provided for, diverse
and repugnant statements, embodied in massy and imposing volumes, in pointed and glittering editorials, in
gusty and delusive partisan harangues (*the wordy wonders of an hour*), in solemn, didactic discourses, in labored
official documents, and in innumerable reports of sanguinary battles, of obstinate and long-continued sieges,

of the fearful and heartrending devastation of large and
populous districts, or brilliant and sudden assaults and
captures upon land or water, and fierce marauding incursions—a necessary concomitant of war, and yet how
shocking and deplorable—have awakened and diffused
such clashing and intensely-cherished prejudices and pre-
dilections as naught would be of power to remove, save,
perchance, the toilsome diligence of such discriminating
writers as some future age may supply, and the ever
softening and effacing influence of *Time.* If this be true
in regard even to distant nations, how much more forcibly must the statement just made be found applicable to
the different parts of our own country, within whose territorial limits all these momentous events have been taking place, and where all the multiplied sources of *error*
referred to have had their original location. But, even
were those who are now upon the stage of action, in our
own and in other lands, ever so ready to *receive the truth*
in relation to occurrences so irritating and so recent, there
would seem to be but little reason to expect that a suitable writer would be found to record, in language worthy
of general credence and respect, scenes which the powers
of a Livy or a Tacitus would have been scarcely able to
depicture, and of a nature well calculated to discompose
even the philosophic serenity of a Gibbon or a Hume.
With such views as these, and with no exorbitant conception of my own ability as a writer, it will not be held
surprising that I have chosen to indicate in advance, by
the title which I have thought proper to prefix to this
work, that I do not at all aspire to be recognized as the
Historian of the most momentous conflict of arms, viewed

in its various aspects and bearings, that the world has yet known. In truth, I shall aim only to present, in as simple and perspicuous language as possible, a series of remarkable occurrences, running through a period of some twenty years or more, accompanied by sober and impartial delineations of character, and personal anecdotes, more or less illustrative of public events, with some account of the rival movements of parties, and the characteristic acts and utterances of acknowledged party leaders. Having, at a period in my past life not yet remote, been thrown into contact, in the councils of the nation, with a large number of our public men of great distinction and influence, and having held relations more or less familiar with a few of the most eminent among them, I am not without a hope of being able to revive some gratifying and instructive *reminiscences* of illustrious personages now no longer living, as well as of others yet fortunately surviving, which will not prove altogether uninteresting to such as may glance over these pages. It having been my fortune, though born in a Southern state, to have resided for considerable periods in both the great sections of our *now reconciled country*, and having contracted the most delicate and endearing ties, both social and domestic, in each of them, I dare to presume that, in the execution of the task which I have assumed, I shall be able, in a great degree, if not altogether, to avoid the exhibition of any thing like a decided *local bias*. I shall at once give notice that I do not by any means agree in opinion with those who assert that the gigantic military struggle from which we have but just emerged was, to any considerable extent, the result of what has been so

vociferously bruited as an "irrepressible conflict of antagonisms imbedded in the very nature of our heterogeneous institutions;" and, with all proper courtesy and
deference, I shall venture to make direct issue with those,
wheresoever they shall be found, who undertake to promulgate the notion that "the successive compromises
whereby" civil war, with all its attendant horrors, "was
so long put off," were, after all, but "deplorable mistakes,
detrimental to our national character."* I shall, on the
contrary, endeavor to maintain, more by an array of irresistible *facts* than by any effort of over-subtle reasoning,
or by ingenious appeals to long-standing prejudices, that
the fearful domestic troubles in which our noble republic
has been so recently involved could not possibly have
arisen but for the most unskillful and blundering management of men in power—the incessant agitation of sectional factionists, both in the North and in the South, and
the unwise disregard of that august spirit of *conciliation
and compromise* in which our complex frame of government is known to have had its origin, and to the faithful
cultivation of which, if it be destined to endure for future
ages, it must undoubtedly owe both its preservation and
its maintenance.

Without in the least degree calling in question the patriotism or sincerity of others, I may be permitted to say
that no dogma more fraught with mischief could possibly
have been set afloat among the American people, or one
better calculated, if widely diffused, to undermine the sacred compact of union established by our fathers, than
that which has just been alluded to.   Let two considera-

* Extract from Mr. Greeley's " American Conflict."

ble segments or classes of a free and enlightened people any where be once induced conscientiously to believe that such an irremovable incompatibility of essential interests exists between them that the permanent repose and happiness of the whole, or of certain of its parts, will be *impossible*, except by a great and fearful sacrifice on the one side or on the other, and it is most obvious that exciting thoughts and schemes of *separation*, and even of armed collision, would not be very long in making themselves manifest. Such, in fact, is known to have been the precise condition of things in the early days of the Roman republic, between the Patricians and the Plebeians; and hence certain noted attempts on the part of the weaker class in Rome, and the one which deemed itself oppressed, to provide security against future injuries by *secession* to Mons Sacer. So it was also with the people of the American colonies in the last century, when, becoming convinced that it was not at all consistent with their safety and happiness that they should remain longer under British rule, they boldly erected the all-inspiring standard of *independence*. The successful propagation of this theory of an "irrepressible conflict" of hostile forces, in two different sections of the same country, it is evident, must generate "*geographical parties;*" against the formation of which, Washington, in his Farewell Address, so solemnly and so pathetically warned his countrymen. The continued existence of these geographical parties, when once fairly organized, as our melancholy experience has now demonstrated, must naturally beget schemes of *territorial partition;* which, however peacefully and quietly put in execution, if *resisted* on the part of those

who shall chance to feel that they would be deeply injured thereby, more especially if the latter party shall
suppose itself to possess adequate means of *prevention*,
must inevitably lead to a civil war, more or less serious
and protracted. And it is plain that the danger of such a
result must be very greatly increased, if, in addition to
the influences described, the opinion should be given
currency that the *antagonism* asserted to exist is *organic*
and *permanent* in its character, not growing out of interests superficial and *temporary* in their nature, and therefore subject to easy processes of modification and amelioration in one mode or another, but solid, enduring, and
"imbedded in the very nature" of "*institutions*" thus solemnly adjudged to be "*heterogeneous.*" Washington and
his illustrious associates of a former age taught no such
perilous and visionary doctrine; nor did the great statesmen who succeeded them in the administration of the
government for several successive generations at all suspect the existence of any such fatal tendency to discord
and domestic feud to be lurking in the very vitals of our
civil system. I am not prepared to assert that this "irrepressible conflict" theory *originated* either in the North
or in the South *exclusively*. I know that a distinguished
citizen of the State of New York has been given credit
for the first formal promulgation of it; and recent occurrences would seem to indicate that this gentleman still
firmly adheres to his well-known declaration on this subject. Certain it is, though, that I have heard this same
radical incompatibility of interests between the Northern
and Southern states of the Union—between that portion
of the republic recognized until recently as the slave-

holding one, and that which was non-slaveholding in its character—as earnestly urged, and as elaborately insisted upon also by certain well-known sectional politicians south of Mason and Dixon's line, as it ever could have been by individuals of the most extreme opinions on this subject to the north of that same mystical parallel of latitude. I only assert what I know to be true when I state that, for several years antecedent to his death, John C. Calhoun, one of the most intellectual and pure-minded men that has ever lived, habitually gave expression among his friends to the opinion (which there is no doubt he most conscientiously entertained) that the slaveholding states of the South and the free states of the North would never be able again to live in harmony with each other after the abolition agitation had been for several years in progress, and that the former would soon find it indispensable to the preservation of their own domestic peace and safety to resort to the expedient of separation. Early in the eventful year of 1850 he avowed to me and to certain others, some of whom are yet living, his own painful and firmly-riveted conviction on this subject, and declared, in language of extraordinary emphasis, that he regarded a *peaceful* withdrawal from the Union as altogether practicable, provided its execution should be attempted under the lead of Maryland and Virginia; making known at the same time that he had already drawn out a Constitution for the new republic which he contemplated, in which the slaveholding principle had been given a predominant influence. Once, while discussing this interesting matter, he grew more enthusiastic than I ever saw him on any other occasion,

and exclaimed in language something like the following:
"In looking back upon the history of past ages, I have
sometimes been disposed to envy the glory of such men
as Brutus, and Cato, and others; but if this project of
peaceful separation can be accomplished, and my new
Constitution shall be adopted by the people of the South,
I shall feel that I too will have done something, in my
own day and generation, to deserve the gratitude and
veneration of the friends to a well-ordered system of confederative freedom."

The truth is, that between sectional factionists of the
North and of the South, however conscientious many of
them doubtless have been in the views supported by
them, and in the measures from time to time by them
propounded, there was oftentimes to be discerned a most
singular and striking exhibition of similitude in regard
both to general theories of government, and in reference
to their action, in and out of Congress, upon several of
the most exciting questions which have ever disturbed
the public repose. Special evidences in proof of what
has now been asserted will be hereafter adduced. I propose at present to bring forward what all America will,
I fancy, deem as high an authority as could well be cited.
The following memorable words were uttered in my
hearing in the national Senate in the month of July,
1850, when the celebrated measures of compromise were
under discussion in that body, by one of the wisest and
most patriotic statesmen, as well as one of the most consummate orators that the world has known; whose profound and salutary counsels, had they been since that
period faithfully observed by those for whose benefit he

then spoke, would have infallibly saved our country from all those scenes of unfraternal strife, and fierce, sanguinary conflict, to avert which was the most cherished wish of his whole long and useful public life. Mr. Webster, upon the occasion referred to, said:

"Sir, this measure is opposed by the North, or some of the North, and by the South, or some of the South; and it has the remarkable misfortune to encounter resistance by persons the most directly opposed to each other in every matter connected with the subject under consideration. There are those (I do not speak, of course, of members of Congress, and I do not desire to be understood as making any allusion whatever, in what I may say, to members of this House or of the other), there are those in the country who say, on the part of the South, that the South by this bill gives up every thing to the North, and that they will fight it to the last; and there are those, on the part of the North, who say that this bill gives up every thing to the South, and that they will fight it to the last. And really, sir, strange as it may seem, this disposition to make battle upon the bill by those who never agreed in any thing before under the light of heaven, has created a sort of fellowship and good feeling between them. One says, Give me your hand, my good fellow; you mean to go against this bill to the death, because it gives up the rights of the South. I mean to go against the bill to the death, because it gives up the rights of the North; let us shake hands, and cry out, 'Down with the bill!' and then unitedly raise the shout,

      "'A day, an hour of virtuous liberty,
       Is worth a whole eternity in bondage!'

such is the consistency of the opposition to this measure."

· Having thus incidentally alluded to Mr. Webster, I
shall seize the opportunity of expressing frankly my own
opinion of this remarkable personage, together with a few
of the considerations upon which this opinion is bottom-
ed. It will fall within the scope and compass of this
volume to make frequent references to this truly conservative and patriotic statesman; in consideration of
which fact, and by reason of the additional fact that one
of the most gifted of his numerous admiring friends* has,
some years ago, published an analysis of Mr. Webster's
life and character, more masterly, perhaps, than any other production of that class which the present age has produced, I shall confine myself at present to a very brief
statement of my own recollections of a man who has filled
the world with his fame, and the glories connected with
whose public career are as imperishable even as those
solid granite hills of New England, amid which he came
into existence, and in sight of which it was his fortune to
be afterward nurtured in all the arts of true greatness.
I saw Mr. Webster for the first time in the summer of
1825, while he was sojourning for a few days at the celebrated Saratoga Springs, on his way to the Falls of Niag-
ara, which stupendous wonder of Nature he was then
about to visit for the first time, and in company with his
esteemed and life-long friend Justice Story. An acquaintance of mine, Colonel White, then a representative
in Congress from Florida, did me the honor of presenting
me to Mr. Webster a few days after the publication, in

* Mr. Choate.

pamphlet form, of the first of his Bunker Hill orations;
which masterly and thrilling oration I had just read with
weeping eyes and soul on fire. Never shall I cease to
remember, and with a pleasure not unmixed with veneration, the impression then made upon my youthful and
untutored sensibilities by the solemn and imposing aspect, the grave yet courteous demeanor, and the simple,
cordial, and unassuming conversational tone and manner
of this extraordinary individual. After reading the marvelous speech to which I have alluded, on being thus
ushered into the august presence of him by whom that
speech had been delivered, and after listening with fixed
and silent admiration to his noble colloquial utterances,
I could scarcely feel surprised that his fellow-citizens of
Boston had named him "the God-like;" and I am not
at all ashamed to confess that I do, even at the present
moment, hold Daniel Webster to have been far better
entitled to this swelling appellation than was the famed
Pericles of old to that of "the Olympian," which his im-
aginative countrymen are known to have bestowed on
him. Years rolled away before I again saw Mr. Webster, and was able to renew my former personal acquaintance with him. Meanwhile, his renown, both as a statesman and orator, had greatly extended. He had successfully contended for mastery with the ablest forensic rea-
soners that had ever graced the bar of the highest judicial tribunal of the country; he had delivered numerous
grand and instructive popular discourses, which Cicero,
of all the ancients, might alone perchance have been able
to equal, and which neither Burke, nor Bossuet, nor Fisher Ames, nor Massillon could have been expected to sur-

pass; and he had met in exciting and stormy debate
some of the most consummate parliamentary speakers
that the country had produced upon questions involving
alike the fundamental principles of all government, and
the varied and conflicting interests of our own growing
republic. In all these contests, the world had given him
credit for displaying the highest oratorical powers, deep
and far-reaching views, and a knowledge of all that apper-
tains to the affairs of a free and self-governing people, of
which few if any of his contemporaries had ever shown
themselves to be possessed. After meeting with Mr.
Webster in the Senate, I had the good fortune to be associated with him on the Committee of Foreign Affairs
of that body, and to act as chairman of the same committee while he was Secretary of State during Mr. Fillmore's
administration, and I thus enjoyed an opportunity of becoming somewhat familiar with the particular views
which he entertained touching the great international
questions of the age. I saw much of him also at his own
hospitable mansion, as well as in social life elsewhere, and
I am now prepared to declare that he was, in my judgment, one of the few public men whom it has been my
fortune to know who did not suffer some loss of dignity
upon a near personal approach. In all my intercourse
with him, I beheld constant and ever-increasing evidences of the purity and elevation of his sentiments, his
steady devotion to principle, his lofty disinterestedness of
motive, his kind and charitable temper, and his entire exemption from every thing like low personal rivalry. I
am quite certain that he never cherished feelings of rancorous malevolence toward any human being in his life;

and it is quite remarkable, that I never heard from his
lips a single unkind allusion to any of those whom he
might naturally regard as, in some degree, his competitors
for political advancement. After the moment of heated
conflict had once passed by, he seemed always both to
forgive and to forget all the irritating collisions which
had occurred. In proof of the exceeding kindness and
magnanimity of his nature, I will cite a single evidence,
but one that shall be *conclusive*. Mr. Calhoun was, of all
the eminent statesmen who were in public life at the
same time with Mr. Webster, and who were occasionally
thrown into serious and painful conflict with him, undoubtedly the most potential. These gigantic champions
of opposite and hostile political creeds were, in truth, for
a long period the veritable Achilles and Hector of the
Senate; yet, upon the sudden decease of Mr. Calhoun in
the summer of 1850, behold what his truly high-minded
and chivalrous opponent said of him! No knight of
the Middle Ages, not Sir Philip Sydney himself, nor the
world-renowned Bayard, nor even the famous Black
Prince, when holding King John of France as a prisoner
of war, could have been expected to display a more high-
bred courtesy, a more manly and tender sympathy toward a former adversary, or a more generous oblivion of
former contentions in arms, than is evinced by Mr. Webster in the following beautiful effusion. Let the puny
and heartless traducers of entombed greatness, whom our
own unfortunate times have temporarily brought into
notice, read the funeral eulogy pronounced by this august
son of New England on the occasion referred to, and
blush, if indeed the sense of shame has not become en-

B

tirely extinct in their cold and icy bosoms, over the consciousness of their own deep and ineffaceable dishonor.

"I hope the Senate will indulge me in adding a very
few words to what has been said. My apology for this
presumption is the very long acquaintance which has
subsisted between Mr. Calhoun and myself. We were
of the same age. I made my first entrance into the
House of Representatives in May, 1813. I there found
Mr. Calhoun. He had already been a member of that
body two or three years. I found him there an active
and efficient member of the House, taking a decided part
and exercising a decided influence in all its deliberations.
From that day to the day of his death, amid all the strifes
of party and politics, there has subsisted between us always and without interruption, a great degree of personal kindness.

"Differing widely on many great questions respecting
our institutions and the government of the country, those
differences never interrupted our personal and social intercourse. I have been present at most of the distinguished instances of the exhibition of his talents in debate. I have always heard him with pleasure, often with
much instruction, not unfrequently with the highest degree of admiration.

"Mr. Calhoun was calculated to be a leader in whatso-
ever association of political friends he was thrown. He
was a man of undoubted genius and of commanding talent. All the country and all the world admit that. His
mind was both perceptive and vigorous; it was clear,
quick, and strong.

"Sir, the eloquence of Mr. Calhoun, or the manner in

which he exhibited his sentiments in public bodies, was part of his intellectual character; it grew out of the qualities of his mind; it was plain, strong, terse, condensed, concise; sometimes impassioned, still always severe. Rejecting ornament, not often seeking far for illustration, his power consisted in the plainness of his propositions, in the closeness of his logic, and in the earnestness and energy of his manner. These are the qualities, as I think, which have enabled him, through such a long course of years, to speak often, and yet always command attention. His demeanor as a senator is known to us all—is appreciated, venerated by us all. No man was more respectful to others, no man carried himself with greater decorum, no man with superior dignity. I think there is not one of us, when he last addressed us from his seat in the Senate, his form still erect, with a voice by no means indicating such a degree of physical weakness as did in fact possess him, with clear tones, and an impressive and, I may say, an imposing manner, who did not feel that he might imagine that we saw before us a senator of Rome survived.

"Sir, I have not, in public nor in private life, known a more assiduous person in the discharge of his duties. I have known no man who wasted less of life in what is called recreation, or employed less of it in any pursuits not connected with the immediate discharge of his duty. He seemed to have no recreation, but the pleasure of conversation with his friends. Out of the chambers of Congress, he was either devoting himself to the acquisition of knowledge pertaining to the immediate subject of the duty before him, or else he was indulging in those social interviews in which he so much delighted.

"My honorable friend from Kentucky (Mr. Clay) has spoken in just terms of his colloquial talents. They certainly were singular and eminent. There was a charm in his conversation not often equaled. He delighted especially in conversation and intercourse with young men. I suppose that there has been no man among us who had more winning manners, in such an intercourse and such conversation, with men comparatively young, than Mr. Calhoun. I believe one great power of his character, in general, was his conversational talent. I believe it is that, as well as a consciousness of his high integrity, and the greatest reverence for his talents and ability, that has made him so endeared an object to the people of the state to which he belonged.

"Mr. President, he had the basis, the indispensable basis, of all high character, and that was unspotted integrity and unimpeached honor. If he had aspirations, they were high, and honorable, and noble. There was nothing groveling, or low, or meanly selfish, that came near the head or the heart of Mr. Calhoun. Firm in his purpose, perfectly patriotic and honest, as I am sure he was, in the principles that he espoused and in the measures that he defended, aside from that large regard for the species of distinction that conducted him to eminent stations for the benefit of the republic, I do not believe he had a selfish motive or selfish feeling. However he may have differed from others of us in his political opinions or his political principles, those principles and those opinions will now descend to posterity under the sanction of a great name. He has lived long enough, he has done enough, and he has done it so well, so successfully, so honorably, as to

connect himself for all time with the records of his country. He is now an historical character. Those of us
who have known him here will find that he has left upon
our minds and our hearts a strong and lasting impression
of his person, his character, and his public performances,
which, while we live, will never be obliterated. We shall
hereafter, I am sure, indulge in it as a grateful recollection, that we have lived in his age, that we have been his
contemporaries, that we have seen him, and heard him,
and known him. We shall delight to speak of him to
those who are rising up to fill our places. And when
the time shall come that we ourselves must go, one after
another, to our graves, we shall carry with us a deep
sense of his genius and character, his honor and integrity,
his amiable deportment in private life, and the purity of
his exalted patriotism."

CHAPTER II.

Early colonial Settlements in North America.—Character of the People very nearly identical.— Similitude of Customs, Language, Religion, Laws, and Mode of Life.—No Conflict of Sentiment then between the Colonists of the North and South in regard to African Slavery.—Testimony of Mr. Greeley on this Point.—Kindly social and commercial Intercourse between the Colonists North and South. — Their united Defense of the infant American Settlements against Indian Violence and the hostile French.—Early Suggestion of a confederate Union between all the British Colonies in North America.—Strange Interpretation of a Portion of the Language of the Declaration of Independence. —Mr. Jefferson's important Statement as to the Action of the Confederate Congress in regard to Slavery at the Time the Declaration was adopted.—Mr Webster's important Recital of historic Facts connected with this Subject in his 7th of March Speech.

THOSE who are best acquainted with the early history of our forefathers upon the American Continent will be most inclined to concur in the opinion that, though the various colonial settlements effected by them were made under circumstances which upon a superficial view might be regarded as materially different, and though the course of historic events in these settlements was not uniformly similar, yet that, in regard to all those influences which were to impart a distinctive character to infant communities, there were no such *radical diversities* as, to a philosophic mind, would have been held worthy, in the least degree, of grave and thoughtful consideration. In all the colonies the same language predominated. In all of them the same religion prevailed, and in most of them the same *form* of that religion. The same literature was in all of them the source of intellectual cultivation and of refinement in manners. In all of them it was necessary to employ the same means of warding off the violence of the savage tribes who encompassed them; of felling and displacing the great trees which overshadowed the surface of the wilderness in which their primeval huts were established, and of reducing the virgin soil to a state fitted for profitable culture. The growth of the various colonies, whether by natural increase or by immigration from abroad, was for many years nearly the same. The social usages and customs which sprang up in the different settlements were, from the operation of similar causes, very nearly identical. Even in their relations with the mother country the same resemblances were apparent; in all of them the imperial power of the British government was, in somewhat varying forms, very distinctly acknowledged, and enforced, also, with a marked uniformity. At different periods while the colonial condition continued, the same collisions with the authority of the parent country occurred, and with substantially similar results. Even in relation to a matter which some assert to have supplied grounds for an essential discrimination among the residents of the different colonies—to wit, *the introduction of slaves from Africa*, it will be found, on examination, that many of those who have most freely written and spoken upon this subject have been guided far more by fanciful conjectures, put in action by an eager desire of sectional ascendency, than by a proper and becoming regard for the deductions of sober historic truth. Without dwelling on a subject the prominent topics con-

nected, with which have been already thoroughly exhausted by innumerable disputants, most of whom are
too furious to be fair, and too much interested to be honest, I shall content myself with quoting a pregnant paragraph from a work of great respectability, which has recently issued from the press, and with the author of
which I shall be always glad to agree when I shall be
able to do so without disparagement to my own conscientious convictions.   Mr. Greeley, in "*The American Conflict*," expresses himself thus: "The austere morality and
democratic spirit of the Puritans ought to have kept their
skirts clear from the stain of human bondage.   But, beneath all their fierce antagonism, there was a certain kin-
ship between the disciples of Calvin and those of Loyola.
Each were ready to suffer and die for God's truth as they
understood it, and neither cherished any appreciable sympathy or consideration for those they esteemed God's enemies, in which category the savages of America and the
heathen negroes of Africa were so unlucky as to be found.
The Puritan pioneers of New England were early involved
in desperate life or death struggles with their aboriginal
neighbors, in whom they failed to discover those poetic
and fascinating traits which irradiate them in the novels
of Cooper and the poems of Longfellow.   Their experience of Indian ferocity and treachery, acting upon their
theologic convictions, led them early and readily to the
belief that these savages, and, by logical inference, all
savages, were children of the devil, to be subjugated, if
not extirpated, as the Philistine inhabitants of Canaan
had been by the Israelites under Joshua.   Indian slavery, sometimes forbidden by law, but usually tolerated,

if not entirely approved by public opinion, was among the early usages of New England; and from this to negro slavery—the slavery of any variety of pagan barbarisms—was an easy transition. That the slaves in the Eastern colonies were few, and mainly confined to the sea-ports, does not disprove this statement. The harsh climate, the rocky soil, the rugged topography of New England, presented formidable, though not impassable barriers to slaveholding. Her narrow patches of arable soil, hemmed in between bogs and naked blocks of granite, were poorly adapted to cultivation by slaves. The labor of the hands without the brain, of muscle divorced from intelligence, would procure but a scanty livelihood on those bleak hills. He who was compelled for a sub- · sistence to be by turns farmer, mechanic, lumberman, navigator, and fisherman, might possibly support one slave, but would be utterly ruined by half a dozen. Slaveholding in the Northern States was rather coveted as a social distinction, a badge of aristocracy and wealth, than resorted to with any idea of profit or pecuniary advantage."

Under such circumstances as have been stated, it is certainly not at all surprising that constant friendly intercourse, both social and commercial, was cultivated between the various American colonies, whether in the northern or southern divisions of the continent; that they should have cordially aided each other in repulsion of Indian hostilities; that, under the advice and protection of the parent country, they should have sturdily co-operated in the defense of all colonial territory against invasions from abroad, and in even attempting the con-

B 2

quest of adjoining territory belonging to France, in what
is now known as Canada, at the period when the kings
of France and of Great Britain were warring for exclusive dominion on this continent. Nor should we be astonished, either, to find that, long before the Declaration
of American Independence in the year 1776, there should
have been more than one attempt to bring about a confederation of the American colonies under the protection
of the British crown.

It is sufficiently apparent, one would think, that, up to
the era of our deliverance from British rule, no fancied
heterogeneousness of institutions, or fixed repugnances
of opinion or sentiment, seriously divided those whose
posterity were destined soon to form a still closer compact of union, and, by the common dangers and sufferings of a long and sanguinary war, to become endeared
to each other by ties of the most solid and enduring character. Such is the unconquerable truth of history, let
him deny it who may.

It has been contended by some, of late, that the Declaration of Independence itself asserted a fundamental principle of universal application even at the time of its adoption, which was understood by our forefathers as drawing
a serious line of distinction between those citizens of the
newly-formed American Union who were then friendly
to the continued existence of African slavery, and those
who were unfriendly to it; and as the greater part of the
former have been constantly located in the states of the
South, it has been sagely inferred that a permanent conflict of sentiment between slaveholders and non-slaveholders was thus recognized from the beginning, and

among those who had just declared themselves *one peo-ple, both in peace and in war.* Persons who undertake to make good this position assume that, when the authors of the Declaration of Independence declared "all men are created equal," they meant to include the sons of Africa as well as those of European origin; and these contro-versialists do thus contend, in the face of the undeniable fact, that no such interpretation of the instrument was either suggested or thought of any where in Christendom until within a few years past; and notwithstanding the facts that the efforts of the Emancipationists were not, until very recently, professedly founded upon any such overstrained view; that language substantially similar is used in the Virginia Bill of Rights, penned by the cel-ebrated George Mason, one of the most open and strenu-ous supporters of slavery who participated in the forma-tion of the Federal Constitution; and that Mr. Jefferson himself, the acknowledged draughtsman of the Declara-tion of Independence, though friendly to the adoption of a system of gradual emancipation, never in any way indi-cated that the universal freedom spoken of was absolute-ly provided for in this important document, or that such a thing was even thought of or suggested. The truth is, that Mr. Jefferson, in his works, p. 170, vol. i., asserts the fact that there were persons in Congress at the time, both from the North and from the South, who were not only not hostile to the continuation of African slavery as then existing, but who were unwilling to embody in the Dec-laration any language strongly denunciatory even of the continued importation of slaves from the coast of Africa; his words on this point being as follows: "The clause, too, reprobating the enslaving the inhabitants of Africa was struck out in complaisance to *South Carolina* and *Georgia*, who never attempted to restrain the importation of slaves, and who, on the contrary, still wished to continue it. Our Northern brethren also, I believe, felt a little tender under those censures; for, though their people had few slaves themselves, yet they had been pretty considerable carriers of them to others."

The conclusion to which the mind is irresistibly driven by the mass of evidence adduced is, that the American people, at this early period of their history, were in all respects sufficiently *homogeneous*, both in regard to local interests and in relation to all questions likely to arise under any common government which they might choose thereafter to establish, as to justify a reasonable hope of reciprocal kindness and permanent concord between them. So far is it, indeed, from being true that any such "antagonisms imbedded in the very nature of our heterogeneous *institutions*" then existed, as the accomplished author of "The American Conflict" has so emphatically asserted, that it may be safely affirmed that, strictly speaking, African slavery did not any where at that period exist in an *institutional* form; in relation to which point I shall again cite the language of one who will ever be regarded as the highest authority, in reference to a question of this nature, by all men whose minds are not altogether given up to sectional prejudice or party bigotry. Mr. Webster, in his speech delivered in the national Senate in the year 1848, upon the "EXCLUSION OF SLAVERY FROM THE TERRITORIES," uses the following language:

"The Constitution of the United States recognizes it

(slavery) as an existing fact, an existing relation between the inhabitants of the Southern States. I do not call it an *institution*, because that term is not applicable to it; for that term seems to imply a *voluntary* establishment. When I first came here, it was a matter of frequent reproach to England, the mother country, that slavery had been established upon the colonies by her against their consent, and that which is now considered a cherished institution was then regarded as, I will not say an *evil*, but an entailment on the colonies by the policy of the mother country *against their wishes.*"

The state of public sentiment in regard to slavery in the colonies remained the same throughout the war of the Revolution. With a few exceptions here and there, there were none in the South who were anxious to *extend* its existence and influence, and there were as few in the North who were inclined to interfere with or complain of its presence wheresoever it had already taken root; so that, when the men of '76 began to take measures for their future safety in the separate and independent condition which they had deemed it wise to assume, they were prepared, with the fullest deliberation, to adopt articles of confederation which *in terms* provided for the establishment of a "perpetual Union" between those who had then become fraternally associated in the war against the mother country. Nor is it apparent that there was any material change in the feelings and opinions of any portion of the people of the United States in regard to African Slavery up to the year 1789, when the Federal Constitution was adopted. In proof of this fact, I shall again lean upon the authority of Mr. Webster, whose accuracy in relation to all matters of this kind is so well established that I am not aware that any deliberately uttered statement of his touching points of disputed American history has ever been by any one directly called in question. In that memorable 7th of March speech which he delivered in the Senate of the United States for "the Constitution and the Union," and which, at the time of its being pronounced, as I well recollect, awakened sentiments of respect and gratitude among conservative and enlightened patriots throughout the length and breadth of the republic—in that speech, for the delivery of which Mr. Calhoun is known, on his dying bed, to have thanked him in the most solemn and formal manner—Mr. Webster thus explicitly covers the ground which I am at present discussing: "Let us, therefore, consider for a moment what was the state of sentiment North and South in regard to slavery at the time this Constitution was adopted. A remarkable change has taken place since; but what did the wise and great men of all parts of the country think of slavery *then?* In what estimation did they hold it at the time when this Constitution was adopted? It will be found, sir, if we will carry ourselves by historical research back to that day, and ascertain men's opinions by authentic records still existing among us, that there was then *no diversity of opinion* between the North and the South upon the subject of slavery. It will be found that both parts of the country held it equally an evil—a moral and political evil. It will not be found that, either at the North or at the South, there was much, though there was some, invective against slavery as inhuman and cruel. The great ground of objection to it was *political;* that it weakened the social fabric; that, taking the place of free labor, society became less strong and labor less productive; and therefore we find from all the eminent men of the time the clearest expression of their opinion that slavery is an evil. They ascribed its existence here, not without truth, and not without some acerbity of temper and force of language, to the injurious policy of the mother country, who, to favor the navigator, had entailed these evils upon the colonies. I need hardly refer, sir, particularly to the publications of the day. They are matters of history on the record. The eminent men, the most eminent men, and nearly all the conspicuous politicians of the South, held the same sentiments—that slavery was an evil, a blight, a scourge, and a curse. - There are no terms of reprobation of slavery so vehement in the North at that day as in the South. The North was not so much excited against it as the South; and the reason is, I suppose, that there was much less of it at the North, and the people did not see, or think they saw, the evils so prominently as they were seen, or thought to be seen, at the South."

CHAPTER III.

Continuation of the same Subject.—Cession of Northwestern Territory by Virginia and other States in 1784.—Ordinance of 1787.—Federal Convention.—Correlative and contemporaneous Action of that Body and of the Confederate Congress upon the Subject of African Slavery.—No Conflict worth mentioning then existed between the States of the North and the South in regard to African Slavery.—Action of Congress upon Abolition Petitions in 1790.—Congressional Resolution on the Subject of non-interference with Slavery in the States by the general Government for many Years faithfully observed in the North.—Mr. Webster's uncontradicted Statement on this Subject in the Debate between Mr. Hayne and himself.—Washington's Administration.—Election of John Adams; his stormy Administration.—Mr. Jefferson and Mr. Madison, and Virginia and Kentucky Resolutions of 1798, '9.—Nullification and Secession growing out of these.—John C. Calhoun.—Confederate Constitution professedly based upon the absolute Sovereignty of the States. —This Principle shamefully abandoned by the Confederate Government itself.—Successive Administrations of Mr. Jefferson, Mr. Madison, and Mr. Monroe.—Rise of the Missouri Question, and violent Agitation consequent thereupon.—Wise and salutary Compromise of that Question. —Remarks upon the Value of legislative Compromises in general, with Mr. Calhoun's Views of the same.

THERE are one or two remarkable facts in addition to be brought forward in support of this view of the subject, which I will now concisely state. In the year 1784, Virginia and other states ceded to the United States all the territory northwest of the Ohio River. In the year 1787, the celebrated ordinance was adopted in the Congress then holding its session in the city of New York, by which slavery was forever excluded

• from the whole of that vast dominion. At the very moment of its adoption, the Federal Convention, sitting at the time in Philadelphia, was engaged in the consideration of the subject of slavery in its various aspects. Constant intercourse, by mail and otherwise, was going on between these two great commercial marts. Some of the most eminent members of Congress were likewise members of the Convention, and were of course sometimes engaged in the deliberations of one of these bodies, and sometimes in those of the other. The ordinance was *unanimously* adopted, every Southern member present and every Northern member voting for it. With such facts staring us in the face, surely he would be a bold man, and far more bold than discreet, who would assert that at this memorable period in American annals any serious *antagonism*, either of sentiment or of policy, in regard to slavery, was apparent. But other evidence in corroboration is easily adducible. In the Federal Constitution under which we now live, two other points were distinctly and definitively settled : 1st. Provision was made for the *prospective*, not the immediate prohibition of the African slave-trade—that is to say, Congress was, by the clearest implication, empowered to pass laws for the suppression of this nefarious traffic by the clause which provides that no legislation by this body for the purpose specified should take place anterior to the year 1808. 2d. The Convention, in language to which, until recently, only one interpretation has been any where affixed, not only *guaranteed* to the states wherein slavery then existed the right to regulate it according to their own discretion, without any foreign interference whatev-

er, but moreover guaranteed in a manner deemed at the
time sufficiently explicit, the return of fugitive slaves to
the service of their recognized masters.

No moon-struck political philosopher then undertook
to declare that the constitutional clause guaranteeing to
each of the states a "republican form of government"
was designed by its framers to provide for the universal
manumission of bondmen and bondwomen of African descent.

I now assert, what no fair-minded man will deny, that
the existence of slavery in the states still choosing to retain it did not, for many years after the foundation of
the present government, become a source of excitement
and unbrotherly feeling. The injunctions of the Constitution were every where understood in the same way,
and were every where faithfully observed. A few abolition petitions were sent forward by a portion of the inhabitants of Pennsylvania to the first Congress, the appearance of which produced no serious irritation, and
these petitions were at once quietly disposed of and forgotten, but not until the adoption of the following important resolution:

"*Resolved*, That Congress have no authority to interfere in the emancipation of slaves, or in the treatment of
them in any of the states; it remaining with the several
states alone to provide rules and regulations therein,
which humanity and true policy may require."

For many years, and, indeed, up to the year 1835,
slavery in the South did not become a subject of unkind
discussion any where.

Justice demands the admission that, up to a period

comparatively recent, the spirit of this resolution was most faithfully adhered to; so that Mr. Webster was perfectly justified in what fell from his lips on this subject in the memorable debate in the United States Senate between himself and Mr. Hayne, when he said, referring to the resolution above cited,

"The fears of the South, whatever fears they might have entertained, were allayed and quieted by this early decision; and so remained, till they were excited afresh, without cause, but for collateral and indirect purposes. When it became necessary, or was thought so, by some political persons, to find an unvarying ground for the exclusion of Northern men from confidence and from lead in the affairs of the republic, then, and not till then, the cry was raised, and the feeling industriously excited, that the influence of Northern men in the public councils would endanger the relation of master and slave. For myself, I claim no other merit than that this gross and enormous injustice toward the whole North has not wrought upon me to change my opinions, or my political conduct. I hope I am above violating my principles, even under the smart of injury and false imputations. Unjust suspicions and undeserved reproach, whatever pain I may experience from them, will not induce me, I trust, nevertheless, to overstep the limits of constitutional duty, or to encroach on the rights of others. The domestic slavery of the South I leave where I find it—in the hands of their own governments. It is their affair, not mine. Nor do I complain of the peculiar effect which the magnitude of that population has had in the distribution of power under this Federal government. We know,

sir, that the representation of the states in the other House
is not equal. We know that. great advantage, in that
respect, is enjoyed by the slaveholding states; and we
know, too, that the intended equivalent for that advantage, that is to say, the imposition of direct taxes in the
same ratio, has become merely nominal—the habit of the
government being almost invariably to collect its revenue
from other sources and in other modes. Nevertheless,
I do not complain, nor would I countenance any movement to alter this arrangement of representation. It is
the original bargain, the compact: let it stand; let the
advantage of it be fully enjoyed. The Union itself is too
full of benefit to be hazarded in propositions for changing
its original basis. I go for the Constitution as it is, and for
the Union as it is. But I am resolved not to submit in
silence to accusations, either against myself individually
or against the North, wholly unfounded and unjust—accusations which impute to us a disposition to evade the
constitutional compact, and to extend the power of the
government over the internal laws and domestic condition of the states. All such accusations, wherever and
whenever made, all insinuations of the existence of any
such purposes, I know and feel to be groundless and injurious. And we must confide in Southern gentlemen
themselves; we must trust to those whose integrity of
heart and magnanimity of feeling will lead them to a desire to maintain and disseminate truth, and who possess
the means of its diffusion with the Southern public; we
must leave it to them to disabuse that public of its prejudices. But, in the mean time, for my own part, I shall
continue to act justly, whether those toward whom jus-

tice is exercised receive it with candor or with contumely."

Nothing can be more undeniable than the proposition that, during the eight years' administration of Washington, there was not in existence any where what has since become so mischievously known as a sectional party organization, though much opposition was in various quarters presented to the measures of policy recommended by this most venerated of all our presidents. That this opposition was mainly of a factious and reprehensible character can not now be doubted, and it would seem to have owed its origin in a considerable degree to the eager desire entertained by certain ambitious statesmen to secure their own advancement to the highest official position known to our form of government, to the exclusion of others whom they suspected of possessing a larger share than themselves of the confidence and friendly wishes of the exalted personage who was even then preparing to return to private life. The election of John Adams, of Massachusetts, to the Presidency, and of Thomas Jefferson, of Virginia, to the Vice Presidency of the United States, would appear to prove conclusively that sectional jealousies had not yet gained much strength in either of the two great divisions of the republic. The passage of the Alien and Sedition Acts, during the administration of the elder Adams, and the questions connected with the then anticipated war with France, furnished a plausible occasion for the array of opposition to the new administration, and supplied an opportunity far too tempting to be passed by of calling into existence a party organization which, under proper tutelage and training, it was hoped might be of sufficient power to prevent the election of the then incumbent for a second presidential term, and secure the elevation in his stead of one of the most accomplished statesmen, as well as one of the most astute and skillful political managers that has yet made his appearance any where upon the public stage. With a view to attaining the interesting end then held in view, it was necessary that steps should be immediately taken to aggregate all the elements of political opposition in one cohesive and potential mass, that the same might be wielded with adequate efficacy against those who were then seated in the highest stations of Federal trust. Hence the adroit preparation of the celebrated Virginia and Kentucky Resolutions of 1798, '9, the former of which are now known to have been drawn by Mr. Jefferson, and transmitted to certain trusted political friends of his in Kentucky, while the latter were drafted by Mr. Madison, under the counsels of the same distinguished personage (always recognized by the former thereafter as his veritable political Magnus Apollo), and placed in the willing and ever facile hands of the celebrated John Taylor, of Caroline, for presentation to the Virginia Legislature. I have not time now to analyze either of these famous sets of resolutions, nor have I the smallest inclination to do so. They answered admirably well the purposes for which they had been originally fabricated; and though the dogmas embodied in these resolutions were not sufficiently fortunate to find general sanction in the co-states of the Union, yet they undoubtedly constituted, in a great degree, the basis upon which that great political party was then brought into existence, which was

soon to raise to the presidency three eminent personages
in succession, all of whom will go down to future generations as representatives of a school of politics which
owes its origin and long-retained ascendency mainly to
the subtle and prolific genius of him to whom his numerous admirers have been long accustomed to refer as "the
sage of Monticello." That the fearful doctrine of *nullification*, which was more than twenty years subsequent to
this period so imposingly blazoned forth to the world by
Mr. Calhoun and his enthusiastic political disciples, and
that of *secession* likewise, which has been recently subjected to the severest of all earthly tests, may be directly
traced to these same resolutions, though perchance not
set forth in either of them with all the precision and
clearness that an Aristotle or a Locke would have required, no discerning and unprejudiced man will be
much inclined to dispute. That either set of these resolutions contains sound and salutary principles, and is in
strict unison with the Constitution framed by our fathers,
few, it is to be presumed, will be hereafter heard to assert. It is certainly not a little remarkable that Mr. Madison, who, in the Federal Convention, was the close ally
of Hamilton and Governeur Morris in claiming for the
new government which he was aiding to build up powers wholly inconsistent with the practical enforcement
either of nullification or secession, and who had said on
one occasion, according to his own report of the matter,
that he " was of opinion, in the first place, that there was
less danger of encroachment from the general government than from the state governments; and, in the second place, that the mischiefs from the encroachments

would be less fatal," should have not only consented to
draw up the Virginia Resolutions of '98, but should have
also agreed to be the draftsman, one year later, of an
elaborate report prepared expressly for the purpose of
explaining and enforcing these same resolutions. It is
true that in after life he disavowed any intention on this
occasion to yield his sanction either to nullification or secession, and I have certainly no inclination either to call
in question the sincerity of this eminent personage, or to
accuse him of gross forgetfulness as to the operations of
his own clear and well-balanced intellect; but I repeat
that the language of his resolutions, as well as those
drawn by Mr. Jefferson, as already noticed, must be regarded as inculcating all the perilous doctrines now recognized as specially appertaining to the South Carolina
school of politicians. However objectionable these doctrines may be in practice, I am not aware that their promulgation, at the close of the last century, in the manner
described, had the effect of calling into action feelings of
sectional jealousy, or of impressing upon the public mind
in either section sentiments of acerbity, alienation, or distrust. It is indeed probable that the effect of the exciting struggle for political ascendency in 1801 was chiefly
to cause the depositories of Federal power to be a little
more on their guard against the perpetration of encroachments on the reserved rights of the states and people
than they might otherwise have been, and that, in point
of fact, it may in this way have contributed rather to prevent than to instigate collisions calculated to endanger
the domestic peace.

I can not well refrain from remarking here, in passing,

that, during the four years just elapsed, the Southern States of the Union have had the most conclusive evidence supplied to them, and in forms eminently impressive in every way, of the utter futility and worthlessness of all the ultra states-rights governmental theories; since, in less than a twelve-month after a Constitution had been agreed upon at Montgomery, framed especially with a view to indicating the intention of its framers to set forth and promulgate to all the world a "compact among sovereign states," to which compact each of said states should be recognized as having "acceded as a state, its co-states forming, as to itself, the other party;" providing, too, that the "government created" by said compact should not be "the exclusive or final judge of the extent of powers delegated to itself;" and providing still farther, that "as in all other cases of compact among powers having no common judge, each party" should have "a right to judge for itself, as well of infractions as of the mode and manner of redress;" since, I repeat, in less than a twelve-month after this same boasted states-right Constitution was put in operation, its very framers notoriously, and in spite of all remonstrances, succeeded in consolidating all governmental power in the central agency at Richmond, and, upon the stale plea of *military necessity*, shamelessly trod under foot all the reserved rights of the states and people, and organized an irresponsible military despotism in the very bosom of the Ancient-Dominion, as harsh and grinding in its character as has ever heretofore existed in any age of the world. On this subject I shall in due season bring forward such damning evidences as will profoundly shock the sensibilities of all

C·

the friends of orderly and well-regulated government,
and all the honest upholders of true constitutional liberty.
Of the intermediate period which elapsed between the
inauguration of Mr. Jefferson as President, on the 4th of
March, 1801, and the year 1819, when the celebrated
Missouri question shook the republic to its centre, I have
only to observe that, with the exception of the period of
excitement which intervened when the Embargo measure was upon its trial, and the war of 1812 with Great
Britain was in progress, the country, and every portion
of it, enjoyed an almost halcyon repose.   However fierce
may have been the denunciations of the Embargo policy
in certain quarters, as well in Congress as out of it, whatever insane and indecent menaces may have been fulminated by Hartford Convention zealots, and others of a
similar complexion, the tranquillity of the republic was
at no time dangerously disturbed; the waves of popular
excitement were again and quickly calmed into a state
of complete serenity, and all angry and unkind feeling
was seen once more to disappear.   Never were any people in the enjoyment of a more happy, and, to all appearance, a more *assured* state of domestic quietude than were
our honored fellow-countrymen on the 4th of March,
1817.   This period of our history is borne in pleasant
recollection by persons who still survive, and continues,
to some extent, yet to be referred to by them as "the
era of good-feeling."

   But soon came the Missouri struggle, that "*fire-bell of
the night*," as Mr. Jefferson figuratively entitles it.   Upon
this oft-discussed topic I shall here only hazard a few
suggestions, and gladly would I refrain from alluding to

it altogether, could I do so consistently with the faithful execution of the task which I have assumed. The historic details which belong to this famous contest are already, indeed, sufficiently well known to most of those who may glance over these pages, and recent occurrences have rendered it altogether impossible for men even of ordinary intelligence to avoid some little acquaintance with them.

The principal facts are capable of being concisely stated as follows: The people of the Missouri Territory, in the early part of the year 1818, memorialized Congress for its admission into the Federal Union as a state. This memorial was at first favorably received, and a bill for the admission of the new state was quickly reported to the House of Representatives from the appropriate committee in that body. There was not sufficient time for the bill to become a law before Congress adjourned, to meet again in the month of November of the same year, when the measure of admission was taken up for consideration. An amendment thereto was now offered by a representative of the State of New York, providing against "the introduction of slavery or involuntary servitude" in said territory after it should have become a state, and had been admitted into the Federal Union as such. This restriction was incorporated with the bill in the House, and the bill as amended was sent to the Senate for its consideration. The latter body struck out the restrictive amendment, and adopted the bill as a simple act of admission.

In the form which it had thus assumed in the Senate the bill again made its appearance in the House, when a motion for its indefinite postponement having failed, upon the question which then arose of concurrence in the territorial amendment, a small negative majority was the result, and the bill, embodying again the restriction mentioned, a second time reached the Senate, when, the latter body insisting upon its amendment, it was once more sent back to the House, where a motion that the House should adhere to its vote of disagreement prevailed. Missouri was not, therefore, then admitted. Again the measure was brought forward in the Congress which commenced its session in December, 1819. After much altercation in both Houses, and various movements of curious political adroitness not needful to be here specified, with an intense excitement ever on the increase alike in Congress and in the whole country, a *compromise*, as it was called, was finally agreed upon, whereby the State of Missouri was given admission as a slave state, with its territorial extent limited to the North by the line of 36 degrees 30 minutes north latitude; and in all the remaining territory belonging to the government of the country acquired by purchase from France in the year 1803, slavery or involuntary servitude was *forever prohibited*.

Such is the substance of the celebrated Missouri Compromise, devised by able statesmen and devoted patriots nearly a half century ago, for the purpose of saving the republic itself from ruin then most seriously menaced. And who shall now censure this wise and noble act, which restored peace once more to a disturbed country, and perchance averted the horrors of war as fierce and terrible as that which we of the present generation have just so painfully realized?

As to the power of Congress, under the Federal Constitution, to *exclude slavery* from any portion of the public
domain of which it has been given control, I have at present little to say. Whether, under the clause of the Constitution giving to Congress "power to make needful rules
and regulations respecting the territory of the United
States," that body may adopt, as one of these regulations,
such a prohibitory clause as that embodied in the Missouri Compromise, thus assimilating the whole of the vacant
territory of which it has been given the administration
to that portion merely to which a similar prohibition was
extended under the authority of the confederation, is a
question exceedingly difficult to be satisfactorily solved;
upon which the ablest and purest statesmen, and the most
astute and erudite jurists that the country has known
have been long most painfully divided in opinion, and
one which (perhaps happily for us all) has been now forever settled by the sternest and most inexorable arbiter
to whose decision it is possible that the earth-born affairs
of mortals can be submitted. But, I again ask, who of
us now of the present generation will presume to condemn the peace-makers of 1819? Who is at this moment
inclined to bring harsh and undeserved opprobrium upon
the great and good men, whether of the North or of the
South, who risked their fame, their popularity, and perchance in some instances, also, their repose in social life,
for their country's safety at a moment so full of peril?
Where is the man that will undertake to deny that, in
nearly all the most difficult concerns of human society,
when great public interests are at stake, and when questions shall arise for decision eminently dark and difficult

in their character, and which stand surrounded on all sides
with considerations of grave and vital expediency, so urgent in their nature as imperiously to demand that all the
nobler instincts of the soul should be put in exercise, as
well as all the higher faculties of the understanding, for
the ascertainment of the true pathway of duty—where is
the man, I ask, who will deny that *compromise*—yes, *compromise*, a little giving and taking, here and there, on both
sides of the line of controversy—a little conciliation, forbearance, yea, and of *sacrifice* too, if need be, of cherished
opinions, of loved personal interests, and of the ambitious
desires for local ascendency, may be both wise and patriotic, if any.or all of these shall be found to stand in the
way of a nation's salvation? Were not such the views
of Washington and his compeers of the last century? Is
it not in support of such views as these that some men of
our times, little less worthy of love and veneration than
the men of '76 themselves, have been known to act on
more than one critical occasion? *Compromise! Compromise!* that term hateful to the dreamers and cold abstractionists of the present vapid and shallow generation, but
which is, notwithstanding, oftentimes grandly typical of
the utmost attainable perfection of human reasoning, when
that reasoning may be said to partake least of the discred-
iting taint of mortality, and to approach most nearly to the
unerring and unfathomable wisdom of the Deity himself!

I propose to conclude this chapter with an apt and
pregnant quotation from a work of a deceased American
statesman on *Government*, which I fear has been far too
little read since its first appearance, about fifteen years
ago, even in the very region in .which it had its origin,

and among the avowed disciples, too, of a truly great and
patriotic personage, who, I can not doubt, is destined to be
much better understood and much more accurately appreciated hereafter than it was his fortune to be by many in
his own age.

Thus speaks John C. Calhoun, as it were, from the tomb
wherein he lies inurned:

"Constitutional governments, of whatever form, are, indeed, much more similar to each other in their structure
and character than they are, respectively, to the absolute
governments even of their own class. All constitutional
governments, of whatever class they may be, take the
sense of the community by its parts, each through its appropriate organ, and regard the sense of all its parts as
the sense of the whole. They all rest on the right of
suffrage, and the responsibility of rulers, directly or indirectly. On the contrary, all absolute governments, of
whatever form, concentrate power in one uncontrolled
and irresponsible individual or body, whose will is regarded as the sense of the community. And hence the
great and broad distinction between governments is not
that of the one, the few, or the many, but of the constitutional and the absolute.

"From this there results another distinction, which, although secondary in its character, very strongly marks
the difference between these forms of government. I refer to their respective conservative principle—that is, the
principle by which they are upheld and preserved. This
principle, in constitutional governments, is *compromise*,
and in absolute governments is *force*, as will be next explained.

"It has been already shown that the same constitution

of man which leads those who govern to oppress the governed, if not prevented, will, with equal force and certainty, lead the latter to resist oppression, when possessed of
the means of doing so peaceably and successfully. But
absolute governments, of all forms, exclude all other
means of resistance to their authority than that of force,
and, of course, leave no other alternative to the governed but to acquiesce in oppression, however great it may
be, or to resort to force to put down the government.
But the dread of such a resort must necessarily lead the
government to prepare to meet force in order to protect
itself; and hence, of necessity, force becomes the conservative principle of all such governments.

"On the contrary, the government of the concurrent
majority, where the organism is perfect, excludes the possibility of oppression, by giving to each interest, or portion, or order, where there are established classes, the
means of protecting itself, by its negative, against all measures calculated to advance the peculiar interests of others
at its expense. Its effect, then, is to cause the different
interests, portions, or orders, as the case may be, to desist
from attempting to adopt any measure calculated to promote the prosperity of one or more, by sacrificing that of
others; and thus to force them to unite in such measures
only as would promote the prosperity of all, as the only
means to prevent the suspension of the action of the government, and thereby to avoid anarchy, the greatest of all
evils. It is by means of such authorized and effectual resistance that oppression is prevented, and the necessity of
resorting to force superseded, in governments of the concurrent majority; and hence compromise, instead of force,
becomes their conservative principle.

"It would perhaps be more strictly correct to trace the conservative principle of constitutional governments to the necessity which compels the different interests, or portions, or orders to compromise, as the only way to promote their respective prosperity and to avoid anarchy, rather than to the compromise itself. No necessity can be more urgent and imperious than that of avoiding anarchy. It is the same as that which makes government indispensable to preserve society, and is not less imperative than that which compels obedience to superior force. Traced to this source, the voice of a people—uttered under the necessity of avoiding the greatest of calamities, through the organs of a government so constructed as to suppress the expression of all partial and selfish interests, and to give a full and faithful utterance to the sense of the whole community in reference to its common welfare —may, without impiety, be called *the voice of God*. To call any other so would be impious.

"In stating that force is the conservative principle of absolute, and compromise of constitutional governments, I have assumed both to be perfect in their kind; but not without bearing in mind that few or none, in fact, have ever been so absolute as not to be under some restraint, and none so perfectly organized as to represent fully and perfectly the voice of the whole community. Such being the case, all must, in practice, depart more or less from the principles by which they are respectively upheld and preserved, and depend more or less for support on force, or compromise, as the absolute or the constitutional form predominates in their respective organizations."

C 2

CHAPTER IV.

Happy Cessation of Excitement after the Adoption of the Missouri Compromise.—Era of good Feeling during the Remainder of Mr. Monroe's
Administration.—Presidential Contest of 1824.—Mr. Adams's Election by the House of Representatives to the Presidency.—Inaugural
Speech of Mr. Adams.—Interesting Scene in the White House on the
Occasion of President Monroe's taking Leave of his Friends to return
to his private Home in Virginia.—Intense Excitement growing out of
Mr. Adams's Election, but without any Intermixture of sectional Feel-
ing.—Violent and illiberal Opposition to his Administration.—Defeat
of Mr. Adams for Re-election in 1828, and Elevation of General An-
drew Jackson in his Stead.—Rise of Nullification in South Carolina in
1832.—General Jackson's Proclamation against South Carolina.—Mr.
Clay's successful Scheme of Pacification, known as the Compromise
Tariff Bill.—Origin of Abolition Societies in 1835.—Minute historical
Account of these Societies given in Mr. Greeley's "American Conflict."
—Mr. Webster's striking Remarks upon these Societies in his 7th of
March Speech.—Author declines any special Notice of the Presenta-
tion of Abolition Petitions, and the excited Discussions growing out of
the same.—Notice of the Acquisition of Texas with the general Con-
sent of the American People.—Breaking out of the Mexican War, and
Presentation of the Wilmot Proviso in the Midst thereof.—Author's
Election to the United States Senate, with Jefferson Davis as his official Colleague. — Serious political Disagreements between them. —
Sketch of President Davis's Character, with some Notice of his History.—Session of the United States Senate commencing in December,
1847. — Mr. Dickinson's Non-intervention Resolution, and Mr. Calhoun's extreme Opposition to it.—Curious colloquial Scene in the Senate.—General Cass's Nicholson Letter.—Complimentary Notice of General Cass.

In taking a retrospect of the past, it is alike surprising
and gratifying to observe how soon after the adoption of

the Missouri Compromise it was that the public mind became every where once more tranquil.

The majestic ship of state, which Longfellow has so beautifully depictured, was seen careering again over the surface of the now untroubled deep, whose waves had no longer power to disturb the regularity of its movements, or impede the celerity of its course. Those of us who remember the three years of happy quietude which our country enjoyed under the upright and truly conservative administration of Mr. Fillmore, are best able to understand how magically efficacious are sometimes found to be the healing balsams furnished by a judicious and liberal pharmacopœia, when these shall be applied in season to wounds inflicted by unfriendly hands upon the most vital parts of the body politic. I shall ever hold it to have been a most fortunate circumstance for our country's welfare that a few of those experienced and gifted statesmen who had been prominently instrumental in saving the republic from menaced overthrow in 1819 lingered still upon the public stage after full thirty years had rolled away, and that they were found alike ready and willing to lend their inspiring presence, as well as their priceless monitions, to a rash and froward generation, who at one moment seemed bent upon making sudden shipwreck of those moral treasures which, once lost, are in general found to be completely past recovery. But let us proceed with our rapid historic review.

During the remainder of Mr. Monroe's administration party excitement was almost unknown, and indeed at the close of it there was only one party designation known in all the broad republic. It was during the continuance

of this political calm that four presidential candidates
were seen to present themselves to popular consideration, all of whom professed to be of the same creed, and
claimed the same political associations—Mr. Crawford,
Mr. Clay, General Jackson, and Mr. John Quincy Adams,
about the shoulders of the last of whom was the presidential mantle destined to be ultimately cast.

On the 4th day of March, 1825, the writer of these
pages, then a mere novice in the great world of national
politics, had the honor of seeing John Quincy Adams for
the first time, and of listening to that inaugural speech
of his which was fated to call forth so much of sharp and
biting criticism, and of ungenerous objurgation. I was,
an hour or two afterward, one of the numerous visitants
who thronged the presidential mansion in order to take
leave of Mr. Monroe and to greet the incoming of his
successor, and well do I remember the bland and cheerful aspect of the venerable man who, then in a state of
green old age, was gracefully casting off the harness of
official labor and responsibility, as well as the solemn and
care-marked visage of his successor, who, under embarrassing and unprecedented circumstances, and with the
prospect opening upon him of a long course of virulent
and relentless assailment from a thousand heretofore
friendly quarters, was about to take upon himself duties
the performance of which I am sure no truly sagacious
man has ever yet eagerly coveted, who at the same time
expected to perform them with a true and vigorous fidelity.   Though Mr. Adams very soon found a fierce and
energetic party organized for his overthrow, and though
the most strenuous efforts were used by his zealous oppo-

nents in order to effect his defeat in the next presidential election, I am not aware that this opposition to him has been heretofore asserted to have been at all of a *sectional* cast. When General Jackson succeeded him in 1829 there were no indications any where that a political organization merely *sectional* in its character was at all likely to make its sinister appearance either in the North or in the South. After the second election of this remarkable personage had occurred, though, and perhaps a little before the close of his first official term, such an organization did arise in the State of South Carolina, which very soon ramified itself into several other states. The grounds assumed for the formation of this party were plausible enough in the beginning, but it never had a perfectly healthful and vigorous existence, and would, in in all probability, have ultimately perished from its own intrinsic feebleness, even had it not been promptly and energetically dealt with by the heroic and sagacious man then occupying the chair of state. The local movements which at that period occurred in South Carolina; the dangerous political theories disseminated then among her sensitive and mercurial people; the conventional ordinances solemnly adopted, but which were destined never to be enforced; the excited and long-continued discussion which these various movements brought on in the halls of the national Congress; Mr. Webster's several august and triumphant refutations of the absurd theory of nullification; General Jackson's paralyzing and crushing proclamation, are all yet fresh in the memories of millions. I hope it is not yet forgotten either, that in 1832, Mr. Clay, the great *pacificator*, as he has been so aptly entitled, was, fortunately, then in the national Senate, and that, being earnestly pressed from various quarters, as I have myself more than once heard him declare to be the fact, to undertake the work of *conciliation* then so much needed, this gentleman, with that clear judgment and lofty moral courage for which he was so celebrated, brought forward and quickly secured the passage of what is known as the *Compromise* Tariff Bill, which measure proved satisfactory to fair and just-minded men every where, extinguished the local excitement yet lingering in South Carolina, and diffused peace and brotherly kindness once more over the whole republic.

About the year 1835, as has been generally agreed, a new and serious danger to the quiet of the country began to disclose itself: I allude to organized opposition, in some of the free states of the North, to slavery as it then existed in the South. For many reasons, some of which are of a nature which I do not deem it expedient here to unfold, the united force of which, though, will give to them a controlling influence over my action in this particular, I shall decline entering into a minute examination of all the painful particulars connected, in one way or another, with the origin and speedy multiplication of associations set on foot in the free states for the destruction of the slaveholding system of the South. Those who are desirous of obtaining information upon this subject, both ample in volume and minute in detail, embellished with frequent delineations of character, and numerous scenes not unsuited to appear in the pages of a well-written romance, or as portions of some stately production inspired by the historic muse, will be able to gratify their curiosity on this subject most fully by looking through the first volume of Mr. Greeley's "American Conflict." I may be permitted, I trust, without giving serious offense in any respectable quarter, to say that, while I am disposed to give full credit to many of the prominent champions of abolition, whose virtues and achievements the author just referred to has so glowing-ly depictured, for entire conscientiousness of *motive*, and for having also done more or less *good* in their day and generation (good unfortunately not unmixed with evil), yet I can not but agree with Mr. Webster in what he is reported to have said in regard to the same associations in his great 7th of March speech, which contains the fol-lowing weighty declarations :

" Then, sir, there are the abolition societies, of which I am unwilling to speak, but in regard to which I have very clear notions and opinions. I do not think them *useful.* I think their operations for the last twenty years have produced nothing good or valuable. At the same time, I believe thousands of their members to be honest and good men, perfectly well-meaning men. They have excited feelings, they think they must do something for the cause of liberty; and in their sphere of action they do not see what else they can do than to contribute to an abolition press, or an abolition society, or to pay an abolition lecturer. I do not mean to impute gross mo-tives even to the leaders of these societies, but I am not blind to the consequences of their proceedings. I can not but see what mischiefs their interference with the South has produced. And is it not plain to every man? Let any gentleman who entertains doubts on this point recur to the debates in the Virginia House of Delegates in 1832, and he will see with what freedom a proposition made by Mr. Jefferson Randolph for the gradual abolition of slavery was discussed in that body. · Every one spoke of slavery as he thought; very ignominious and disparaging names and epithets were applied to it. The debates in the House of Delegates on that occasion, I be-, lieve, are all published. They were read by every colored man who could read, and to those who could not read those debates were read by others. At that time Virginia was not unwilling or afraid to discuss this question, and to let that part of her population know as much of the discussion as they could learn. That was in 1835. As has been said by the honorable member from South Carolina, Mr. Calhoun, these abolition societies commenced a new course of action. It is said, I do not know how true it may be, that they sent incendiary publications into the slave states; at any rate, they attempted to arouse, and did arouse a very strong feeling; in other words, they created great agitation in the North against Southern slavery. Well, what was the result? The bonds of the slaves were bound more firmly than before; their rivets were more strongly fastened. Public opinion, which in Virginia had begun to be exhibited against slavery, and was opening out for the discussion of the question, drew back and shut itself up in its castle. I wish to know whether any body in Virginia can now talk openly, as Mr. Randolph, Governor McDowell, and others talked in 1832, and sent their remarks to the press? We all know the fact, and we all know the cause; and every thing that these agitating people have done has been, not to enlarge, but to restrain, not to set free, but to bind faster, the slave · population of the South."

I shall cheerfully leave to others the unwelcome task of describing those scenes of crimination and recrimination which have heretofore taken place in the two Houses of Congress in connection with the presentations of abolition petitions, and which are known to have been marked with ebullitions of rancor and ill-will, which no true friend to the future repose and concord of the republic can desire to withhold from oblivion. I should be of all men most unwilling to do or say aught on this delicate and exciting subject to inflame ancient irritations, or provoke the fresh discussion of questions which are now most emphatically *res judicata*. That there has been much of needless and unprofitable zeal manifested in times past, both on the one side and the other, upon the occasions referred to, no reasonable man would now be inclined to deny. For my own part, I am not a little gratified to feel that, in order to develop the true *causes* which have led to so much shedding of fraternal blood in civil strife as we have been of late compelled to witness, it will not be necessary to dwell to the extent which some of our contemporaries have judged it right to do upon various topics which I have determined, for the reason just suggested, altogether to pretermit.

After much and painful scrutiny, I have become entirely satisfied that *twenty years ago* there was no earthly danger that abolition hostility would ever be able to accomplish the downfall of African slavery on this continent. Under the protecting ægis of the Federal Constitution, with the exercise of a sound practical discretion on the part of its professed friends and supporters, it would doubtless have survived for many generations yet to come, and would have been only in the end dispensed with when those connected with its control and management should have found that its continued existence was no longer desirable either to themselves or to the world at large. *Twenty years ago,* Mr. Polk had been triumphant over his great competitor, Mr. Clay, mainly upon what was known as the issue of Texan annexation, and was vigorously and successfully running that career which has so justly endeared his name to all who feel a proper interest in the future territorial extension and moral ascendency of the American republic in this hemisphere. *Twenty years ago,* the slaveholding system of the South seemed to be well-nigh as solid and likely to endure even as the Federal Union itself. *Twenty years ago,* the now prostrate and exhausted states of the South were prosperous, free, and happy, and those who dwelt therein possessed the respect and sympathy of the enlightened and liberal-minded in every country where the honored name of *America* had itself been pronounced.

The prejudices of men on both sides of the Atlantic in regard to every thing *Southern,* either in its location or origin, so far as their prejudices had made themselves apparent, were fast giving way under the influence of great commercial considerations, and of that surest of all teachers—*Time.* The then recent acquisition of Texas, obtained with the general consent of the American people, North as well as South, mainly, as we all vividly remember, with a view to defeating the anti-slavery policy of Great Britain, then aiming to undermine the cotton-growing system of the South by converting Texas into a *free* British province, had supplied a new bulwark to that system, and.a wider area for African slavery, then generally supposed to be so desirable. The thrice happy and exultant South, in despite of the solemn teachings of her sagest and most sagacious statesman, was then, like the youthful Alexander, "*sighing for new* worlds to con-quer," and was preparing, with the apparent sanction of millions dwelling far to the north of the celebrated Ma-son and Dixon's line, to plunge the country into a war with *contiguous* Mexico.

Just then movements originated which, though they at-tracted less attention at the time than they should have done, were opening the way to occurrences the influence of which will be felt for a thousand generations yet to arise. Soon the Wilmot Proviso cloud, at first "no big-ger than a man's hand," was, before it should disappear, to cover the whole heavens with blackness. Presently a second cloud, sometimes, and aptly, entitled "the Wil-mot Proviso South," was to make its appearance, and aid in precipitating the coming storm. At this period of the country's history I had the fortune to be sent to the United States Senate from the State of Mississippi, as the colleague of one whose name is now a familiar word in the languages of all nations. A portion of what I *saw* and *heard* in that high position, and of what I have au-thentically learned from miscellaneous sources, both in Washington and elsewhere, I shall now proceed to bring forward, with such occasional reflections as shall occur to me. Aware how difficult it is, as Mr. Gibbon has finely

remarked, for "a man to speak gracefully of himself," I
shall yet have to incur the hazard of being accused by
some of unbecoming egotism in undertaking to narrate
occurrences of great dignity and importance, in which,
though always acting a very subordinate part, I had necessarily, to some extent, an official participation. Hoping that what I shall now attempt to impart will at least
receive a liberal interpretation, I shall proceed to the task
before me.

As would be naturally expected, I shall essay, as a
preliminary proceeding, to describe, in as concise a manner as I can, and with as much impartiality, I trust, as if
he had lived a thousand years ago, the personage whom
the accidents of public life had now given me for a senatorial colleague. Mr. Davis was born, as I have repeatedly heard from his own lips, in the State of Kentucky,
where he was afterward in part educated. His boyish
days were spent chiefly in the State of Mississippi, whence
he was sent, in due season, to West Point, as a cadet of
that institution. On graduating there, he joined the regular army, as is usual in such cases, and I saw him first
in the city of Vicksburg, more than thirty years ago, as
Lieutenant Davis. He was then a young man of modest
and pleasing aspect and manners, but gave slight indications of any abilities likely to lead to future distinction.
He married, left the army, and settled himself on a plant-
ation of respectable dimensions in the southern part of
the County of Warren, some twenty miles from the city
of Vicksburg, where he has constantly resided since, until he became President of the Confederate States. I saw
him rarely after his retirement, being myself a good deal

engaged at this period in professional and other pursuits; but I have learned that Mr. Davis lived a very secluded and studious life for a series of years, until about the year 1843 he visited the city of Jackson as delegate to a Democratic Convention; during the session of which body I met him once more, and heard from his lips a formal and elaborate eulogy upon Mr. Calhoun's character and principles, which impressed the Convention very favorably indeed. In 1844, Mr. Davis and myself, as Democratic co-electoral candidates upon the Polk and Dallas presidential ticket, traversed the State of Mississippi together, and addressed in connection numerous large popular assemblages, by whom, in general, he was most kindly and respectfully received, and attentively listened to. He was afterward nominated for Congress, and elected to a seat in the House of Representatives, which he occupied for several months of one session only, having been chosen, in his absence at Washington, colonel of a new volunteer regiment which had been a short time before raised in Mississippi for the Mexican War, which was then in progress. The regiment which Mr. Davis commanded as colonel won much *éclat* both at Monterey and Buena-vista, at the latter of which places he was severely wounded in the foot, and, returning home on a visit, Governor A. G. Brown, with general popular approval, appointed him to the seat in the United States Senate from the State of Mississippi, which had recently become vacant by reason of the decease of General Speight. Mr. Davis and myself journeyed to Washington City together in the autumn of 1847, and arrived there several days before the session of Congress commenced. Very soon after taking our seats as senators from the same state, it became apparent that serious incompatibilities, both of taste and temper, as well as exceedingly conflicting views of men and measures, forbade all reasonable hope of our being able to harmonize as would have been every way so desirable. My opinion of Mr. Davis then was pretty much as it is at present, and may be expressed in a few words. He is, in the ordinary sense of those terms, a high-minded and well-bred man. In domestic life, I do not doubt that he is amiable and exemplary. In his temper, as displayed on public occasions, he is arbitrary and exacting. His personal ambition is most intense and exorbitant. He is overtenacious alike in his public resolves and in his personal partialities and prejudices. He doubtless always *intends* to do *right*, but is often in gross *error*, both as to men and to affairs. His disposition, naturally irritable and unquiet, has been much sharpened and embittered of late years by long-continued and severe nervous disease, and by numerous disappointments. His intellect is certainly above mediocrity, both in strength and activity, and his general literary attainments are respectable; but it will be admitted by all who have approached him nearly, and who are themselves competent to judge, that his mind is not at all remarkable either for comprehensive force or for a rich fecundity of ideas. With the particular branches of science belonging to a strictly military education he is more than ordinarily familiar; in other departments of learning he is decidedly deficient. As a party tactician, he is astute, subtle, and plausible; but he is sadly deficient in judgment, in a politic turn for conciliation, and in the exercise of a liberal allowance for

trivial differences of opinion. His public course is about
as consistent as could be well expected among politicians
more solicitous of obeying party obligations and securing
personal advancement, than of maintaining principles and
promoting the public welfare. Upon the whole, those
who have judged him capable of *originating* a grand revolutionary movement, and of conducting it forward to
success, are as much in error as are those, if there be any,
who suppose him capable of such cold-blooded and cruel
atrocities as those which have been of late so trippingly
attributed to him.

One of the most agreeable reminiscences of my past
public life is the first interview which occurred in Washington City about this time between the Hon. Daniel S.
Dickinson and myself. I saw this gentleman first in the
spring of 1847. When we met a few months afterward,
and just before the assemblage of the Congress of 1847, '8,
Mr. Dickinson did me the honor of submitting to my
consideration the following resolutions, which he informed me he had previously laid before General Cass, then
the acknowledged leader of the Democratic party in Congress, and I learned from him also that this gentleman
had heartily endorsed the same :

" *Resolved*, That true policy requires the government of
the United States to strengthen its political relations upon
this continent by the annexation of such contiguous territory as may conduce to that end, and can be justly obtained ; and that neither in such acquisition, nor in the territorial organization thereof, can any conditions be constitutionally imposed, or institutions be provided for or established inconsistent with the rights of the people thereof

to form a free sovereign state, with the powers and privileges of the original members of the confederacy.

"*Resolved*, That in organizing a territorial government
for territory belonging to the United States, the principles of self-government upon which our federative system
rests will be best promoted, the true spirit and meaning
of the Constitution be observed, and the confederacy
strengthened, by leaving all matters connected with the
domestic policy therein to the Legislature chosen by the
people thereof."

It will be found, on examination, that these resolutions
state, in very clear and unambiguous language, the great
and salutary principle of *popular sovereignty* and *non-intervention*, as it has been denominated, which was afterward embodied in the Democratic presidential platform
of 1848, and which was afterward retained therein, without material modification, so long as the strength of that
party was maintained, and it was yet able successfully to
ward off the assailment of sectional factionists and preserve the peace of the republic. It will be hereafter seen
that this same principle constituted the leading feature
of the compromise measures of 1850, and imparted to
them their chief value. I read the resolutions with attention, and stated to Mr. Dickinson my warm approval
of them, when he told me that he had made up his mind
at some early day to offer them for adoption in the Senate, which he accordingly did some two weeks thereafter,
when a curious and somewhat characteristic scene occurred. Mr. Dickinson's resolutions having been presented,
were then lying on the clerk's table ready to be printed,
after which that gentleman, as he had already announced,

intended calling them up for consideration, when Mr. Calhoun walked up to the place where they were deposited, took them from the table for perusal, and, after having read them over, walked behind the Vice President's chair and beckoned me to come to him. I joined him accordingly, whereupon he, in a very excited manner, called my attention to the phraseology of Mr. Dickinson's aforesaid resolutions, and said that they were worse than the Wilmot Proviso; that the constitutional doctrine set forth in them was infinitely dangerous, and concluded by declaring that he intended to denounce them in the most emphatic manner whenever Mr. Dickinson should call them from the table. I was most deeply and painfully surprised, conceiving, as I did, that the adoption of just such resolutions as Mr. Dickinson had offered by the two Houses of Congress, and the speedy acquiescence in the declaration of principle which they contained, would effectually guard the quiet of the country by defeating the Wilmot Proviso policy, or the policy of excluding slavery from the territories of the Union by congressional action, and would thus rescue the South and her cherished local interests from menaced subversion. I expostulated mildly and respectfully with Mr. Calhoun against pursuing the course which he had avowed his determination previously to adopt, and, without incurring the hazard of inflaming him additionally by informing him that my adhesion to the resolutions of Mr. Dickinson had been already pledged, I proceeded to the seat of General Cass, informed him of what had just occurred, and this gentleman, at my instance, went with me to the seat of Mr. Dickinson, and united his efforts with mine in persuading

D

him that he would decline pressing the Senate to a vote upon his resolutions until a better understanding could be had, so as, if possible, to avoid any division among those who were united in opposing the adoption of any restrictive legislation in regard to slavery in the territories. Mr. Dickinson, with a display of that conciliatory and obliging temper for which all who know him are prepared to give him credit, declared at once that he would not urge the Senate to action upon his resolutions immediately, that he would call them up in a few days for consideration; and that, after having concisely discussed them, as he had it in contemplation to do, and after having thus set himself right in the view of his own particular constituents, he should be willing that the resolutions should then lie upon the table until all interested in preserving the peace of the country should be ready to take some decided legislation on the matters embraced therein. This arrangement being made known to Mr. Calhoun, he acquiesced therein, and thus for a short period an extended and unprofitable controversy in the Senate upon the territorial question was avoided. It is due to Mr. Dickinson to state here that he afterward was heard at considerable length in exposition of the true meaning of the resolutions which he had offered, and in vindication of the principle of *non-intervention* which they set forth, and that he delivered on that occasion a manly, well-reasoned, and eminently patriotic speech, which greatly enhanced his reputation both as a statesman and orator.

I should mention here that, early in the session of Congress, General Cass, in an interview which I had with

him, informed me that he had just received a letter from
Mr. Nicholson, of Tennessee, then an ardent political
friend of his, as I certainly was myself, requesting an
expression of his views on the question just noticed, and
that he had drawn up a reply thereto, which he desired
me to read. I read it accordingly, made several comparatively immaterial suggestions in regard to the phraseology, which he kindly consented to modify, when I
urged him to give publication to the correspondence at
once, being well satisfied that it was eminently important
that all proper efforts should be made to get the general
mind of the country matured as soon as possible upon
the new and difficult question so ably discussed by General Cass in that now far-famed letter. He agreed, in
case his political friends generally in Congress should
regard the publication of the letter as desirable, to allow
it to be inserted in the newspapers without delay. I
then drew up a formal letter to General Cass, asking the
publication of this letter, to which I took care to obtain
the signatures of a considerable number of congressional
members alike from the North and from the South, and
it was thereupon given to the public.

Much has been said at different times both in censure
and in commendation of this letter—far more, perhaps,
than was either needful or advantageous. It has been
accused of vagueness and ambiguity by some, while others have not hesitated to speak of it as one of the hap-
piest emanations of its distinguished author. For my
own part, though I have never for a moment regretted
my instrumentality in procuring its publication in the
manner described, and though I do yet most fully con-

cur in the leading idea embodied in it, that the question
of whether slavery should or should not be allowed to
exist in the new territories, might safely and properly
have been "left to the people of the confederacy in their
respective local governments," yet have I never thought
that the Nicholson Letter was in all respects so explicit
in its phraseology as it might have been, or equal, in
point of mere literary finish, to many of the numerous
productions of its venerable author's most gifted pen.
General Cass certainly owed his nomination for the presidency by the Democratic party in 1848 in some degree
to the sound and conservative doctrine which he had
dared thus seasonably to avow, and I shall ever feel
proud of having zealously sustained him in the presidential contest which soon ensued, as the bold and uncompromising champion of the principle of *non-intervention;*
which principle was destined, in the perilous crisis of
1850, to become the distinguishing feature of those measures of compromise and adjustment, the introduction and
successful advocacy of which were to gild the evening
of Mr. Clay's eventful life with a moral effulgence which
can never become extinct.

I should gladly close this chapter with the tender of
my humble tribute of applause to the venerable octoge-
narian statesman who has been thus incidentally alluded
to.   No one admires him more than I do, and no one has
more reason to cherish for him a fervent and solid attach-
ment.   But what can my humble pen record, either of
his rare moral graces or his eminent public services,
which is not already familiarly known to his grateful
and admiring countrymen or to the world at large?   He

has himself written and spoken so often and so ably, he has so long been the honored incumbent of high official positions, and has so little at any time sought to conceal either his conduct or his motives from the view of men, that I might justly despair, were I even sufficiently presumptuous to hazard the effort, to add in the least degree to the fullness and brightness of that fame which already challenges the admiration alike of his own countrymen and of the dwellers in other lands, and before the mild and simple grandeur of which even the living calumniators of party and of faction have been at last completely humbled into silence.

" Serus in cœlum redeas !"

CHAPTER V.

Proceedings upon the Wilmot Proviso during the Congressional Session of 1847, '8.—Mr. Clayton's Compromise Bill, and its unfortunate Defeat in the House of Representatives.—General Cass as the Presidential Candidate of the Democratic Party in 1848. — The Contest between himself and General Taylor by no means of a sectional Character.— Election of the latter.—Appearance of William L. Yancey at the Baltimore Convention of 1848, and the prompt Rejection by that Body of his celebrated Protection Proposition. — Unfortunate Division of the Strength of the Democratic Party in 1848 between the Hunkers and Barnburners, resulting in the Nomination of Martin Van Buren and Charles Francis Adams by the Buffalo Convention.—Mr. Gott's Resolution.—Declaration, as early as 1843, by Messrs. Adams, Slade, Giddings, and others in Favor of dissolving the Federal Union in the Event of the Annexation of Texas.—Inflammatory Address issued by these Gentlemen.—Author's first acquaintance with John Quincy Adams and his accomplished Lady.—Commendatory Notice of his Life and Character.—Parallel between John Quincy Adams and John C. Calhoun.

EARLY in the congressional session of 1847, '8, a test vote upon the Wilmot Proviso had been taken in the House of Representatives, and the proposition embodying the essential feature of that Proviso had been laid upon the table on the motion of Mr. Broadhead, a member from Pennsylvania. This result was looked upon by the friends of domestic quiet at the time as a most favorable symptom; but it was supposed by some of the most judicious and experienced personages then in Congress that it would be best to guard against future danger by having the vexed territorial question submitted for adjudication, at as early a period as practicable, to the Supreme Court of the United States; it being then hoped that the decision of that high tribunal, touching the *constitutionality* of legislative measures of *restriction*, would command the respect of the great body of the American people, and render the clamors of sectional demagogues, whether in the North or in the South, thenceforward powerless. Accordingly, Mr. John M. Clayton, of Delaware, after advising extensively with senators and representatives of the greatest weight and influence in their respective states, and whom he knew, at the same time, to be solicitous to do what they could to suppress the spirit of discord then visibly manifesting itself in various quarters, as a member of a select committee of the Senate, to whom had been referred the Oregon Bill, reported said bill back to the Senate, with amendments establishing territorial governments for New Mexico and California in addition, and containing a clause, likewise, providing, in a very careful and precise manner, for the *judicial arbitrament* referred to in relation to all three of said territories. It is obvious that, could this bill have become a law, sectional agitation would have been, at least for a while, suppressed. *Faction* had not then grown strong enough, either in the North or in the South, successfully to resist the deliberate adjudication of that grave and solemn tribunal where a Marshall and a Story had so recently sat, and where there were still judges to be found worthy of the better and purer days of the republic.

But the Clayton Compromise Bill, after passing the Senate by a vote of 33 yeas to 22 nays, was fated to receive its quietus in the House from a hand least expected to in-

flict a blow so unfortunate. Mr. Stephens, of Georgia,
having moved that the said bill *do lie* upon the table, the
motion prevailed by what was very nearly a sectional
vote, only eight Southern members having yielded their
support to it. I have never heard from Mr. Stephens
himself what particular reasons influenced his course on
this occasion, but have been repeatedly told, and suppose
such to have been the case, that this gentleman, having
maturely arrived at the conclusion that African slavery
in all the recently acquired territory had been uprooted
by antecedent Mexican legislation, and that therefore if
the question propounded by the Clayton Bill should be
submitted to the Supreme Court, a decision was to be apprehended which would prove fatal to the policy then so
warmly cherished by a portion of the Southern people
of extending slavery into the vacant territories, deemed
it unsafe to risk the action thereof. I have also heard
that the course of Mr. Stephens and his distinguished colleague from Georgia, Mr. Toombs, in refusing to vote for
the appropriation of money for carrying into effect the
then recently ratified treaty with Mexico, was controlled
by similar views. However this may be, both Mr. Stephens and Mr. Toombs were for a time very much cen-
sured by certain overheated persons in the South on account of their conduct at this period, and motives were in
several quarters charged to each of them, the operation of
which I rejoice never myself to have suspected, and which
all just-minded men must now admit to have been wholly
unmerited. I can not doubt now, though, any more than
I did sixteen years ago, that even had the Supreme Court
of the republic at that time decided that slavery had no

legal and authorized existence in New Mexico and California, and that even had Congress, acquiescing in that decision, refused to adopt enactments for its establishment therein, the people of the South would have rested quiet under this determination, and the painful scenes through which we have been lately passing, as well as the fearful agitations which preceded them, might have been happily avoided.

The Democratic party, of which General Cass was now the acknowledged chief, and whom they put in nomination for the presidency in the Convention held in the city of Baltimore in the month of May, 1848, adopted a resolution at the same time which pledged that party, and the candidates chosen to represent it in the pending presidential contest, to "a vigilant and consistent adherence to those principles and *compromises of the Constitution* which are broad enough and strong enough to uphold the Union as it was, as it is, and as it shall be, in the full expansion of the energies and capacity of this great and progressive people."

At this precise moment indications first clearly display themselves, not of "an irrepressible conflict" between antagonistic elements imbedded in the Constitution, but between two rampant and reckless local factions, neither of which was truly friendly to the compromises of the Constitution or the permanent repose of the republic; which two factions, as will be seen in the sequel, were thereafter to struggle with each other and with the two great conservative parties then existing; and while gaining from time to time fresh accessions to their respective ranks, or losing a portion of their strength temporarily, from the operation of accidental causes, were in a few years to grow strong enough to shake the republic to its foundation, and to make themselves responsible before all generations for the most absurd, unnecessary, and un- natural war that the combined wickedness and folly of man have ever yet waged upon this terrestrial planet. I will make myself more plain on this point by a short historic recital. While the Democratic Convention was in session in Baltimore, a gentleman from the State of Alabama appeared therein, whose name is now familiar to the ears of all intelligent men on both sides of the At- lantic. I saw this personage in Washington on his way to Baltimore, and I learned by accident what was the nature of his mission to the latter city. This gentleman (of course I am alluding to Mr. William L. Yancey) offered to the consideration of the Convention the following res- olution :

"*Resolved*, That the doctrine of non-interference with the rights of property of any portion of the people of this confederacy, be it in the states or territories thereof, *by any other than the parties interested in them*, is the true re- publican doctrine recognized by this body."

It is evident that it was intended by this adroit move- ment to get the whole Democratic party *committed* against any legislation in the territories, either on the part of Congress or the local Legislatures, and to prevent even any action by conventions called for the purpose of form- ing state constitutions with a view to admission into the Federal Union in any of said territories, which should be of a nature to affect the rights of property in slaves, un- less with the consent of the individual owners. A proposition so absurd and dangerous could receive but few votes in a Convention constituted of such intelligent and patriotic men as were then assembled in Baltimore, and accordingly, out of 252 votes, only 36 persons were found radical enough to follow Mr. Yancey's lead. The *Trojan horse* brought into the Democratic citadel was driven beyond its ramparts before the armed warriors which it inclosed could be disgorged from its sides for the perpetration of the mischief contemplated. We shall after a while see this same cunningly-constructed *equine* machine make its ominous appearance in the cities of Charleston and Baltimore under the care of the self-same political groom, and shall see it unhappily accorded there a very different reception indeed.

While this attempt was making to transform the Democratic party into a secession faction, another effort was in progress, in an opposite quarter, to convert the same party into a mere Free-soil organization. I shall cite here the short and precise description of the latter movement, of which the Democratic nominating Convention in Baltimore was likewise the chosen theatre, from the pages of Mr. Greeley's Conflict. " Two delegations from New York presenting themselves to this Convention— that of the Free-soilers, Radicals, or Barnburners, whose leader was Samuel Young, and that of the Conservatives, or Hunkers, whose chief was Daniel S. Dickinson—the Convention attempted to split the difference by admitting both, and giving each half the vote to which the state was entitled. This the Barnburners rejected, leaving the Convention, and refusing to be bound by its conclusions. The greater body of them heartily joined in the

Free-soil movements, which culminated in a National Convention at Buffalo, whereby Martin Van Buren was nominated for President, with Charles Francis Adams, of Massachusetts, for Vice-President."

The last of the series of resolutions adopted at this same Buffalo Convention shortly afterward raised, in a very sharp and distinct manner, the issue between the Radicals or Sectionalists of the North and the Radicals or Sectionalists of the South, which was to remain a standing and unsettled issue for a series of years, and was to grow, in the imaginations of some, into an "irrepressible conflict," but which, in point of fact, was never either a necessary, safe, or expedient issue, and has since wrought incalculable mischiefs to the whole land, the vestiges of which a century will scarcely be able to efface.

In the month of December, 1848, a resolution was introduced into the House of Representatives by Mr. Gott, of New York, the object of which was to prohibit the trade in slaves in the District of Columbia. This resolution, in itself, was perhaps not justly subject to objection or censure, but its discussion, in connection with the circumstance that certain slaves in the ownership of members of Congress from the South were about that time illegally abstracted from their possessors, begot very fierce and acrimonious discussion, and induced a number of the Southern senators and representatives then in Washington to hold a meeting for *consultation* purposes, which meeting appointed a committee to draft a suitable address to the people of the South. This address was drawn up by Mr. Calhoun, was exceedingly calm and decorous in its tone, indulged in no menacing language whatever, and took the

ground emphatically in behalf of the South, that all which
the slaveholding section demanded was *to be let alone;*
asking no special *protection* for slaves at the hands of
Congress, and only desiring that the well-known guaranties of the Constitution should be faithfully executed.
Certain public writers have bitterly denounced this proceeding, charging even that it was a rank *disunion* movement, when it was, in truth, precisely the reverse; and
yet it is a most noticeable fact that these same writers
have taken care never to apply the language of reproach
to John Quincy Adams, William Slade, Joshua R. Giddings, and others, who, as early as 1843, in an able and
eloquent address to the people of the free states, did not
hesitate to declare, in connection with the measure of
Texan annexation then under contemplation, that "annexation effected by any act or proceeding of the Federal
government, or any of its departments, *would be identical
with the dissolution of the Union*," and adding, "it would
be a violation of our national compact, its objects and designs, and the great elementary principles which entered
into its formation, of a character so deep and fundamental, and would be an attempt to eternize an institution
and a power of a nature so unjust in themselves, so injurious to the interests and abhorrent to the feelings of the
people of the free states, as, in our opinion, not only *in-.
evitably to result in a dissolution of the Union, but fully to
justify it;* and we not only assert that the people of the
free states *ought not to submit to it,* but we say with confidence *they would not submit to it.*"

I seize with pleasure the opportunity presented of expressing frankly some opinions which I have long enter-

tained in reference to *John Quincy Adams.* I was not so fortunate as to be upon the list of his personal and confidential friends. I had been introduced to him in the lobby of the House of Representatives on one occasion, without holding any conversation with him, a circumstance which I shall now forever regret; but I had for some years felt for his character and abilities a profound respect. On the New Year's day immediately preceding his decease I had gone to his hospitable mansion, with a large number of his fellow-citizens besides, to pay the customary respects to Mrs. Adams and himself. The appearance of both these venerable personages on that occasion painfully indicated the pressure of increasing years, and both of them went through the tiresome scene of receiving the miscellaneous greetings of the thousands who had come to do them deserved homage with an evident sense of weariness and exhaustion. It had chanced that, as early as the year 1824, when I had scarcely attained to manhood, I had met Mrs. Adams at the Bedford Springs, in the State of Pennsylvania, whither she had gone for the restoration of her health, which was then supposed to be more or less impaired. The condition of my own health at the time had brought me to this place also; and as the fashionable season had not then commenced, and there were but few visitants at the Springs, I was one of seven or eight persons, including Mrs. Adams, her fair niece, Miss Hellen, and her son John, who for several weeks had seats at the same private table. A more high-bred, intelligent, and affable lady I do not remember at any time to have encountered. The next time I saw Mrs. Adams was at a levee given by the French minister in Washington, just two days before the inauguration of her husband as President of the United States. Mr. Adams was then President elect by the recent action of the House of Representatives. He himself was not at the levee, but, as was certainly to have been expected, his accomplished better half was the great centre of attraction—all the political friends of the incoming President especially being disposed to evince the satisfaction which they felt at the recent promotion of their favorite by the rendition of fitting homage to Mrs. Adams, and many others being attracted to her presence by her own engaging qualities. More than twenty years then glided by before I beheld this esteemed lady again, on the New Year's occasion already referred to. Nor did I then make known to her that we had ever before met, as I could scarcely suppose that she would bear in remembrance thus long the humble and undistinguished youth with whom she had so accidentally formed a passing acquaintance at the renowned Pennsylvania watering-place.

To return to Mr. Adams. I saw him on the day before his death, or perhaps two or three days antecedent, in the hall of the House of Representatives, on Sunday, attending divine service there, and was very much struck with his pale and feeble appearance, as I know many others besides to have been. A day or two after his sudden decease, a gentleman who has since filled several highly respectable official positions, Caleb Lyon, of Lyonsdale, called on me at my residence on the Georgetown Heights, and handed me for perusal a light and vivacious, but highly humorous and piquant poetic effusion, which he

told me Mr. Adams had addressed to a charming young
lady of his acquaintance only forty-eight hours before his
decease. The aged author had, as Mr. Lyons informed
me, at the request of the latter, supplied him with a copy
of these verses, which he seemed, and most naturally too,
to prize very highly.

In my judgment, the country has produced but few
men who have left behind them more multiplied evidences of elevated patriotism, of *private* virtue, and of
varied ability and attainments than the eminent statesman of New England to whom I am now referring. This
much all unprejudiced men must, I think, every where
admit. I can certainly not suspect myself of being deluded by feelings either of personal partiality or identity
of political opinions. I was, according to my ability, a
zealous opponent of the administration of Mr. Adams
while that administration was yet in progress, and it is
known by my acquaintances that I was far from approving many of his public acts during the closing years of
his life. But a laborious and dispassionate examination
of the leading incidents in his long official career has effectually vanquished early prejudices, and will now enable me to speak of him, I believe, with something of the
cool impartiality which the future historian may be expected to display. More than thirty years have gone by
since Mr. Adams was defeated by his distinguished military rival for the first office in the gift of the American
people; and it may be now safely asserted, that never
since that striking period in American annals, has any
citizen occupied the chair of state who, while performing
the varied and complex duties of President, offered clear-

er and more numerous proofs of inflexible honesty of purpose, a thorough knowledge of affairs, unremitting industry in the performance of official duty, entire exemption from mere party or personal prejudice, moderation, mingled with firmness, in all critical emergencies, mild and unassuming urbanity both in official and social intercourse, with a vigilance that never winked, and an energy that never knew exhaustion. Mr. Adams was, perhaps, upon the whole, the most highly cultivated public man, in many respects, that our country has yet known, and it is understood that he labored strenuously to the last moment of his protracted life to increase his stores of useful knowledge. There was no department of science of which he was altogether ignorant. He had traversed the whole wide domain of general literature; his knowledge of history, both ancient and modern, was alike thorough and minute; his imagination, like that of Mr. Burke, seemed to grow more fertile, vigorous, and resplendent as he advanced in years; his memory, as well of men as of things, was such as it has been seldom given man to possess; his oratorical powers, not supposed, I have heard, to have been very remarkable in early life, were such, during the last fifteen years of his congressional existence, as compelled even his bitterest political foes to acquiesce in his claim to be recognized as "The Old Man Eloquent," and ever secured to him the unbroken and interested attention of those who hated him with an acrimony never yet surpassed, but who felt awed into unmurmuring respect under the magical influence of his unpremeditated and truly electrical utterances. That Mr. Adams was much, and unjustly, embittered toward the

South in the evening of his remarkable career, I think
will hardly be now in any quarter denied. That he had
some *cause* for *alienation* and for *unkindness* seems to me
to be equally apparent. His opinions in regard to the
baneful influence of African slavery, and his zealous opposition to its future *extension* into the vacant domain of
the republic, were not less sincerely entertained than were
precisely opposite views by his sectional adversaries; and
perhaps his prejudices toward the South were not stronger than those of Mr. Calhoun toward the North, who,
throughout his whole public career, was never known, as
I have learned, to place his feet for a moment upon Northern soil; and from whose lips I heard the declaration,
more than once, during the year 1848, when General Taylor and General Cass were contesting for the presidency
of the Union, that he would prefer the election to that
place of *any respectable'Southern planter* whatever to any
man *of Northern birth and residence;* though it is possible
that Mr. Calhoun was, after all, not altogether so averse
to his fellow-citizens of the free states as he seemed to imagine himself to be, inasmuch as I remember his declaring to me on one occasion, and about the period just referred to, that he should be quite content to see George
M. Dallas elevated to the presidency, as his political opinions were known to be in the main such as Southern men
were inclined to approve, and as he was not only a *gentleman* himself, in character, person, and demeanor, but
also *the son of a gentleman* — he (Mr. Calhoun) having
known in former days very intimately, as he said, the
father of Mr. Dallas, for whom he ever cherished a very
special esteem and kindness.

Between John C. Calhoun and John Quincy Adams there were remarkable points both of resemblance and of dissimilitude. They were both men of undoubted personal integrity; alike amiable and exemplary in domestic and in social life; fervent lovers of their country, yet of decided local bias; assiduous and untiring in their application to business, and cherishing equally the strictest notions of *frugality* in the appropriation and expenditure of the public money. So far were both these statesmen from being personally tainted with *fraud*, or even suspected of a disposition to participate in corrupt bargaining and traffic in connection with concerns of government, that it may be now safely asserted that no man who justly suspected himself of gross obliquity of purpose would have even ventured to challenge familiar intercourse with either of these sternly upright men. One of them was principally a profound logician, while the other was a spirited and powerful debater, not pre-eminently distinguished for argumentative power, nor yet, indeed, wholly deficient therein. Mr. Calhoun was profoundly metaphysical in his habits of thought, and had penetrated deeply into all the mysterious arcana connected with the fundamental principles of government; and he poured forth occasionally, in his moments of highest exertion, such a continued series of massive and strongly interlinked deductions, constantly advancing from one Alpine height of argument to another, that the mind of the ordinary hearer was often most painfully exercised in attempting to follow his giant intellectual strides, and even the reporters themselves complained that, with aching and overpowered brain, they were often compelled to re-

linquish in despair the arduous and impossible task of
marking down the successive steps of his Herculean
progress. Both Mr. Adams and Mr. Calhoun were members of Mr. Monroe's cabinet, and are understood to have
there differed, though not unkindly, upon several questions of no little magnitude and importance. Mr. Adams
has left behind him the charge that Mr. Calhoun voted in
that cabinet for yielding the Executive sanction to what
is known as the Missouri Compromise; while Mr. Calhoun asserted, more than once, in the Senate, in my hearing, that his formerly official associate had, in making this
statement, committed a grave and surprising error of
memory. Who can believe now that either of these illustrious statesmen *intended* TO violate *truth?*

At this moment, when African slavery has been swept
from the face of this continent by the remorseless scythe
of war, and when all of us must distinctly recognize
the fact that every vestige even of its former existence
must inevitably soon disappear forever, surely, both on
the one side and on the other, the proper time may be
regarded as having arrived when even what may have
been deemed gross errors of judgment in regard to the
dark and difficult constitutional question involved in
the policy of *restriction* may at last be forgiven. When
such men as Adams, Webster, Clay, Van Buren, Story,
M'Lane, and Curtis assert the *power* of Congress to prohibit the entrance of slavery into the territories of the
Union, and when such men as Calhoun and Douglas,
Taney, Grier, Campbell, and Nelson assert exactly the
contrary, it seems to me that ordinary Christian charity,
and a becoming deference to acknowledged intellectual

power and indisputable integrity of character, might prompt a decent and civil avoidance of rude and acrimonious invective, either on the part of the advocates of slavery restriction, or on the part of those who were formerly its adversaries.

CHAPTER VI.

Session of Congress closing on the 3d of March, 1849.—Important Test Question raised by Mr. Douglas, of Illinois, in Connection with the Oregon Bill, which was then pending.—Defeat of Mr. Douglas's Proposition by the unexpected but effective Interposition of Mr. Wm. H. Seward, who had not yet taken his Seat as a Senator from New York. —Mr. Seward at that Time opposed to all Compromise of the Slavery Question.—Extract from a memorable Speech of his, delivered in the United States Senate in the Year 1850, having Relation to this Subject. —Mr. Seward's Cleveland Speech in 1848.—Important Extracts therefrom.—General Taylor's Administration.—Violent Excitement beginning to rage both North and South upon the Slavery Question, and in Connection with the Admission of California.—Unfortunate non-action Policy of General Taylor's Administration.—Alarming Condition of the Country.—Election of Messrs. Gwin and Fremont United States Senators from California.—Attempt of Colonel Thomas H. Benton to revive his decaying Popularity by becoming the Champion of Californian Admission.—Efforts of the Author to defeat this Scheme of selfish Ambition. — Retrospect of Colonel Benton's Attempt, about the Close of Mr. Polk's Administration, to bring about the Rescission of the Treaty with Mexico, by which all the territorial Domain recently acquired would have been lost to the United States but for the Defeat of that Attempt.—Signal Defeat of this unpatriotic Scheme, and remarkable Particulars connected therewith not heretofore divulged.— Colonel Benton deprived in Democratic Caucus of the Chairmanship of the Committee of Foreign Affairs in the Senate on the Motion of the Author, after a two-days' Struggle, by a Majority of one Vote only.— Mr. Benton's extraordinary Attack on Mr. Calhoun and Others in his public Speech delivered in Missouri in the Summer of 1848, and Mr. Calhoun's overwhelming Response thereto, drawn up at Author's earnest Instance.—Short Sketch of Colonel Benton's public Character, and Delineation of his intellectual Qualities.

In the last days of the session of Congress terminating on the night of the 3d of March, 1849, Mr. Douglas, of Illinois, raised an important *test* question in connection with the bill then on its passage for the organization of the new Territory of Oregon, by the introduction of the following amendment thereto:

"That the line of thirty-six degrees and thirty minutes of north latitude, known as the Missouri Compromise line, as defined in the eighth section of an act entitled 'An Act to authorize the people of the Missouri Territory to form a Constitution and state government, and for the admission of such state into the Union on an equal footing with the original states, and to prohibit slavery in certain territories, approved March 6th, 1820,' be, and the same is, hereby declared to extend to the Pacific Ocean; and the said eighth section, together with the compromise therein effected, is hereby revived, and declared to be in full force and binding for the future organization of the territories of the United States, in the same sense and with the same understanding with which it was originally adopted." This amendment was carried in the Senate, but defeated in the House by an almost strictly sectional vote; so that the author of "The American Conflict" would seem to be justified in the following declaration which he has made in the thirteenth chapter of his voluminous and interesting work: "So Oregon became a territory consecrated to free labor *without compromise or counterbalance*, and the Free States gave notice that they would *not* divide with slavery the vast and hitherto free territories then just acquired from MEXICO."

In a well-known letter published in the National In-

telligencer, a few weeks after the close of the session of
Congress which had now just terminated, Mr. William H.
Seward, a newly-elected senator from the State of New
York, but who had not then taken his seat as such,
claimed much, and doubtless deserved credit for the success of his efforts on the last night of the session to defeat
all compromise of the territorial question in the various
modes proposed, preferring to keep it open for settlement
by the incoming administration of General Taylor. This
gentleman, it would seem, had never believed in the value
of legislative compromises, and afterward, in a speech delivered by him in the month of March, 1850, when the
compromise enactments of that period were under discussion, he used the following memorable words: "It is
insisted that the admission of California shall be attended by a compromise of questions which have arisen out
of *slavery. I am opposed to any such compromise, in any
and all the forms in which it has been proposed*, because,
while admitting the purity and the patriotism of all from
whom it is my misfortune to differ, I think all legislative
compromises which are not absolutely necessary radical-
ly wrong and essentially vicious. They involve the surrender of the exercise of judgment and conscience on
distinct and separate questions, at distinct and separate
times, with the indispensable advantages it affords for
ascertaining truth ; they involve a relinquishment of
the right to reconsider in future the decisions of the present on questions prematurely anticipated ; and they are
acts of usurpation as to future questions of the province
of future legislators."

This gentleman had delivered a speech at Cleveland,

Ohio, in 1848, in which he had doubtless stated his conscientious convictions, the spirit and character of which will be made sufficiently evident by the citation of the following striking extracts: "There are two antagonistical elements of society in America, freedom and slavery. Freedom is in harmony with our system of government, and with the spirit of the age, and is therefore passive and quiescent. Slavery is in conflict with that system, with justice, and with humanity, and is therefore organized, defensive, active, and perpetually aggressive.

"Freedom insists on the emancipation and elevation of labor; slavery demands a soil moistened with tears and blood—freedom a soil that exults under the elastic tread of man in his native majesty.

"These elements divide and classify the American people into parties. Each of these parties has its court and its sceptre. The throne of the one is amid the rocks of the Alleghany Mountains, the throne of the other is reared on the sands of South Carolina. One of these parties, the party of slavery, regards disunion as among the means of defense, and not always the last to be employed; the other maintains the Union of the States one and inseparable, now and forever, as the highest duty of the American people to themselves, to posterity, to mankind."

I have no acrimonious strictures to apply to what has just been cited. Perhaps, though, the eminent personage who delivered, with so much apparent deliberation, the celebrated Cleveland speech, will not take special offense if I venture to suggest that what is reputed as having fallen from his lips on this very memorable occasion

E

is not altogether in unison with that fine admonition of
Mr. Burke's, for which he expresses his own warm regard in another one of his public addresses: "*We ought
to act in political affairs with all the moderation which does
not absolutely enervate that vigor, and guard that fervency of
spirit without which the best wishes for the public good must
evaporate in empty speculation.*" I will also add here that,
ten years subsequent to the delivery of this anti-compromise speech, Mr. Seward, as will be seen hereafter, distinguished himself not a little as a champion of compromise.

It was now evident,—that is to say, on the 4th of March,
1849—that a conflict of sectional forces was impending
which it would require all the vigilance, wisdom, and
energy of the best and ablest men that the whole republic contained to bring to a peaceful termination. *Sectionalism*, fierce and uncompromising, and which some began
to fear might prove *irrepressible* also, was now rampant
alike in the North and in the South, and redoubted chieftains on either side of Mason and Dixon's line were industriously organizing their forces for the coming collision.

General Taylor's administration, then occupying the
seats of executive trust in Washington, mainly, as was
very soon ascertained, under the influence and counsels
of Mr. Seward, whose energy, zeal, and adroitness as a
party tactician secured him an ascendency exceedingly
difficult to counteract, was not slow in marking out the
policy which it would adopt in regard to the vexed territorial question, which, as has been seen, had been *pur-
posely* left in an unsettled condition, with a view to the

attainment of ends which the light of subsequent events
has relieved from the obscurity which originally en-
shrouded them. The highest historic authority which
could be cited on this interesting point (Mr. Greeley's
American Conflict) contains the following precise and
important statement:

"The new administration appears to have promptly
resolved on its course. It decided to invite and favor an
early organization of both California and New Mexico
(including all the vast area recently ceded by Mexico,
apart from Texas proper) as *incipient states*, and to urge
their admission as such into the Union at the earliest
practicable day. Of course it was understood that, being
thus organized, in the absence of both slaveholders and
slaves, they would almost *necessarily* become *free states.*"

It will not be denied that this was the very first occasion in our annals in which an American president had
regarded himself as justified in intermeddling with territories in an incipient and as yet only partially organized
condition, for the purpose of swelling the number of sovereign members of the confederacy; and the precedent
was justly felt to be one of most alarming import by
many who were, upon other and independent grounds,
quite willing to see California enter the Union, by reason
of the fact that both California and New Mexico were
yet *under strict military rule*, and could be scarcely expected to act in this most important transaction with that
independence and exemption from exterior influence
which is in all such cases confessedly so eminently desirable. In response to a special congressional call for
information on this subject, the frank and outspoken sol-

dier then in the executive chair did not hesitate to confess that he had declared to the people of the territories
in question his "desire that they should, if prepared to
comply with the requisitions of the Constitution of the
United States, form a plan of a state Constitution, and
submit the same to Congress, with a prayer for admission
into the Union as a state." It was not to be expected
that the territories thus encouraged to act would long delay the putting on of the *wedding garment*, preparatory to
the political banquet to which they had been thus affec-
tionately invited. General Riley, then military govern-
or of California, under instructions from Washington, issued a proclamation calling into existence a convention '
of the people of California, the delegates to which body
were in a few weeks elected, after which, with all practicable dispatch, they came together, and proceeded to
frame their state Constitution. It must be confessed
that no one at all acquainted with the general character
of the soil in California, and its extraordinary and wide-
ly-diffused mineral riches, would at all censure the enterprising and astute population of that fair and teeming region for preferring to exclude slave labor altogether from
their newly-organized state, to the introduction of myriads of the dusky sons of Africa, probably under the control and direction of selfish and mercenary owners, into
the most attractive and profitable mining districts, thus
crowding out the enterprising and hardy pioneers from
the old states, and stamping upon their honest industrial
labors the inevitable brand of *discredit*.

It is a curious and not altogether uninstructive fact,
that of the two United States senators from the new State

of California, Messrs. Fremont and Gwin, the latter a
large slaveholder at the time in the State of Mississippi,
was the mover and most prominent advocate of the *slavery prohibition clause* in the new Constitution, while his
senatorial colleague, destined to be in a few years the selected candidate of the Republican party for the presidency, was by far the most zealous *opponent* of that
clause!!

During the summer of 1849, Colonel Thomas H. Benton, who is well known to have been originally an open
opposer of General Taylor's plan providing for the admission of California and New Mexico as states into the
Federal Union, was seen to undergo a very sudden and
mysterious change, and commenced making in the State
of Missouri earnest and laborious speeches in favor of
that same policy. Circumstances presently to be narrated had awakened in my mind serious and painful distrust touching the movements and designs of this remarkable personage, whose bitter, but somewhat covert
opposition to Mr. Polk's administration (growing mainly
out of the fact that this gentleman had declined appointing him *lieutenant general* during the Mexican war over
the head of General Scott, and thus enabling him to mo-
nopolize the glory of conquering Mexico), had been for a
short time sufficiently manifest to those officially associated with him. His astounding attempt to procure the
nullification of the Mexican treaty, and thus deprive the
United States of the whole of that valuable domain recently acquired in California and New Mexico, by an extraordinary and unprecedented proceeding, the history of
which has not been heretofore sufficiently made known,

induced me to feel exceedingly anxious, and, as I yet think, very naturally, to aid in defeating his new scheme of reviving a decaying popularity by putting himself forward as the most prominent advocate of the measure of Californian admission, which it was already quite easy to perceive could not but prove otherwise than one of great, as well as deserved popularity. With such views I wrote a newspaper article addressed to a very eminent citizen of Virginia (not at all deserving to be inserted here, but to which the accidents of legislative contestation subsequently imparted a sort of semi-documentary stamp), in which I endeavored, in a very free and formal manner, to guard the public mind of the country against Mr. Benton's subtle devices, after which I addressed an earnest letter to Mr. Calhoun, who had been most virulently assailed by Mr. Benton a few weeks before in one of his public speeches in Missouri, communicating to him intelligence of this attack upon him, and urging him to lose no time in vindicating himself against what I could not but recognize as unprovoked and unmerited aspersions. Mr. Calhoun very soon wrote the desired response, a proof-sheet copy of which having been transmitted to me by its author, with a request that I would cause the same to be inserted in the Union newspaper in Washington; it made its appearance accordingly, without delay, in the columns of that journal. In my letter to Mr. Calhoun already referred to, I urged him most warmly to be himself the introducer and chief champion at the coming session of Congress of the measure of admission, giving him my reason for supposing that California would be, and ought to be admitted, and suggesting the *impolicy*, as well as *injustice* of opposing that measure, and the earnest desire which I felt that California should come into the Union, if possible, under *Southern auspices*, with a view to guarding against the invigoration of the sectional opposition to the South already, to some extent, existing, and with a view also to the building up for himself a truly national standing and popularity, which I thought could not be otherwise than beneficial to the whole country.   Though Mr. Calhoun consented, as has been stated, to write in response to Mr. Benton as I had requested, and gave to the world on that occasion the most finished and telling specimen of dialectic power that had ever emanated from his pen, yet I regret to say that he declined altogether the support of the admission policy, expressing the opinion that California, if allowed to enter the Union, would eventually become an enemy to the South and her cherished interests, and would completely destroy the political *equipoise* then so happily existing between the states of the North and those of the South. He added that he should have no objection whatever to seeing Utah admitted, since the Convention which had just held its session in that territory for the purpose of providing a state Constitution had *refused* to adopt a clause prohibitory of slavery, and inasmuch as he had satisfactorily learned that there were already in Utah some five or six hundred slaves of African derivation. Thus this negotiation ended; but I did not desist still from the efforts which I had initiated to secure the admission of California in a manner not to give increased irritation to the South; and hoping still that Mr. Calhoun might be induced to change his mind in regard to this

important matter before the approaching session of Congress would commence, I drew up a long and comprehensive bill covering the whole territorial subject, which,
after submitting the same to a few judicious and discerning friends, and obtaining their approval of it, I offered
to Mr. Calhoun, when he reached Washington, for his examination, declaring to him that I did not wish personally to move in the affair, but did still most intensely desire that he should take the *lead* on the question of admission, believing, as I did, that members of Congress
from the South would cordially acquiesce in any policy
touching California and the other new territories which
Mr. Calhoun might judge wise and proper. He returned
the bill which I had handed to him in a day or two,
promising still to examine its provisions at some early
moment more carefully; but finding him afterward resolutely opposed to the admission of California upon any
terms whatever, with great chagrin I relinquished all
hope of his complying with my wish in regard to this important matter, and afterward brought forward the same
bill in the Senate, as the Congressional Globe of that period will attest.

Before I proceed farther with congressional details in
connection with this very exciting question, I will now
narrate in a very concise manner the particulars of the
extraordinary conduct of Colonel Benton, which has been
above referred to, at the close of Mr. Polk's administration, and which I am sure it is high time that all AMERICA
should learn.

One morning, a gentleman of remarkable astuteness
and penetration, and who had been formerly a member

of Congress, but whose name it is needless that I should
at present disclose, called upon me at my room in the
Capitol, and laid before me facts showing very conclusively that Colonel Benton was then in collusion
with the Mexican minister resident in Washington for
the purpose of procuring the *rescission* of the Mexican
treaty, as heretofore indicated. I learned from him that
these individuals were constantly interchanging visits,
and that official letters signed by the Mexican minister
had been received at the Department of State, wherein
Mr. Buchanan was presiding at the time, urging, with singular ingenuity and force, that the treaty with the Mexican republic, by the instrumentality of which California
and New Mexico had both been obtained, was of no
earthly validity whatever, by reason of the fact that
what was somewhat loosely called a *protocol*—an official
paper subscribed by the ministers of the United States
who had previously negotiated the treaty—was so palpably repugnant to the provisions thereof, as necessarily, if
enforced, to effect its abrogation. I was farther advised
that Mr. Benton would very soon introduce this important subject in the Senate while that body should be in
executive session, and would offer a resolution for adoption correspondent with the views set forth in the letters
of the Mexican minister to the Secretary of State, which
have been already referred to. This extraordinary dis-
closure, fortified as, it was by numerous surrounding circumstances, awakened in my bosom mingled feelings of
indignation and of alarm. Great national interests seemed to be in jeopardy. Mr. Benton's peculiar political position at the time (that gentleman not having yet lost all

E 2

his former influence with the Democratic party, and having done much, of late, of a nature to soften down and conciliate his former party adversaries the Whigs), together with the weight and influence which he still possessed in the country at large, furnished, as I thought at the time, and as I yet think, ground for serious anxiety and apprehension. After consultation with several considerate friends, being mindful of the noted *test* to which Hamlet is described as subjecting his usurping uncle by an extemporized dramatic entertainment fitted to develop aught of "rottenness" which might perchance be lurking "in the state of Denmark," I delivered one morning in the Senate a short address (which may be found in the Congressional Globe of that period), accompanying the same, as far as I was capable, with appropriate glances and gestures, so as at least to shadow forth to any guilty conscience which might chance to be in presence the painful suspicions which I had conceived, and "probe it" also, if possible, "to the very quick." This address concluded with the following well-known couplet from Pope:

"Who would not *smile*, if such a man there be?
Who would not blush, if *Atticus* were he?"

Whether there was real "blenching" or not in the distrusted quarter, I shall leave it to those present on the occasion specified to decide. I was, I confess, exceedingly desirous that the aged senator from Missouri should desist from the execution of his scheme of territorial spoliation, if he could be induced to do so either by his own fears of personal disgrace or by the persuasions of friends; and I awaited the result of events with patience, though certainly not without carrying forward diligently the scrutiny which I had already commenced. In a day or two thereafter Mr. Polk ceased to be president, and General Taylor became domiciliated at the White House. Having unlimited confidence in the love of country which glowed in the pure bosom of this time-worn chieftain, and entertaining a high personal esteem for the members of his cabinet, I resolved to make an early appeal to those then in power to aid, with whatever of influence they possessed, in defeating any measure which Mr. Benton might introduce in the Senate looking to the doing away of the Mexican treaty. Before this intention could be fully executed, two Democratic senators from the West, whose names, were I to mention them, would not fail to command the most profound homage, came to me at the Capitol, directly from the presence of Mr. Buchanan, bearing to me a message from that gentleman requesting that I should lose no time in calling upon him, for the purpose of being made acquainted by him with all the particulars connected with the correspondence which had several weeks before taken place between this personage as Secretary of State and the Mexican minister. It should be here observed that Mr. Buchanan yet occupied the State Department, having been requested by General Taylor to continue therein until it might become convenient to Mr. Clayton, then otherwise much occupied, to relieve him. I will here mention an additional fact, which I could not consider altogether immaterial. The two senators who had thus summoned me to the presence of Mr. Buchanan had been, up to that time, the ardent admirers of Mr. Benton, and had frankly de-

clared, in this very interview, that they had before that
time been often disposed to find fault with what they had
deemed my over-censorious course toward Mr. Benton.
The interview with Mr. Buchanan did accordingly take
place, but barely in time to prevent mischievous consequences in the Senate. The adroit and skillful engineer
had already commenced his work in that body with all
the artistic skill which his great Parliamentary experience could put in use, and it had now become an intensely interesting question whether or not this same wily engineer could be "*hoist on his own petard.*" Mr. Buchanan
informed me that he felt well satisfied that General Taylor and his cabinet fully approved the position which he
had assumed in the correspondence already referred to in
regard to the "protocol;" that they would do all in their
power (as he thought) to uphold the treaty, and to preserve the national domain against the dangers to which
it stood exposed from the course of Mr. Benton; but
suggested, in addition, that he and I should visit the
White House in the morning anterior to the meeting of
the Senate (then in special session), and procure, if we
could, a formal official declaration from the President or
his expected premier, Mr. Clayton, which, when exhibited
to the Whig members of the Senate, would advise them
fully as to the views and wishes of the existing administration. Early on the following morning, before yet the
hour of ten o'clock had arrived, Mr. Buchanan and myself were on our way to the presidential mansion. Just
as the carriage which was conveying us thither drove opposite the Department of State, Colonel James Watson
Webb, formerly editor of the New York Courier and

Enquirer, made his appearance, told us he knew what was taking us to the presence of General Taylor, and requested to be allowed to accompany us upon our patriotic mission. To this proposition we cheerfully acceded, and our carriage took us without delay to the place of destination. When we reached the White House we learned that the cabinet was then in session. We sent our names to Mr. Clayton, and asked for an immediate interview, which having been accorded to us, we proceeded to lay the matter so near our hearts before this courteous and accomplished personage. His conduct on the occasion was most proper and becoming. He told us that the subject of the treaty and the protocol had been before the President and his cabinet; that they could see no repugnance whatever between the said treaty and the protocol. He said he had thoroughly examined the official correspondence which had taken place, and that he was prepared to endorse most fully every line and sentence in Mr. Buchanan's letters to the Mexican minister. After this declaration had been made, I requested Mr. Clayton to embody, or cause to be embodied in a short resolution, the views which he entertained on this important subject, and accordingly he dictated such a resolution, which one of our company took down in pencil-marks from his lips. This resolution I took back to the Senate, and exhibited it to several Whig members of that body, who seemed very much gratified therewith; but, to make assurance "*double sure*," the then attorney general, the Hon. Reverdy Johnson, was dispatched by General Taylor to the Senate, and, long before the discussion of the morning was commenced, this great question of state was virtualy

settled.   Mr. Webster came to me, I well remember, in
his most solemn and formal manner, and declared, in
more zealous and pointed language than he was at all
accustomed to use on ordinary occasions, his disgust and
indignation at what he understood Mr. Benton was attempting to effect, and assured me that there was no
Whig member of the Senate who would not vote with
the Democratic members of that body in defense of our
territorial interests under the treaty.   Not knowing
whether yet the injunction of secrecy in relation to the
proceedings then pending has been removed, I shall only
say now that, whatever may have been the nature of the
proposition then pending in the Senate, there were only
two speeches made in that body — one in favor of and
one in opposition to this proposition, and that the Senate
then voted it down at once, *with only one dissentient vote.*
Whose vote that was I leave to be conjectured.

It will surprise no one now, I presume, to learn that I
considered myself justified by such facts as I have mentioned, and which various of the senators then upon the
stage of action, and who yet survive, are prepared to attest, in doing what I could legitimately and fairly do to
weaken Mr. Benton's influence in the country, and to cir-
cumscribe his capacity for public mischief.   Hence my
assailment of him in the newspapers in the summer of
1849, as already stated, and my anxiety to prevent his
obtaining the lead on the California question of admission.   But my opposition to Mr. Benton did by no means
stop here.   I determined to deal him an additional blow,
which, if the Democratic members of the Senate should
prove as mindful of the honor of the country, as well as

of their own individual dignity, as I hoped, could not but be fatal to him. On the first day of the approaching session of Congress I determined to enter the Democratic senatorial caucus, which was uniformly convoked on that day, and move that Mr. Benton, upon charges which I was prepared to array against him, should be discontinued as chairman of the Committee on Foreign Affairs, well knowing that if this movement should be successful in caucus, the Democratic party having a decided majority in the Senate, Mr. Benton would be of necessity ousted from his position as the head of that important committee. In point of fact, I afterward pursued this very course. I moved in caucus that William R. King, of Alabama, should be chairman of the Committee on Foreign Affairs instead of Thomas H. Benton, which motion, after two mornings spent in earnest controversy, was carried by a majority *of a single vote;* soon after which Mr. Benton resigned his place as a member of said committee. Whether these proceedings had any influence in Missouri afterward in securing Mr. Benton's defeat for senatorial re-election from that state, which occurred during the subsequent winter, I have never specially inquired, and it is not at all important now that this question should be settled. It is a respected maxim that *the dead should not be spoken of but with commendation.* I am not at all disposed to violate this maxim upon the present occasion; but, as Mr. Benton was accustomed to observe when living, "*The truth of history must be vindicated.*"

I shall decline saying any thing as to the *motives* by which he was actuated in this strange affair of the protocol, nor shall I now descant upon the moral qualities, whether good or bad, which entered into his character, either as a public man or as a private citizen. He was certainly a man of much natural strength of intellect, and of a most capacious and retentive memory. He possessed much knowledge of various kinds, and as a writer of pure and nervous English he had few equals. He was exceedingly deficient in extemporaneous oratorical power, had a bad voice, a forbidding, dogmatical, and unconciliatory manner, showed but little respect for the feelings of others whom he met in debate, and, as a politician, was not over-scrupulous as to the means which he employed for the attainment of his ends. He never spoke in the Senate except upon the most deliberate preparation, and then always from copious notes, and his principal speeches were generally written out in full before their delivery. While General Jackson was in the presidential office, and Mr. Blair was editing the Globe, he was eminently successful as a party leader in the Senate. When another Pharaoh arose "who did not know Joseph," and when the Globe was fated to give way to the Union, under the direction of the venerable Thomas Ritchie, the renowned champion of the celebrated expunging resolution seemed to have forever lost his political *equipoise*, and his conduct as a senator was thenceforth such as not only to grieve his remaining friends most sorely, but seriously to impair his legislative usefulness, as well as to enfeeble his claims to influence the opinions and conduct of such as had looked up to him at one time with sentiments of profound esteem and admiration. In view of these sad and painful scenes, we may well exclaim with Mr. Burke, "*What shadows we are, and what shadows we pursue!*"

CHAPTER VII.

Review of General Taylor's non-action Policy.—Painful and exciting Rumors in regard to the Instrumentalities employed by him to carry that Policy into Operation.—Intense Alarm awakened among Patriots as to the Fate of the Country. — Mr. Clay leaves his own Home, and comes to Washington upon a Mission of Pacification.—He is met upon his arrival there with general Cordiality and Respect.—Mr. Benton attempts to inveigle him into a false Position in regard to the Measure of admitting California, and is for a time successful.—Mr. Clay's Programme of Adjustment, and the "five bleeding Wounds."—This Gentleman severs his Alliance with Mr. Benton, and becomes the Champion of the famous Omnibus Scheme.—His magnanimous waver of certain abstract Opinions with a View to general Conciliation.—First meeting of the Nashville Convention.—Great Excitement consequent upon its Proceedings.—Anti-slavery Movements about the same Period, and Mr. Seward's anti-compromise Speech.—Resolution introduced by the Author, several weeks before, for the raising of the famous Committee of Thirteen, finally pushed to a Vote at the Instance of Mr. Cass.—Eminently patriotic Conduct of Mr. Webster on this Occasion.—Resolution finally carried.—Mr. Clay appointed Chairman thereof, who speedily brings in his Report, upon which an animated Discussion occurs.

THE scheme of policy which, in the summer of 1849, it was generally known that the administration of General Taylor had deliberately adopted, by which it was expected that by an adroit and subtle process, for which there had been then no example, slavery would be at once and forever shut out from the territories recently acquired (it being " understood," as is now frankly confessed, " that being thus organized, in the absence of both slaveholders and slaves, they would almost necessarily be-

come free states"), leaves no ground for surprise that, in
the condition of the popular mind at that period existing throughout the South, intense excitement and alarm
should have every where prevailed. It was discovered
that, within a month or two, in some mysterious manner,
one of the great parties to the "*irrepressible conflict*,"
which had been so oracularly announced, had already
put on the armor of war and regularly taken the field;
that all the appliances which government could muster
were ready to be used, yea, were *being at that moment* used
to render that party ultimately triumphant; and that the
boasted equiponderance of power upon which the South
had so long confidently relied was about to disappear forever. Popular meetings were immediately called in every Southern state, and indeed almost in every neighborhood of each state, for the purpose of remonstrating respectfully but earnestly against the menaced infraction
of slaveholding rights. Inflammatory resolutions were
adopted at all these meetings, and from some of them
strong and eloquent addresses went forth, calculated to
produce alarm, distrust, and alienation in bosoms where
quiet, and confidence, and fraternal affection had been
formerly wont to dwell. Grave and thoughtful statesmen were grieved and astonished at the prospect of coming evils; and fierce sectional demagogues, the pest of
all extended republics, were every where engaged in fan-
ning the embers of dissatisfaction; ambitiously hoping,
doubtless, that in the whirlwind which seemed to be now
coming on, even such miscreants as themselves might
perchance be tossed into positions of airy and lofty elevation. The whole republic was convulsed as by a moral

earthquake, and desponding patriots began to look forward to those scenes of civil ruin against which Washington in his Farewell Address had so impressively warned his countrymen. In looking back now to that fearful
period in American annals, the votary of classic lore is
almost irresistibly reminded of that almost unequaled
picture in the Æneid in which the bard of Mantua de-
scribes with so much vivacity and force the fierce and
tumultuous waves of the tempest-raised ocean. For our
consolation, amid the perils which his imagination con-
jures into existence, the great Latin poet presently brings
forward Neptune, with his all-potent trident, to compose
the vexed waves of his watery domain—likening the sea-
god, in his auspicious coming, to "some man of earth re-
vered for his purity and worth," who, suddenly presenting himself to the view of the seditious multitude stirred
up to violent commotion, "by persuasive eloquence rules
their passions and calms their breasts." So was it precisely in 1850, when the venerable Henry Clay, of Kentucky, left his own loved and peaceful home upon a sacred mission of peace, and visited the Capitol of the republic, where he beheld, on his arrival, all the elements
of discord and unfriendly feeling fiercely at work. He
at once addressed himself to the mighty task before him,
and happily, in a few months, by the employment of mild
and pacific expedients, saved his country from that threatened "conflict" which, most fortunately for that same
country, this admired statesman did not by any means
regard as of a hopelessly "*irrepressible*" character.

From the day of Mr. Clay's arrival in Washington, it
was evident that all in Congress who were the sincere

and enlightened friends of the Union recognized him as
their leader. All seemed to accord to him the purest and
most patriotic motives; though it is true that there were
selfish and designing factionists to be found here and
there, who, perceiving that he was in the way of their
own cherished schemes, affected to apprehend mischief
to the public weal from his influence. Mr. Webster
met him in the most cordial and deferential manner, as
was due to his superior years; and I saw Mr. Calhoun,
after consulting a friend or two about him touching the
propriety of his making the first approach to one from
whom, a few years earlier, he had parted with some unkindness, advance with manly stride toward the seat of
the great statesman of the West and offer to him his most
affectionate salutations. I had the honor of being presented to Mr. Clay, in his own parlor at the National Hotel, by my venerated friend from Michigan, General Cass.
The meeting between these two illustrious citizens was
marked with much affection and respect on both sides,
and it would seem that both of them even then anticipated the new ties of enduring affection which were soon
to spring up between them. That the relations between
Mr. Clay and General Cass did in a few weeks grow most
kind and confidential is known already to many. It is
perhaps not so well known to all, though, or is at least
perhaps not now so vividly remembered by them, that
each of these personages displayed, in the progress of a
few months, a most magnanimous and self-sacrificing temper toward the other. I recollect well that when, on one
occasion, the warm political friends of General Cass, anticipating that much popularity would accrue to the indi-

vidual who should be most conspicuous in effecting a fair
and honest settlement of existing sectional difficulties,
urged this gentleman to allow his name to be used in
connection with the position of chairman of the celebrated
Committee of Thirteen, suggesting that, should Mr. Clay
be allowed to become chairman of that committee, he
would, in all probability, be elevated to the presidency at
the next election, General Cass at once declared, "Well,
be it so; Mr. Clay is entitled on every ground to be the.
chairman of the committee; he alone can rescue the
country from its present dangers; and if he shall succeed in doing it, I shall vote for him for President with
the greatest pleasure myself." In the winter of 1851, '2,
I heard Mr. Clay repeatedly declare that, while Mr. Fillmore was his first choice for president, in the event of
this latter gentleman's failing to obtain the nomination
of his party, he should then prefer General Cass for the
presidency to any man in the republic. These rare examples of disinterestedness and elevated patriotism are
worthy to be borne eternally in the minds of their countrymen of the present and of all future generations.

Mr. Clay had hardly reached Washington City before
Mr. Benton, not recognizing, as did all others, the peculiar sacredness of his mission to the capital, made early
and prodigious efforts to appropriate his well-earned influence and popularity to the accomplishment of his own
favorite designs. With this view he very soon flattering-
ly informed him that he and his son-in-law, Colonel Fremont, had determined to rely mainly upon his efforts for
securing the early admission of the newly-formed State
of California, and requested him, indeed, to *initiate* the

measure. Mr. Clay, as he afterward frankly acknowledged, had not duly examined all the surrounding circumstances, nor become convinced yet, as he subsequently was, that the attempt to force hastily and prematurely the act of admission as a *separate* measure, while the other outstanding questions growing out of slavery remained unadjusted, might add seriously to the existing troubles of the country, and be productive of many injurious consequences of a permanent character. He agreed, therefore, to introduce the bill as requested, and at an early day; which he in fact afterward did, and in a most graceful and impressive manner.

It was evident to many members of both Houses of Congress, in the condition of things then existing, that, for the reasons already stated, any attempt to bring California in as a *separate* measure would be productive of much mischievous wrangling and contention in these bodies, and might, in addition, produce far more serious consequences elsewhere. Mr. Clay, in a very eloquent speech delivered by him in the Senate, had referred to *five bleeding wounds* then existing in the body politic, and had insisted upon the necessity of stanching all of them as soon as possible. He was known, when he used this figurative language, which has at different times been the subject of so much pointless criticism, to have had in view the five following points: 1st, the admission of California; 2d, the settlement of the Texan boundary; 3d, an adequate amendment of the existing Fugitive Slave Law; 4th, the doing away with the traffic in slaves in the District of Columbia; 5th, the establishment of a territorial government for all the domain acquired from Mexico outside of the boundaries to be assigned to California. He was sincerely anxious to settle all these questions, and was fully resolved to leave none of them open, if he could avoid it, to prove thereafter a source of needless irritation. His desire was to adjust all the points of dispute existing between the two sections upon equitable and satisfactory principles, and leave no heart-burning or discontent remaining in any quarter. He did not perceive at first that, in order to effect a settlement so comprehensive as he desired, it would be indispensable to *conjoin* the various measures, so as to get through Congress several enactments which were in themselves not a little odious to a portion of the states and people of the Union, by force of the overwhelming popularity in certain other states, of the measure of Californian admission; and that there was great danger, if California should be admitted, as Mr. Benton and others were so unwisely and illiberally urging, *as a separate measure*, and in advance of all the other enactments the adoption of which he aimed to procure, that the other enactments referred to, or at least some of the most essential of them, might thereafter never pass at all. Besides, he had been authentically informed that the state of party feeling in the House of Representatives was daily getting more and more excited and acrimonious, and that some scenes had already occurred in that body which more or less portended even the spilling of blood in unfraternal strife — an occurrence which he could not but feel might be made to result in extended civil war. Under these circumstances, Mr. Clay came to the conclusion that a *single measure of compromise and adjustment*, embracing all the contested points, would be the most wise and sal-

utary expedient which could be devised; and he was
farther persuaded by certain friends of either House of
Congress in whose good sense and disinterested patriotism he reposed the utmost confidence that no good could
possibly arise, but, on the contrary, in all probability,
much of evil, from pertinaciously insisting that Congress
should come to a distinct vote upon the two *abstract* questions touching the constitutional authority of the Federal
government to abolish slavery in the District of Columbia, and to exclude it from the territories. Never did
Mr. Clay evince more true statesmanship, more elevated
patriotism, and a nobler moral courage, than he did in
consenting to change his attitude in the manner mentioned, in view of all the imperious considerations which
have been specified; and yet this, the noblest act perhaps
of his long public life, has been the subject of most vehement and acrimonious reproach in numerous quarters,
and was, in a short time also, to bring him once more
into fierce collision with his ancient antagonist, Mr. Benton, with whom he had been at variance for some twenty
years or more, until they had been persuaded, about two
years antecedent, by mutual friends, to resume their early relations of kind social intercourse.

As soon as Mr. Clay consented to take this course, I
lost no time in bringing forward a resolution in the Senate which proposed to raise a committee of thirteen, to
which should be referred the several sets of resolutions
embracing the subject of slavery then pending in the
Senate; and I continued to urge, morning after morning,
the adoption of the resolution for the formation of said
committee for several weeks before success was eventually achieved.

Meanwhile several movements were in progress elsewhere, of which I deem it expedient now to take a passing notice.

The excitement in the South had culminated in the assemblage of the celebrated Nashville Convention, where much was said and done which seemed indicative of coming troubles. Another session of the same body was expected soon to occur, which might or might not, according to the course of events, yet painfully uncertain, adopt extreme measures for the preservation of cherished Southern rights, supposed by not a few to be in danger of speedy immolation. In another and opposite quarter the Abolition caldron was beginning most ominously to seethe and bubble, emitting copious effusions of cloudy vapor, and was in fact almost ready to overboil from the intense heat which the breath of fierce agitators, with capacious, bellows-like lungs, was fast kindling beneath it. The doors of Faneuil Hall had not yet refused to turn upon their "golden hinges" to let into that famed sanctuary of fervent and sublime patriotism in the olden time, the noblest, the wisest, and most renowned of all the glorious defenders of the Constitution and the Union. But the praise of Daniel Webster was no longer universally upon the lips of his once almost idolizing fellow-citizens of Boston, and his great heart was almost ready to break under the mingled influence of the fears which he felt for his country's safety, and the profound chagrin and anguish which he could not but experience when every mail from the East brought to him fresh intelligence of the ingratitude of some whom he had so long faithfully served, and the profound delusion of not a few from

F

whose former steadiness of temper and calm equipoise of intellect he had confidently expected that encouragement and support, amid the painful and perplexing labors in which he was then involved, which it is indeed melancholy to recollect were *not* accorded to him.   It must be confessed. though, that there were some then in Congress, both from the North and from the South, who did not seem to feel any serious alarm for the fate of the country. Among these, Mr. Seward, of New York, in so many ways distinguished in the latter years of the republic, was apparently as calm and unexcited as he could have been in times most free from commotion and conflict; and I well recollect about this period that this gentleman expressed himself as follows: "And this brings me to the great and all-absorbing argument that the Union is in danger of being dissolved, and that it can only be saved by *compromise.*   I do not know what I would not do to save the Union, and therefore I shall bestow upon this subject a very deliberate consideration.

"I do not overlook the fact that the entire delegation from the slave states, although they differ in regard to the details of the compromise proposed, and, perhaps, in regard to the exact circumstances of the crisis, seem to concur in this momentous warning.   Nor do I doubt at all the patriotic devotion to the Union which is expressed by those from whom this warning proceeds.   And yet, sir, although such warnings have been uttered with impassioned solemnity in my hearing every day for near three months, my confidence in the Union remains unshaken.   I think they are to be received with no inconsiderable distrust, because they are uttered under the influence of a controlling interest to be secured, a paramount object to be gained, and that is, an equilibrium of power in the republic. I think they are to be received with even more distrust, because, with the most profound respect, they are uttered under an obviously high excitement. Nor is that excitement an unnatural one. It is a law of our nature that the passions disturb the reason and judgment just in proportion to the importance of the occasion, and the consequent necessity for calmness and candor. I think they are to be distrusted, because there is a diversity of opinion in regard to the nature and operation of this excitement. The senators from some states say that it has brought all parties in their own region into unanimity. The honorable senator from Kentucky (Mr. Clay) says that the danger lies in the violence of party spirit, and refers us for proof to the difficulties which attend the organization of the House of Representatives.

"Sir, in my humble judgment, it is not the fierce conflict of parties that we are seeing and hearing, but, on the contrary, it is the agony of distracted parties—a convulsion resulting from the too narrow foundations of both the great parties, and of all parties—foundations laid in compromises of natural justice and of human liberty. A question, a moral question, transcending the too narrow creeds of parties, has arisen; the public conscience expands with it, and the green withes of party associations give way and break, and fall off from it. No, sir; it is not the state that is dying of the fever of party spirit. It is merely a paralysis of parties, premonitory, however, of their restoration, with new elements of health and vigor to be imbibed from that spirit of the age which is so justly called Progress. Nor is the evil that of unlicensed, irregular, and turbulent faction. We are told that twenty legislatures are in session, burning like furnaces, heating and inflaming the popular passions: But these twenty legislatures are constitutional furnaces. They are performing their customary functions, imparting healthful heat and vitality while within their constitutional jurisdiction. If they rage beyond its limits, the popular passions of this country are not at all, I think, in danger of being inflamed to excess. No, sir; let none of these fires be extinguished. Forever let them burn and blaze. They are neither ominous meteors nor baleful comets, but planets; and, bright and intense as their heat may be, it is their native temperature, and they must still obey the law which, by attraction toward this solar centre, holds them in their spheres."

Early one morning at this troublous crisis, General Lewis Cass, ever vigilant and active when the interests of the country demanded that he should be watching and laboring for its welfare, visited me at my boarding-house, and communicated to me the anxiety which he began to feel for the fate of the resolution which I had introduced for raising the Committee of Thirteen, and urged me to bring the Senate to a vote upon it as early as possible, suggesting even that if I could ascertain that there were a sufficient number of the senatorial friends of the resolution then in the city to secure its adoption, to call it up and invoke definite action upon it that very morning. Thus admonished, though feeble in health, I traversed the city of Washington in every direction, in order to ascertain what senators would be probably in attendance; and coming to the conclusion that if Mr. Webster, who had been absent from the Senate for several days, could be induced to occupy his seat that morning, the resolution could, in all probability, be carried through by a meagre majority, I immediately dispatched a note to this gentleman's house by a special messenger, apprising him of the expected movement, and of the desire which I felt for his presence and co-operative aid. He came to the Senate accordingly. No sooner did this gentleman reach his seat than he was surrounded by an earnest crowd of his New England friends, some of whom, as I afterward learned from his own lips, came to dissuade him from voting for my pacificatory resolution. He likewise informed me, in an interview which presently occurred between us, that he had received while in his seat, only a few minutes before, two pressing epistolary missives from political friends in the House of Representatives, urging him not farther to risk his popularity and influence by efforts in support of measures of compromise. Under these trying circumstances, this august personage proposed to me that I should agree to unite with him in supporting a motion which he proposed in an hour or two to offer for taking up for *separate consideration* the California Bill, in consideration of his aiding me in getting my own resolution immediately passed. He stated that, if allowed to make known this arrangement before giving his vote for raising the Committee of Thirteen, he thought it would satisfy certain of his friends whose sensibilities he was unwilling needlessly to wound. To this proposition I could not but ac-

cede, considering, as I did, and as I then explained to
Mr. Webster himself, that if all the measures of compromise, *including the bill for admitting California*, should
have been once referred to the Committee of Thirteen,
there were insuperable parliamentary obstacles to taking
up any one of these bills *separately*, unless a motion for
the reconsideration of the resolution of reference should
be first carried. Immediately after this conversation,
Mr. Webster returned to his seat, when I called up my
resolution. When it was put upon its passage, Mr. Webster rose and stated his intention to vote for raising the
Committee of Thirteen, but took occasion also to mention
in the hearing of the Senate the arrangement which he
and I had entered into, as already described. This immediately called forth language of indignant surprise
from my own senatorial colleague, Mr. Davis, from Mr.
Butler, of South Carolina, and Mr. Clemens, of Alabama,
who seemed to object very strongly to the *private* understanding between Mr. Webster and myself of which they
had just been apprised, and one or the other of them in-
sinuated something about the movement being an *illicit*
one, and threatened even to vote against the resolution.
I went immediately to the seats of these gentlemen, made
such an explanation of what had occurred as the circumstances so easily admitted of, and succeeded in so far
pacifying them that they all voted for the resolution,
which presently passed.

The committee had now to be formed. According to
the terms of the resolution which had been adopted, the
Senate would have to designate the members of the committee by ballot. Senatorial comity allowing the mover

of the resolution the privilege of naming the persons to be placed on the committee, I caused a list of the members thereof to be laid on the desks of the senators, and the following gentlemen were *unanimously* voted into the committee: Henry Clay, of Kentucky, chairman; Dickinson, of New York; Phelps, of Vermont; Bell, of Tennessee; Cass, of Michigan; Webster, of Massachusetts; Berrien, of Georgia; Cooper, of Pennsylvania; Downs, of Louisiana; King, of Alabama; Mangum, of North Carolina; Mason, of Virginia; and Bright, of Indiana. Six of these gentlemen were Democrats, six of them were Whigs; six were Southern men, and six were Northern men; with Henry Clay, the Nestor of the Senate (who was now no longer a party man, and who had emphatically announced himself as knowing "*no North and no South, no East and no West*"), as chairman. A fairer committee was never formed, and no committee was ever better fitted, as the event soon proved, wisely and successfully to execute the important task allotted to it.

In a few days, Mr. Clay, who had retired to the country in order to draw the bills which the committee was expected to report, returned to the Senate, and announced the following *programme* for the future action of the Senate, accompanying the same with an elaborate and well-drawn report, which it is judged unnecessary to insert here:

"1st. The admission of any new state or states formed out of Texas to be postponed until they shall hereafter present themselves to be received into the Union, when it will be the duty of Congress fairly and faithfully to execute the compact with Texas by admitting such new state or states.

"2d. The admission forthwith of California into the Union, with the boundaries which she has proposed.

"3d. The establishment of territorial governments, without the Wilmot Proviso, for New Mexico and Utah, embracing all the territory recently acquired from Mexico not contained in the boundaries of California.

"4th. The combination of these two last measures in the same bill.

"5th. The establishment of the western and northern boundaries of Texas, and the exclusion from her jurisdiction of all New Mexico, with the grant to Texas of a pecuniary equivalent; and the section for that purpose to be incorporated in the bill admitting California and establishing territorial governments -for Utah and New Mexico.

"6th. More effectual enactments of law to secure the prompt delivery of persons bound to service or labor in one state under the laws thereof, who escape into another state; and,

"7th. Abstaining from abolishing slavery, but, under a heavy penalty, prohibiting the slave-trade in the District of Columbia."

CHAPTER VIII.

Great Compromise Struggle of 1850.—Mr. Clay and Mr. Webster the principal Figures in the Picture.—Mr. Webster's 7th of March Speech, and its prodigious Effect upon the Public Mind.—Striking Extracts therefrom.—Mr. Calhoun's last Speech in the Senate, in which he urges that the Admission of California shall be made a *test* Question.—Emphatic Protest by the Author to this Portion of the Speech, and painful Altercation with Mr. Calhoun in Reference to the disputed Point.—Proceedings of the Nashville Convention.—Wise and patriotic Conduct of Judge Sharkey, the President thereof, which prevents immediate Mischief.—Judge Sharkey arrives in Washington, and is offered the Department of War, which he declines.—Some Account of Judge Sharkey's Life and Character.   •

THE contest between the friends of peace and those whose conduct was at this period seriously threatening to disturb the public repose, was now fairly in progress. Of all the champions of the measures of compromise, Mr. Clay and Mr. Webster undoubtedly commanded the largest share of the public respect, and their course in Congress awakened in various quarters much both of commendation and of dispraise. Mr. Clay had delivered at an early period of the session several speeches of marked ability and eloquence, which had called forth gratifying responses in all parts of the republic. It was now evident that old party prejudices were fast giving way to sentiments of a very different character all over the land. Public men of considerable prominence and of no mean influence, who had been the steady and unswerving op-

F 2

ponents of the measures of policy in past times advocated by Mr. Clay even from the commencement of their
political career, were every day approaching him kindly,
and tendering to him their future friendship and support.
Many of the old supporters of Jackson were seen to come
into his presence, and were heard to avow their devotion
to his person and character. Men from whom he had
been estranged for twenty years, and who were known
to have pursued him at a former period with charges of
a nature even to touch his reputation for integrity, were
now heard to disavow these charges formally, and to confess that they had done him the most cruel injustice. It
was most evident to all that no living man could do so
much as Mr. Clay then had it in his power to do to suppress the commotion which was already furiously raging,
and to keep in abeyance, for the present at least, the horrors of intestine conflict. About this time, at Mr. Clay's
instance, I addressed numerous letters to eminent and
well-known persons residing in various states of the
Union, asking their opinion of the compromise measures,
their replies to which were uniformly published in the
Union newspaper, then edited by the veteran Ritchie, and
were supposed by some to have had a more or less beneficial effect in maturing public sentiment, and in removing prejudice from the minds of good citizens.

Mr. Webster's 7th of March speech, delivered, as will
be observed, anterior to the raising of the Committee of
Thirteen, had produced beneficial effects every where,
which effects were displaying themselves throughout the
republic. His statement of facts was generally looked
upon as unanswerable; his argumentative conclusions

appeared to be inevitable; his mild, conciliatory, and persuasive tone had penetrated and softened the sensibilities of all patriots. What reasonable and well-intentioned man could indeed refuse his assent to such prop-' ositions as the following, which are extracted from that same memorable speech? "My opinion has been, that we have territory enough, and that we should follow the Spartan maxim, 'Improve, adorn what you have;' seek no farther. I think that it was in some observations that I made on the Three-million Loan Bill that I avowed this sentiment. In short, sir, it has been avowed quite as often, in as many places, and before as many assemblies, as any humble opinions of mine ought to be avowed.

"But now that, under certain conditions, Texas is in the Union, with all her territory, as a slave state, with a solemn pledge also that, if she shall be divided into many states, those states may come in as slave states south of 36° 30', how are we to deal with this subject? I know no way of honest legislation, when the proper time comes for the enactment, but to carry into effect all that we have stipulated to do. I do not entirely agree with my honorable friend from Tennessee,* that, as soon as the time comes when she is entitled to another representative, we should create a new state. On former occasions, in creating new states out of territories, we have generally gone upon the idea that, when the population of the territory amounts to about sixty thousand, we would consent to its admission as a state. But it is quite a different thing when a state is divided, and two or more

* Mr. Bell.

states made out of it. It does not follow in such a case that the same rule of apportionment should be applied. That, however, is a matter for the consideration of Congress when the proper time arrives. I may not then be here; I may have no vote to give on the occasion; but I wish it to be distinctly understood that, according to my view of the matter, this government is solemnly pledged, by law and contract, to create new states out of Texas, with her consent, when her population shall justify and call for such a proceeding, and, so far as such states are formed out of Texan territory lying south of 36° 30', to let them come in as slave states. That is the meaning of the contract which our friends, the Northern Democracy, have left us to fulfill; and I, for one, mean to fulfill it; because I will not violate the faith of the government. What I mean to say is, that the time for the admission of new states formed out of Texas, the number of such states, their boundaries, the requisite amount of population, and all other things connected with the admission, are in the free discretion of Congress, except this, to wit, that, when new states formed out of Texas are to be admitted, they have a right, by legal stipulation and contract, to come in as slave states.

" Now, as to California and New Mexico, I hold slavery to be excluded from those territories by a law even superior to that which admits and sanctions it in Texas: I mean the law of Nature, of physical geography—the law of the formation of the earth. That law settles for ever, with a strength beyond all terms of human enactment, that slavery can not exist in California or New Mexico. Understand me, sir; I mean slavery as we regard it—the slavery of the colored race as it exists in the Southern States. I shall not discuss the point, but leave it to the learned gentlemen who have undertaken to discuss it; but I suppose there is no slavery of that description in California now. I understand that *peonism*, a sort of penal servitude, exists there, or, rather, a sort of voluntary sale of a man and his offspring for debt, an arrangement of a peculiar nature known to the law of Mexico. But what I mean to say is, that it is as impossible that African slavery, as we see it among us, should find its way, or be introduced into California and New Mexico, as any other natural impossibility. California and New Mexico are Asiatic in their formation and scenery. They are composed of vast ridges of mountains of great height, with broken ridges and deep valleys. The sides of these mountains are entirely barren, their tops capped by perennial snow. There may be in California, now made free by its Constitution, and no doubt there are, some tracts of valuable land. But it is not so in New Mexico. Pray, what is the evidence which every gentleman must have obtained on this subject from information sought by himself or communicated by others? I have inquired and read all I could find, in order to acquire information on this important subject. What is there in New Mexico that could by any possibility induce any body to go there with slaves? There are some narrow strips of tillable land on the borders of the rivers, but the rivers themselves dry up before midsummer is gone. All that the people can do in that region is to raise some little articles, some little wheat for their *tortillas*, and that by irrigation. And who expects to see a hundred black

men cultivating tobacco, corn, cotton, rice, or any thing
else, on lands in New Mexico made fertile only by irrigation ?

"I look upon it, therefore, as a fixed fact, to use the
current expression of the day, that both California and
New Mexico are destined to be free, so far as they are
settled at all, which I believe, in regard to New Mexico,
will be but partially for a great length of time—free by
the arrangement of things ordained by the Power above
us. I have therefore to say, in this respect also, that this
country is fixed for freedom to as many persons as shall
ever live in it by a less repealable law than that which
attaches to the right of holding slaves in Texas; and I
will farther say, that, if a resolution or a bill were now
before us to provide a territorial government for New
Mexico, I would not vote to put any prohibition into it
whatever. Such a prohibition would be idle, as it respects any effect it would have upon the territory; and
I would not take pains uselessly to reaffirm an ordinance
of Nature nor to re-enact the will of God. I would put
in no Wilmot Proviso for the mere purpose of a taunt or
a reproach. I would put into it no evidence of the votes
of superior power, exercised for no purpose but to wound
the pride—whether a just and a rational pride, or an ir-
rational pride—of the citizens of the Southern States. I
have no such object, no such purpose. They would think
it a taunt, an indignity; they would think it to be an act
taking away from them what they regard as a proper
equality of privilege. Whether they expect to realize
any benefit from it or not, they would think it at least a
plain theoretic wrong, that something more or less derog-

atory to their character and their rights had taken place. I propose to inflict no such wound upon any body, unless something essentially important to the country, and efficient to the preservation of liberty and freedom, is to be effected. I repeat, therefore, sir, and as I do not propose to address the Senate often on this subject, I repeat it because I wish it to be distinctly understood, that, for the reasons stated, if a proposition were now here to establish a government for New Mexico, and it was moved to insert a provision for a prohibition of slavery, I would not vote for it.

"Sir, if we were now making a government for New Mexico, and any body should propose a Wilmot Proviso, I should treat it exactly as Mr. Polk treated that provision for excluding slavery from Oregon. Mr. Polk was known to be in opinion decidedly averse to the Wilmot Proviso, but he felt the necessity of establishing a government for the Territory of Oregon. The proviso was in the bill, but he knew it would be entirely nugatory; and since it must be entirely nugatory, since it took away no right, no describable, no tangible, no appreciable right of the South, he said he would sign the bill for the sake of enacting a law to form a government in that territory, and let that entirely useless and, in that connection, entirely senseless proviso remain. Sir, we hear occasionally of the annexation of Canada; and if there be any man, any of the Northern Democracy, or any one of the Free-soil party, who supposes it necessary to insert a Wilmot Proviso in a territorial government for New Mexico, that man would of course be of opinion that it is necessary to protect the everlasting snows of Canada from the foot of slavery by the same overspreading wing of an act of Congress. Sir, wherever there is a substantive good to be done, wherever there is a foot of land to be prevented from becoming slave territory, I am ready to assert the principle of the exclusion of slavery. I am pledged to it from the year 1837; I have been pledged to it again and again, and I will perform those pledges; but I will not do a thing unnecessarily that wounds the feelings of others, or that does discredit to my own understanding.

"Now, Mr. President, I have established, so far as I proposed to do so, the proposition with which I set out, and upon which I intend to stand or fall, and that is, that the whole territory within the former United States, or in the newly acquired Mexican provinces, has a fixed and settled character—now fixed and settled by law which can not be repealed, in the case of Texas, without a violation of public faith, and by no human power in regard to California or New Mexico; that therefore under one or other of these laws every foot of land in the states or in the territories has already received a fixed and decided character."

After referring to the Convention then expected to be held at Nashville, and expressing a hope that if "worthy gentlemen" should meet there in convention, "their object will be to adopt conciliatory measures;" after advising "the South to forbearance and moderation," and advising the North to forbearance and moderation "also," he brings this last of his great parliamentary efforts to a close in the following grand and impressive manner:

"Sir, I wish now to make two remarks, and hasten to a conclusion. I wish to say, in regard to Texas, that if it should be hereafter at any time the pleasure of the government of Texas to cede to the United States a portion, larger or smaller, of her territory which lies adjacent to New Mexico and north of 36° 30' of north latitude, to be formed into free states, for a fair equivalent in money or in the payment of her debt, I think it an object well worthy the consideration of Congress, and I shall be happy to concur in it myself, if I should have a connection with the government at that time.

"I have one other remark to make. In my observations upon slavery as it has existed in this country and as it now exists, I have expressed no opinion of the mode of its extinguishment or melioration. I will say, however, though I have nothing to propose, because I do not deem myself so competent as other gentlemen to take any lead on this subject, that if any gentleman from the South shall propose a scheme to be carried on by this government upon a large scale for the transportation of free colored people to any colony or any place in the world, I should be quite disposed to incur almost any degree of expense to accomplish that object. Nay, sir, following an example set more than twenty years ago by a great man,* then a senator from New York, I would return to Virginia, and through her to the whole South, the money received from the lands and territories ceded by her to this government for any such purpose as to remove, in whole or in part, or in any way to diminish or deal beneficially with, the free colored population of the Southern States. I have said that I honor Virginia for her cession of this territory. There have been received into the

---

* Mr. Rufus King.

treasury of the United States eighty millions of dollars, the proceeds of the sales of the public lands ceded by her. If the residue should be sold at the same rate, the whole aggregate will exceed two hundred millions of dollars. If Virginia and the South see fit to adopt any proposition to relieve themselves from the free people of color among them, or such as may be made free, they have my full consent that the government shall pay them any sum of money out of the proceeds of that cession which may be adequate to the purpose.

"And now, Mr. President, I draw these observations to a close. I have spoken freely, and I meant to do so. I have sought to make no display. I have sought to enliven the occasion by no animated discussion, nor have I attempted any train of elaborate argument. I have wished only to speak my sentiments fully and at length, being desirous, once and for all, to let the Senate know, and to let the country know, the opinions and sentiments which I entertain on all these subjects. These opinions are not likely to be suddenly changed. If there be any future service that I can render to the country consistently with these sentiments and opinions, I shall cheerfully render it. If there be not, I shall still be glad to have had an opportunity to disburden myself from the bottom of my heart, and to make known every political sentiment that therein exists.

"And now, Mr. President, instead of speaking of the possibility or utility of secession, instead of dwelling in those caverns of darkness, instead of groping with those ideas so full of all that is horrid and horrible, let us come out into the light of day; let us enjoy the fresh air of liberty and union; let us cherish those hopes which belong to us; let us devote ourselves to those great objects that are fit for our consideration and our action; let us raise our conceptions to the magnitude and the importance of the duties that devolve upon us; let our comprehension be as broad as the country for which we act, our aspirations as high as its certain destiny; let us not be pigmies in a case that calls for men. Never did there devolve on any generation of men higher trusts than now devolve upon us, for the preservation of this Constitution and the harmony and peace of all who are destined to live under it. Let us make our generation one of the strongest and brightest links·in that golden chain which is destined, I fondly believe, to grapple the people of all the states to this Constitution for ages to come. We have a great, popular, constitutional government, guarded by law and by judicature, and defended by the affections of the whole people. No monarchical throne presses these states tögether, no iron chain of military power encircles them; they live and stand under a government popular in its form, representative in its character, founded upon principles of equality, and so constructed, we hope, as to last forever. In all its history it has been beneficent; it has trodden down no man's liberty, it has crushed no state. Its daily respiration is liberty and patriotism; its yet youthful veins are full of enterprise, courage, and honorable love of glory and renown. Large before, the country has now, by recent events, become vastly larger. This republic now extends, with a vast breadth, across the whole continent. The two great seas of the world wash the one and the other shore. We

realize on a mighty scale the beautiful description of the
ornamental border of the buckler of Achilles:

> " ' Now, the broad shield complete the artist crowned
> With his last hand, and poured the ocean round ;
> In living silver seemed the waves to roll,
> And beat the buckler's verge, and bound the whole.' "

In bringing to notice Mr. Webster's very pointed allusion to the Nashville Convention, I am reminded of a
scene which occurred in the Senate a week or two only
anterior to the death of Mr. Calhoun.   His last extended
speech had been delivered in the Senate the day before,
or, rather, Mr. Mason, of Virginia, had read the speech
from a printed pamphlet in a very slow and emphatic
manner, Mr. Calhoun being himself present, and occasionally imparting additional impressiveness to what was thus
enunciated by particularly significant gestures.   There
were portions of it which struck me at the time it was
read as unfortunate, and as calculated to do much mischief, unless their influence should be promptly met and
counteracted.   I feared that the Nashville Convention,
which was then again in session, might be powerfully
influenced in its action by such a speech, emanating from
a source so distinguished, and embodying the views of a
person so much entitled to respect and confidence as I
could not but hold Mr. Calhoun to be.   It was most painful to me to have the least collision with one whom I
certainly loved and respected as much as I did any man
living, but I did not see how I could get over entering
my emphatic *protest* to that portion of the speech to which
I am now referring.   So, in the morning hour, and before the speech of Mr. Calhoun could be distributed over

the country, I brought the subject to the notice of the Senate, and the following scene occurred, as reported in the Congressional Globe.

Mr. Calhoun had, in the speech referred to, demanded in behalf of the South an amendment of the Federal Constitution, which he urged was the *only mode* left for the settlement of the pending sectional questions. Referring to the North, in connection with the proposition of constitutional amendment, he had said: "Nothing else can, with any certainty, finally and forever settle the questions at issue, terminate agitation, and save the Union. But can this be done? Yes, easily; not by the weaker party—for it can of itself do nothing, not even protect itself—but by the stronger. The North has only to will it to accomplish it, to do justice by conceding to the South an equal right in the acquired territory, and to do her duty by causing the stipulations relative to fugitive slaves to be faithfully fulfilled, to cease the agitation of the slave question, and to provide for the insertion of a provision in the Constitution by an amendment which will restore to the South, in substance, the power she possessed before the equilibrium between the sections was destroyed by the action of the government. There will be no difficulty in devising such a provision, one that will protect the South, and which, at the same time, will improve and strengthen the government, instead of impairing and weakening it."

Apprehending that this new demand of a constitutional amendment might, if it went out to the country in behalf of the South, induce the Nashville Convention to adopt it as a *sine qua non* to settlement, and thus fatally compromise the South, on the next morning I rose up, and respectfully but emphatically entered my protest against it. Mr. Calhoun coming in while I was doing so, rose, and, interrupting me, said:

"I must really express my great regret that a member of this body, in my absence this morning, before the hour for the consideration of this question, should have engaged in commenting on my remarks in reference to the important question that is under discussion.. I had not the advantage of hearing the remarks of the senator from Mississippi. Did he accuse me of disunion? Did he mean to insinuate that?"

To which the Congressional Globe reports me as saying, in reply:

"I regret that the honorable senator was not in his place. My only reason for referring to it at this time was, that I did not expect the honorable senator to be here for many days. I thought that he was too much indisposed to be present; and, believing that I should have no other opportunity for seasonably shielding myself from misjudgment, I determined to seize the present occasion for that purpose. Now, I will say to the honorable senator from South Carolina that I had not the slightest intention of imputing to him designs hostile to the Union. I said that his motives were, doubtless, patriotic. He will find my remarks, when reported in the morning, to be somewhat in bad taste, because so exceedingly encomiastic in regard to himself. All that I said was, that his speech, addressed to us with the best intentions, did contain certain declarations, which, if construed as I feared they would be construed, would be regarded as insisting, on the part of the South, upon demands that had never before been set up, and which might prove fatal to the Union if not abandoned."

After other remarks by me not material to the subject at present under consideration, Mr. Calhoun rose again, and concluded a very animated explanation thus :

" But I will say, and I say it boldly, for I am not afraid to say the truth on any question, that, as things now stand, the Southern States *can not with safety remain in the Union.* When this question may be settled, when we shall come to a constitutional understanding, is a question of time; but, as things now stand, I appeal to the senator from Mississippi, if he thinks that the South can remain in the Union upon terms of equality ?"

To which I am reported as replying,

" We can not, *unless the pending questions are settled ;* but, in my opinion, these questions may be settled, *and honorably settled within ten days' time.*"

Then rejoined Mr. Calhoun,

"Does the senator think that the South can remain in the Union upon terms of equality without a *specific guar-antee* that she shall enjoy her rights unmolested ?"

To which the answer, as reported, was,

" I think she may, *without any previous amendment of the Constitution.* There we disagree."

Mr. Calhoun then frankly responded,

" *Yes, there we disagree entirely; and there, I think, we disagree with our ancestors. I agree with them.*"*

* It has been supposed by some, and even directly charged, that Mr. Yancey's course at Baltimore, referred to in a previous chapter, was prompted by Mr. Calhoun. I am myself satisfied that such was not the

Having incidentally alluded in this chapter to the Nashville Convention, I will offer a few observations upon the

fact. At any rate, he was regarded by his political supporters at that
time to be very distinctly committed to *non-intervention*, though exceedingly hostile to what he and others were accustomed to call the *squatter
sovereignty doctrine*. On the occasion of organizing a territorial government for Oregon in the month of June, 1849, he will be found to have
expressed himself as follows:

"But I go farther, and hold that justice and the Constitution are the
easiest and safest ground on which the question can be settled, regarded
in reference to *party*. It may be settled on that ground simply by *non-action*—by leaving the territories free and open to the emigration of all the
world, so long as they continue so; and when they become states, to
adopt whatever Constitution they please, with the single restriction to be
republican, in order to their admission into the Union. If a party can
not safely take this broad and solid position, and successfully maintain it,
what other can it take and maintain?" (I will here suggest that I remember very well that this portion of Mr. Calhoun's Oregon speech was
regarded at the time as intended to recommend to the Democratic party to
embody the non-intervention principle in its presidential platform, which
was accordingly done.) But he continued: "If it (a party) can not maintain itself by an appeal to the great principles of justice, the Constitution,
and self-government, to what other, sufficiently strong to uphold them,
can they appeal? I greatly mistake the character of the people of this
Union if such an appeal would not prove successful, if either party should
have the magnanimity to step forward and boldly take it. It would, in
my opinion, be received with shouts of approbation by the patriotic and
intelligent in every quarter. There is a deep feeling pervading the country that the Union and our political institutions are in danger, which such
a course would dispel."

He said further,

"There is a very striking difference between the position which the
slaveholding and the non-slaveholding states stand in reference to the
subject under consideration. The former desire *no action of the government; demand no law to give them any advantage in the territory about to be
established;* are willing to leave it, and other territories belonging to the
United States, open to all their citizens so long as they continue to be

action of that body, and upon some interesting occurrences connected therewith. Though a considerable number of individuals attended this Convention as delegates
from various Southern States, of no little distinction and
influence in the communities to which they belonged,
and though there were a few of these who possessed remarkable intellectual power and varied attainments, yet
it is equally true that there were others of a very reckless and disorganizing spirit, and not at all fitted, in any
respect, to perform the difficult and somewhat anomalous
duties which had been assigned them. I am not willing, at this moment, to say any thing calculated to cast
discredit upon persons whose political calculations and
whose individual aspirations have suffered such a cruel
blight by the operation of recent events. But justice to
a very uncommon and meritorious personage who chanced
to be selected to preside over that body, Judge William
L. Sharkey, of Mississippi, whose wise and statesmanlike
conduct as Provisional Governor of Mississippi has attracted to him so much of public respect and sympathy
of late, and stamped his name upon the page of history

territories, and when they cease to be so, to leave it to their inhabitants
to form such governments as may suit them, *without restriction or condition*, except that inferred by the Constitution, as a prerequisite for entering the Union. In short, they are willing to ‘leave the whole subject
where the Constitution and the great and fundamental principles of self-
government place it."

Again he said, in the celebrated Southern Address, "What we propose
in this connection is to make a few remarks on what the North alleges
erroneously to be the issue between us and them. So far from maintaining the doctrine which the issue implies, we hold that the Federal government has *no right to extend or restrict slavery, no more than to extinguish or abolish it.*"

G

in characters of enduring honor, demands of me to declare that, but for his courageous and discreet conduct as
president of the Convention in 1850, great and wide-
spread mischief would inevitably have ensued from the
action of that body. The telegraphic reports which were
received in Washington during the pendency of the
measures of compromise, notifying the friends of the
Union in Congress of the happy effects resulting from
the decided action, and sage and healing counsels of
Judge Sharkey, supplied seasonable and essential aid to
those who were struggling to consummate the work of
national pacification then in active progress; and it is
highly gratifying now both to remember and to record
that President Fillmore was so impressed with the great
value of the service which Judge Sharkey had rendered
to the Union cause while presiding over the deliberations
of the Nashville Convention, and was so well persuaded
of his general merits and qualifications, that he did not
hesitate, on this gentleman's arrival in Washington a few
days subsequent to the adjournment of that body, to tender to him the office of Secretary of War, which station
Judge Sharkey modestly, but with a grateful sense of the
honor intended to be conferred upon him, thought proper to decline. This worthy personage has been recently
elected by the Legislature of the State of Mississippi to
the Senate of the United States, where I venture to predict, upon a more than thirty years' acquaintance with
him, his career will be as brilliant and useful as his reputation in private life is stainless and exemplary.

I should fail to do justice to the great mass of American population at this critical conjuncture did I not

mention the fact that large public meetings were held in every part of the republic, at which eloquent speeches were made and patriotic resolutions adopted, of a nature to supply the most important assistance to those who were struggling to keep the ship of state steady and erect amid the conflicting winds then raging. In the great commercial emporium of the republic, New York, movements occurred during the summer of 1850 which a grateful country can never cease to bear in kind and respectful remembrance. A grand popular assemblage was held, where a large proportion of the intelligence and wealth of the city were represented; resolutions approving in the most enthusiastic terms the efforts of those in Congress engaged in the work of national settlement · were adopted, and a committee of safety, numbering one hundred persons, and composed of some of the most enlightened and influential men on the continent, was appointed, which labored afterward incessantly, in every practicable mode, to aid in the preservation of a Union which was felt to be far too precious to be left exposed to the dangers then besetting it on all sides, and which it was evident could be only rescued from ruin by the combined efforts of all who truly loved it, and who were yet willing to struggle for its preservation.

148 · SCYLLA AND CHARYBDIS.

CHAPTER IX.

Omnibus Bill under Consideration.—Strenuous Opposition of General
Taylor's Administration to its Adoption.—Last Appearance of President Taylor in Public on the 4th of July, 1850, at Monument Square,
in Washington City, and touching Scene which occurred there.—General Taylor's Decease a few Days thereafter.—Mr. Webster's eloquent
Funeral Notice of him.—Mr. Fillmore's Inauguration as President, and
efficient Support of the Compromise Measures.—Official Order found
on General Taylor's Table after his Decease, ordering the forcible Expulsion from New Mexico by the Military of Texan Settlers.—Mr.
Clay's heroic Remonstrance against this coercive Policy, which he regarded as needlessly endangering the Union.—Fierce Opposition to the
Compromise Measures on the Part both of Extremists of the North and
Extremists of the South.—Terrible Struggle over the Omnibus Bill in
the Senate, which is finally broken into Fragments mainly by the Indiscretion of its own Friends, but the integral Portions of which finally
pass both Houses.—The Country quieted under the Influence of this
Measure.—Sage and firm Conduct of President Fillmore in causing the
Compromise Enactments to be every where faithfully executed.—Cel-
ebrated *Rescue* Case in Massachusetts, and interesting Proceedings in
Congress in Connection therewith.

THE compromise measures, in the form of an *Omnibus*
Bill, as it was called at the time, were under discussion
in the national Senate, and various questions connected
with the proposed "*plan of adjustment,*" as Mr. Dallas, in
a letter to myself, written about this period and published
in the newspapers, more aptly entitled them, were calling
forth much acrimonious discussion in both wings of the
Capitol, when General Taylor very suddenly died, early
in the month of July, 1850. The last time I saw this fine

specimen of the honest, blunt, strong - minded, resolute, but, it must be confessed, somewhat self-willed and ob- stinate soldier of the backwoods, was on the Fourth of July, at what is known as the Washington Monument, where I had the honor of delivering, by request of the patriotic association formed for the purpose of erecting the same, the customary anniversary oration. President Taylor and his cabinet had all come forth on this occa- sion, far more, I am sure, to render deserved homage to the memory of the august Father of his Country than to listen to the feeble and unworthy effusion to which they were about to give respectful audience. Never had I seen him look more robust and healthful than while seat- ed under the canopy which sheltered the speaker and the assembled concourse from the burning rays of an almost vertical sun. After the address had been concluded, he kindly beckoned me to approach him, cordially offered me his hand, and tendered me his thanks for what I am painfully sensible very little merited such a compliment- ary notice ;. though I am gratified to know that those who may now choose to look over that same speech will at least find it replete with the most fervent Union senti- ments, and the most enthusiastic wishes for our country's happiness. I think that the veteran President added, "*Why will you not always speak in this way?*" a kind and patriotic *implication of rebuke*, which I will not undertake now to say was altogether unreasonable, and from which I hope I did not fail subsequently, in some degree, to prof- it. In a day or two more the hero of so many battles had gone to his long home, and a grand public funeral was awarded him. The following appropriate and pathetic speech was delivered by Mr. Webster in the Senate, on the occasion of presenting resolutions in notice of his demise:

" Mr. Secretary, at a time when the great mass of our fellow-citizens are in the enjoyment of an unusual measure of health and prosperity throughout the whole country, it has pleased Divine Providence to visit the two houses of Congress, and especially this House, with repeated occasions for mourning and lamentation. Since the commencement of the session, we have followed two of our own members to their last home;` and we are now called upon, in conjunction with the other branch of the Legislature, and in full sympathy with that deep tone of affliction which I am sure is felt throughout the country, to take part in the due solemnities of the funeral of the late President of the United States.

" Truly, sir, was it said, in the communication read to us, that a 'great man has fallen among us.' The late President of the United States, originally a soldier by profession, having gone through a long and splendid career of military service, had, at the close of the late war with Mexico, become so much endeared to the people of the United States, and had inspired them with so high a degree of regard and confidence, that, without solicitation or application, without pursuing any devious paths of policy, or turning a hair's breadth to the right or left from the path of duty, a great, and powerful, and generous people saw fit, by popular vote and voice, to confer upon him the highest civil authority in the nation. We can not forget that, as in other instances so in this, the public feeling was won and carried away, in some degree, by the éclat of military renown. So it has been always, and so it always will be, because high respect for noble deeds in arms has been and always will be outpoured from the hearts of the members of a popular government.

"But it will be a great mistake to suppose that the late President of the United States owed his advancement to high civil trust, or his great acceptableness with the people, to military talent or ability alone. I believe, sir, that, associated with the highest admiration for those qualities possessed by him, there was spread throughout the community a high degree of confidence and faith in his integrity and honor, and uprightness as a man. I believe he was especially regarded as both a firm and a mild man in the exercise of authority; and I have observed more than once, in this and in other popular governments, that the prevalent motive with the masses of mankind for conferring high power on individuals is a confidence in their mildness, their paternal, protecting, prudent, and safe character. The people naturally feel safe where they feel themselves to be under the control and protection of sober counsel, of impartial minds, and a general paternal superintendence.

"I suppose, sir, that no case ever happened in the very best days of the Roman republic when a man found himself clothed with the highest authority in the state under circumstances more repelling all suspicion of personal application, of pursuing any crooked path in politics, or of having been actuated by sinister views and purposes, than in the case of the worthy, and eminent, and distinguished, and good man whose death we now deplore. ·

"He has left to the people of his country a legacy in this. He has left them a bright example, which address- es itself with peculiar force to the young and rising gen- eration ; for it tells them that there is a path to the high- est degree of renown straight onward, steady, without change or deviation.

"Mr. Secretary, my friend from Louisiana* has detailed shortly the events in the military career of General Tay-, lor. His service through his life was mostly on the frontier, and always a hard service, often in combat with the tribes of Indians along the frontier for so many thou- sands of miles. It has been justly remarked by one of the most eloquent men whose voice was ever heard in these houses† that it is not in Indian wars that heroes are celebrated, but that it is there that they are formed. The hard service, the stern discipline devolving upon all those who have a great extent of frontier to defend, often with irregular troops, being called on suddenly to enter into contests with savages, to study the habits of savage life and savage war, in order to foresee and overcome their stratagems, all these things tend to make hardy military character.

"For a very short time, sir, I had a connection with the executive government of this country, and at that time very perilous and embarrassing circumstances ex- isted between the United States and the Indians on the borders, and war was actually carried on between the United States and the Florida tribes. I very well re- member that those who took counsel together on that occasion officially, and who were desirous of placing the

* Mr. Downs.   † Fisher Ames.

military command in the safest hands, came to the conclusion that there was no man in the service more fully uniting the qualities of military ability and great personal prudence than Zachary Taylor, and he was appointed to the command.

" Unfortunately, his career at the head of this government was short. For my part, in all that I have seen of him, I have found much to respect and nothing to condemn. The circumstances under which he conducted the government for the short time he was at the head of it have been such as perhaps not to give him a very favorable opportunity of developing his principles and his policy, and carrying them out; but I believe he has left on the minds of the country a strong impression, first, of his absolute honesty and integrity of character; next, of his sound, practical good sense; and, lastly, of the mildness and friendliness of his temper toward all his countrymen.

" But he is gone. He is ours no more, except in the force of his example. Sir, I heard with infinite delight the sentiments expressed by my honorable friend from Louisiana who has just resumed his seat, when he earnestly prayed that this event might be used to soften the animosities, to allay party criminations and recriminations, and to restore fellowship and good feeling among the various sections of the Union. Mr. Secretary, great as is our loss to-day, if these inestimable and inappreciable blessings shall have been secured to us even by the death of Zachary Taylor, they have not been purchased at too high a price ; and if his spirit, from the regions to which he has ascended, could see these results flowing

from his unexpected and untimely end, if he could see
that he had entwined a soldier's laurel around a martyr's
crown, he would say exultingly, 'Happy am I that, by
my death, I have done more for that country which I
loved and served, than I did or could do by all the devotion and all the efforts that I could make in her behalf
during the short space of my earthly existence.'

"Mr. Secretary, great as this calamity is, we mourn
not as those without hope. We have seen one eminent
man, and another eminent man, and at last a man in the
most eminent station, fall away from the midst of us.
But I doubt not there is a Power above us exercising
over us that parental care that has guarded our progress
for so many years. I have confidence still that the place
of the departed will be supplied; that the kind, beneficent
favor of Almighty God will still be with us, and that we
shall be borne along, and borne upward and upward, on
the wings of his sustaining providence. May God grant
that, in the time that is before us, there may not be wanting to us as wise men, as good men for our counselors,
as he whose funeral obsequies we now propose to cele-
brate !"

It has been already stated that while General Taylor
lived he had not seen the necessity of those measures of
compromise which men of not less patriotism than himself, and of far more civic experience, regarded as essential to the restoration of the public repose. I rejoice to
recollect, though, that I never heard any one call his
motives in question in adhering to his *non-action policy*, as
it was at the time, not very aptly, as I must think, entitled; though I suppose no person will deny that this ex-

cellent and patriotic personage had been induced to regard the conduct of Mr. Clay and those co-operating with
him, in urging the early settlement of all the outstanding questions of sectional differences by *congressional legislation*, with considerable disfavor, if not, indeed, with
stronger feelings. It is certain that he was sometimes
heard to complain that the members of Congress referred
to were ungraciously embarrassing his administration;
and in a newspaper published in Washington City, recognized at the time as the organ of the government, daily
diatribes made their appearance directed at the compromise measures, and even severely arraigning Mr. Clay by
name. Nor was this gentleman at all times patient under such illiberal assaults, and on at least one occasion,
in the morning hour, was his trumpet-toned voice raised
in terrible and withering rebuke of the political *Ther-
sites* who was, as he charged, factiously essaying to keep
alive sectional excitement at the hazard of the public
peace and of the nation's safety. It is perhaps not very
surprising that General Taylor, with his exclusive *military* notions, should have resolved to drive off by force
of arms the Texan citizens who were then reputed to be
upon the disputed territory, claimed alike by Texas, as a
part of her own domain, and by the United States, as a
portion of the territory recently acquired from the Republic of Mexico. Mr. Webster, when Secretary of State, a
month or two subsequent to General Taylor's decease, in
a speech or letter, I do not now remember which, stated
the fact that upon the President's official table, or in the
Department of War, an *official order* was found, after Mr.
Fillmore's induction into the presidency, *directing the*

*United States military commander then in charge of New
Mexico to lose not a moment's time in expelling the alleged
Texan intruders beyond what was deemed by the government
to be the true boundary line of New Mexico.* I was myself
in the Senate one morning when Mr. Seward, of New
York, gave distinct and emphatic premonition of what
General Taylor had then resolved to do upon this subject, and well remember the mingled surprise and indignation which Mr. Clay displayed on that occasion, and
the frank and solemn warning he uttered in reference to
the execution of a measure which he did not hesitate to
declare must, if essayed, inevitably produce *civil war,* if,
indeed, it would not *justify* it.   He declared that nothing
could be, in his judgment, more unwise or more pregnant
with mischief than an attempt to settle by the arbitrament of the sword the disputed question of territorial
boundary, and avowed his apprehension that, should the
interposition of military force occur at a time when so
many millions were confidently expecting the early adoption of measures of pacification by Congress, the first
drop of the blood of Texan citizens shed by the regular
soldiers of the government would wake up a general and
fearful conflagration, which might in the issue consume
all that existed of American liberty.

   I shall not say more at present in regard to the measures of compromise proposed, than that there was not
one of them the *constitutionality* of which could be reasonably disputed; nor do I suppose that any enlightened
man can now be found in the republic, whose mind is
free from the delusion of sectional prejudice, who would
undertake to deny the full power of Congress to leg-

islate precisely in the manner contemplated by these same enactments. Sectional agitators, though, on both sides of Mason and Dixon's line, were for some time heard to complain that Congress had seriously transcended the limits of its power, and that its action was therefore not entitled to popular respect. Extremists in the South freely denounced the Texas Boundary Bill as a *fraud*, as a *bribe* administered to a sovereign state, in order to induce her to sacrifice the general interests of the South; nor would they listen with patience to the prophetic language which was constantly thundered in their ears, that this very measure would enable Texas, by means of the large pecuniary sum which was presently to be paid her in exchange for territory the title to which was admitted to be doubtful, to pay off the large public debt contracted during her revolutionary struggle, thus relieving her people from grinding taxation; supply her, in addition, with ample means for establishing a liberal system of education within her borders, and for overspreading her surface with railways, and thus attracting within her limits myriads of immigrants from other regions, who would, in a few years, convert her into the empire slave state of the Southwest, destined, as such, to become an impregnable barrier to the encroachments of abolition in that direction. These dissatisfied factionists murmured over the congressional enactment which uprooted slave traffic in the District of Columbia, and absurdly insisted that by it slavery was virtually abolished therein; when the truth was, that Congress had only re-enacted the old law of Maryland on this subject which had been on the statute-book of the district for more than a half century, and had not, in fact, provided for the liberation of a single slave from bondage. So these persons also denounced the new Fugitive Slave Law as utterly inefficient, and raised a prodigious clamor over the admission of California, declaring such admission unconstitutional, though they were bound to know that the *form* of admission was just the same as had been adopted some dozen times before. Even the territorial bills were not satisfactory to these blinded and overheated zealots, who alleged that special congressional protection to slavery in the territories should have been accorded.

On the other hand, the extremists from the North also objected, and with some little show of plausibility, I confess, to the paying to Texas from the public treasury for lands the value of which they seriously doubted, and the title to which they alleged was really in the general government already. They found serious fault with the territorial bills, because they did not contain the Wilmot Proviso, though Mr. Webster and others had plainly shown, as has been seen, that slavery was already excluded both by the Mexican laws existing there and the irresistible decree of Nature. They insisted that slavery should have been done away altogether in the District of Columbia, and were extremely indignant that the new Fugitive Slave Law was so constructed as to place its due enforcement exclusively in the power of the general government, without looking thereafter to the free states themselves for such legislation on this subject as would be likely to prove effective.

All intelligent men know that the Omnibus Bill, while on its passage through the Senate, was broken into separate enactments mainly by the gross indiscretion of some of its own professed friends, and that finally the several fragments into which it had been dissolved all passed the two houses of Congress, and became part of the *supreme law of the land.*

Some members of Congress, both from the North and the South, still contended that there was nothing more sacred in the compromise measures thus adopted than in *ordinary* legislative enactments, urging that they were all subject, like other bills which passed Congress, to be amended or repealed at pleasure by succeeding Congresses. With a view to counteracting this view of the matter, upon the advice of various judicious friends I introduced resolutions at the next succeeding session of Congress which asserted the various acts of Congress specified, notwithstanding they had been disjoined from each other in the manner stated, still to constitute, in fact, *one scheme of compromise or adjustment,* for the due enforcement of which the public faith was solemnly pledged, and declared the legislation which had just taken place to be a *final settlement,* in *principle* and *substance,* of all the controverted questions of slavery. Though this resolution was not so fortunate as to receive the sanction of the two houses of Congress, yet it is not a little gratifying to me now to recollect that the great principle of finality asserted therein was afterward unequivocally incorporated both in the Whig and Democratic presidential platforms of 1852.

It is due to Mr. Fillmore to say, that but for his efficient co-operation in securing the passage of the various compromise enactments, it is not probable that they would

have become laws; and his wise and patriotic conduct
afterward, in faithfully enforcing these enactments in both
sections of the Union, constitutes, in my judgment, one
of the brightest pages in American annals. Never did
this conscientious and upright President *knowingly* appoint any man to office who was not already pledged to
stand by and maintain the compromise measures in their
entirety, knowing as he did that if the official patronage
of which he had control was bestowed to any considerable extent upon sectional factionists, upon the heated
agitators of questions which the plan of compromise had
adjusted, there was no probability that the excitement
which had been just allayed would fail to be afterward
renewed. This was the true secret of the almost unbroken quietude which the republic so happily enjoyed
while Mr. Fillmore held the position of president; and it
was the notorious and unpardonable adoption of an opposite principle by Mr. Pierce after he came into office—
the continual agitation of the slavery question by him or
under his direction in presidential messages and otherwise—the illicit arts undeniably practiced by certain persons in his employment for the raising of new slavery
issues—the cruel and shameless persecution which they
brought to bear upon Union men in the South who
chanced to be in Federal employment at the time, either
under the appointment of Mr. Fillmore or otherwise, and
the strange and startling discrimination which was practiced in the North in connection with the distribution of
official patronage in favor of what was known at the time
as Free-soil Democrats, that brought into existence once
more those sectional factions which the operation of the

compromise had suppressed, and which, in the sequel, utterly broke down the popularity of Mr. Pierce's administration, fatally undermined the strength of the Democratic party in the free states, and well-nigh brought about the election of a Republican president in 1856. Mr. Pierce will be held by all sound-thinking men as the more justly deserving reprehension in regard to these matters by reason of the fact that he had been elected upon an unequivocal *finality* platform, and was pledged in every way to administer the government upon purely national principles. How he came to pursue such a course will be, to some extent, hereafter explained, and the consequences of such unwise conduct on his part will be perhaps made somewhat more apparent. I will conclude this chapter by the relation of an anecdote, which will bring very strikingly to view the spirit uniformly displayed by President Fillmore and his cabinet in regard to giving full effect to the compromise measures.

About the middle of the month of February, 1851, I was one morning walking along the Pennsylvania Avenue, in Washington City, when, beholding the arrival of the railway cars from the East, I turned in at the dépôt and purchased a New York Herald of that date. On glancing over its columns, I saw, greatly to my concern and alarm, a graphic and minute account of the celebrated *rescue* scene which had just occurred at Boston, and of the successful contravention of the new Fugitive Slave Act by *mob violence*. Though I had never myself participated in the general feeling of my Southern countrymen that it was very essential to the preservation of the slaveholding system that all negroes who chanced to escape from

their owners should be apprehended and returned to service, and had never seen the day when I would have made
the least exertion to recapture a slave of my own, and, indeed, would rather at any time have been inclined to regard the fact of his having actually *accomplished his escape* as a proof that he was more or less fitted to enjoy
freedom, yet I was well satisfied that in the then existing
condition of the public mind of the South, the occurrence
which was thus reported to have taken place, when duly
made known to our overheated and too mercurial Southern countrymen, would at once call forth intense and
widely-extended excitement, and tend greatly to enfeeble the compromise measures in the slaveholding states,
where a general spirit of *acquiescence* was beginning to
display itself.

I was quite confident, also, that the intelligence which
had just reached Washington would that very day provoke renewed controversial acrimony in the two houses
of Congress, the diffusion of which through the newspapers might be productive of much unkind feeling in
both sections of the Union, which all true patriots could
not fail to deplore. With these views I proceeded at
once to the room of Mr. Clay at the National Hotel,
where I found the venerable patriarch surrounded by a
crowd of youthful visitants, several of whom I understood to be his own grandchildren. He received me
with his usual affability. Apologizing to him for disturbing the pleasant scene which I saw in progress, I asked leave to lay before him the news which I had brought.
He requested me to read aloud the article in the Herald,
which I did; on concluding which, he said, with an em-

phasis which I can never forget, "My dear friend, you are right; this is indeed alarming intelligence, and nothing, in my judgment, can prevent the arising of great mischief but the *immediate* adoption by the government of the most energetic measures for the enforcement of the laws. Let me ask you to hasten to the White House, see President Fillmore as soon as you can, lay these extraordinary facts before him, and make known to him that I will myself be also in his presence in a few moments, only being detained here so long as is necessary to have my carriage brought to the door." I acted promptly as he had advised, went rapidly to the presidential mansion, and was in a few minutes admitted to an interview with Mr. Fillmore. I found him, as usual, calm and composed, but yet did his face indicate a little more than ordinary solemnity and earnestness. I lost no time in announcing the object of my errand. He told me that he had already received the Boston news, and had called a cabinet meeting to consider of it, which was very soon to occur. He in a few words announced his determination to enforce the laws of the land at all hazards, and put down, with the whole power of the government, if need be, any illicit or violent attempt to counteract or overturn them.

I remained with him only a few moments, and when he rose up to take leave of me I ventured to say to him, "Mr. President, I am delighted with this interview; the fate of the republic is in your hands, and I rejoice to believe that you are prepared to do your whole duty at this crisis." Mr. Fillmore having suggested that I should call, on my way to the Capitol, upon Mr. Webster, I pro-

ceeded accordingly to the Department of State. I found
the immortal defender of the Union alone. Immediately
on my bringing the Boston outrage to Mr. Webster's notice, he told me that he had already received full intelligence on the subject, and courteously turning to me,
said, "Well, what ought to be done?" To which I responded that I certainly had no idea of intruding my ad-
monitions upon the individual to whom the country was
now looking for a new "*Life of Washington*." "Ah!"
he exclaimed, "I understand you. You are thinking of
the whisky insurrection in Pennsylvania, and suppose that
a presidential *proclamation* may be proper." I replied
that Mr. Clay had said that he thought a proclamation
ought to be issued. "Well," he resumed, "what do you
think of directing all the military and naval forces in the
neighborhood of Boston to aid in sustaining the law?"
"That would seem to be right," I said. "Very well;
what do you say in reference to calling out the militia
of Massachusetts?" he continued. "That, I really suppose, will hardly be needed," I replied; "for I have met
on the way hither a captain of volunteers in Boston, who
told me that he was then hurrying home to call out his
company, with a view to aiding the Federal marshal in
maintaining the authority of the laws." "I am glad to
hear that," he said; and then, rising up and facing me,
he added, with great solemnity and emphasis, "*Be assured that all these things shall be done, and done without
delay, or Daniel Webster will be no longer a cabinet minister.*"

After these interesting interviews I proceeded to the
hall of the Senate, where I found Mr. Hale* upon his

* The gentleman here referred to deserves to be noticed by me a little

legs, declaiming most lustily against the Fugitive Slave
Law, commending warmly the action of the Abolition

more particularly. He is undoubtedly a person of very uncommon qualities as a speaker.- His remarkable readine‌ss and facility of speech, his
kind and genial temper, and his agreeable colloquial powers, will ever bo
pleasantly recollected by those who served with him in the national Senate. A month or two after I took my seat as a member of that body, I
was suddenly and unexpectedly thrown into collision with him, under circumstances of a very peculiar character. On the very day that the Gott
resolutions (already referred to) were introduced in the House of Representatives, Mr. Hale introduced a bill in the Senate during the morning
hour, and poured forth one of the most fervid and irritating speeches upon
the subject of slavery in the District of Columbia that I ever heard. Mr.
Calhoun was greatly inflamed by it, and came to the seats of my senatorial
colleague, Mr. Davis, and myself, and urged us both to say something in
response to Mr. Hale. Thus prompted, we did both assail Mr. Hale and
his speech in language not a little excited in its character. I must confess
that I entirely forgot myself on this occasion, and delivered a fierce, insulting, and vindictive harangue, wholly unworthy of the place, the memory of which has been ever most painful and mortifying. I even used
terms of indecent menace, and talked about *hanging* the gifted New
Hampshire senator. When the excitement of the moment passed away,
I was full of contrition on account of my grossly unsenatorial conduct,
and offered more than once in my place a formal apology for rudeness
which nothing could excuse. The good-natured and forgiving Mr. Hale
acted a most generous and manly part, and gave me the most distinct assurance that he should harbor no unfriendly feelings toward me on account of my *faux pas*. Not so the unsparing and unforgiving public;
and I continued for full ten years to receive the most insulting and acrimonious anonymous letters referring to this affair, and denouncing me as
"Hangman Foote," accompanied sometimes with caricatural representations of a singularly striking and amusing character. About two months
after this indecent conduct, Mr. Hale came to me and said, one morning,
that he had a personal favor to ask at my hands. I inquired what it
was, when he stated that a young man of tender years, whose family he
knew to be very respectable, had just been convicted in the District Court
of Washington of *forgery*, and was then lying in prison. He stated, in

mob in Boston, and declaring that he had always thought
and asserted that no law which was so much opposed to
local public sentiment as this could ever be enforced.
Upon his ceasing to·speak, I rose and announced to
the Senate the manly and patriotic assurances which I
had just received from the lips of Mr. Fillmore and Mr.
Webster, and concluded by declaring that, before the
termination of the day that was then passing away, all
America would learn that there were high-spirited and
fearless men now in power who would dare to do their
duty to the Constitution and the country, despite all that
sectional factionists might essay to bring the government
and its laws into contempt. I had not taken my seat
before Mr. Clay came in. He rose when I sat down,
and confirmed all I had previously stated in regard to
the intended action of the government, and uttered an
earnest and thrilling invocation in favor of vindicating

addition, that his sister, a charming young lady from New Hampshire,
had just reached Washington for the purpose of procuring, if possible,
her brother's release; and did me the honor to say that he thought that
if I would make personal application to Secretary Walker and President
Polk, this interesting object would be easily attained. Becoming satisfied
from his statement that it was a proper case for executive clemency, I
immediately undertook the duty of visiting my friend, Mr. Walker, and
the President, as he desired, and in an hour or two the young man was
released, and placed in the affectionate custody of his weeping sister, to
be escorted without delay to his own New England home. Before they
departed, though, Mr. Hale said to the young lady, "When you get home,
tell your friends that your brother owes his liberation to the kindness of a
United States senator from the South, who is at this moment receiving a
great deal of unjust abuse in the North. The person who procured your
brother's discharge is the individual so often spoken of as *Hangman*
Foote. Go home and tell your friends to abuse Mr. Foote no more."

the violated majesty of the law. While he was speaking he paused for a moment, beckoned me to his position, and whispered to me that he desired a short legislative proposition to be drawn immediately, which he would offer to the Senate before he yielded the floor, the contents of which he specified. I prepared the rough draft of it at once, had it neatly copied, and handed it to him. Just before closing he presented it for the consideration of the Senate. He declared it to have become necessary to arm the President with fuller powers than he was then supposed to possess, for the enforcement of the law for the recapture and restoration of fugitives from service. A warm debate sprang up upon this proposition, which I remember brought my senatorial colleague, Mr. Davis, and myself into sharp collision. This gentleman indignantly scouted the idea of giving the President any additional power, and declared that he would not vote a dollar or a man for coercing the sovereign State of Massachusetts into respect for the law which had been just violated. When the *final* action of the Senate upon this interesting question occurred I chanced to be absent, having been invited to the city of New York to deliver an oration, on the 22d of February, in honor of Washington; but I well remember being deeply pained, though I was certainly not much astonished at finding, from the publications made in the newspapers, that when the vote was taken at last upon the proposition to sustain President Fillmore in carrying out the commendable policy which he had set forth in a special message, addressed to the two houses of Congress, extremists of the North and extremists of the South *united their efforts to defeat that policy,* being evidently bent upon giving evidence to the world that the "*irrepressible conflict*" so much bruited at the time was not a mere figment of fancy, but a *solid and fearful reality !*

CHAPTER X.

Country completely restored to Quiet under the Compromise Measures, except in several of the Southern States.—Exciting Contest in Georgia and Mississippi in 1850, '1, upon the Disunion Issue, in both of which States the Union Cause is finally triumphant.—South Carolina, failing to obtain co-operative Aid, at last subsides into a State of Quietude.— The Election of Mr. Pierce to the Presidency as an avowed Supporter of the Finality Principle, who calls Mr. Davis to the Department of War, and the Slavery Agitation is at once renewed. — Mr. Pierce's gross Infidelity to his Pledges, by whose Indiscretion and Misconduct the Conflict of sectional Factions is again revived.—Mr. Douglas unfortunately yields to the Counsels addressed to him from various Quarters, and introduces the Kansas-Nebraska Bill.—Sectional Excitement greatly increased and intensified by that Measure. — Notice of the Decease of Mr. Clay and Mr. Webster, and of their commanding intellectual Powers and interesting Traits of Character.

THE compromise struggle terminated in Congress during the summer of 1850, and gradually made its way into the affections of the people every where, a great majority of whom were well pleased with the work performed by Mr. Clay and his patriotic co-operators. Fanatical agitators in several of the Northern States still continued for a time to rail against what had been done, and to accuse the wisest and most conservative statesmen that the republic contained of having perpetrated the most criminal violation of the great and fundamental principles of universal liberty and equality; while in the far South, agitators equally excited, and bent upon disturbing the public peace, were pouring forth fierce and violent harangues for states' rights, secession, and a sep-

H

arate Southern republic. In Virginia, Tennessee, Maryland, Delaware, North Carolina, Kentucky, Missouri,
Arkansas, Louisiana, Texas, and Florida, the compromise
enactments were cordially acquiesced in. In Alabama,
after a very short struggle, the 'governor and Legislature
imitated the noble example of the states just named. In
South Carolina movements soon occurred which clearly
indicated that a majority of her people, misled by the
delusory teachings of some of the most ingenious and
plausible political agitators that our hemisphere has yet
known, were fast making up their mind no longer to
remain in a Federal Union which they had learned to
detest, or submit to the authority of a government which
they regarded as menacing them with intolerable oppression. There were public men even in South Carolina
who were exceedingly opposed to all rash and fatal
measures, and who were by no means ready to try the
rash hazards of such an experiment as that in which they
were now invited to participate. Among these was the
present provisional governor of South Carolina, Mr. Perry, so judiciously selected a few months since by President Johnson to assist in the important work of *reconstruction*, now in such successful progress, and whose conduct in this high and responsible station has gained for
him a position so enviable in the estimation of his countrymen every where. It is a somewhat curious and
pleasing coincidence that Governor Perry, of South Carolina, and Governor Sharkey, of Mississippi, without
knowing each other personally, as I am informed, not
only took the same moderate and patriotic course in
1850 and 1851, but some six or seven years later distin-

guished themselves alike in opposing the reopening of the African slave-trade; and now, for the rendition of similar patriotic services to their country, they have both been called to take a still more prominent part in the councils of the nation as co-members of the United States Senate. Georgia and Mississippi were, in 1850, the only states in the South, except South Carolina herself, who had not yet yielded formal assent to the compromise measures, and whose ultimate action in this regard was at all doubtful. In the former state a Union organization was speedily set on foot, mainly under the auspices of Messrs. Stephens, Toombs, and Cobb, which very soon, in entire disregard of ancient party prejudices and obligations, brought into hearty and effective co-operation all the conservative elements of the state, and a large proportion also of the ability which had previously displayed itself in this intelligent and populous commonwealth. A well-known struggle had at that period its progress in Georgia, which resulted in the signal triumph of Mr. Cobb for the office of governor, and in obtaining an emphatic popular endorsement of the principles embodied in what has been known as the *Georgia platform*. No one can now doubt that, had this important contest resulted differently, the civil war which has of late so unhappily occurred would have had its dark and doleful progress ten years earlier. South Carolina only waited for the co-operation of a single state beyond her own borders, and was prepared to consummate her well-matured project of separation whenever it should be ascertained that she would not stand absolutely alone in the contemplated struggle.

The course of events at the same period in Mississippi is a part of the painful history of the country, and must therefore be passed in review; but I shall labor to be as concise on this branch of the subject as is possible, by reason of my own personal connection with the scenes which then occurred. It had been my fortune to stand alone in Congress in 1850, from the State of Mississippi, as a supporter of the compromise enactments. All my five colleagues in the two houses were zealously opposed to these measures, and closely banded themselves together, in order to make their opposition to them more effectual among the people of Mississippi than it had been in Washington City. The governor of the state, General Quitman, was in close alliance with them, as were more than two thirds of the Legislature, and as large a proportion of all the public officers of the state. The Legislature was persuaded to *censure* me by formal resolutions, which had been most widely disseminated. Nearly every newspaper in the state condemned my conduct in Congress, and I was daily subjected in their columns to such bitter and violent denunciation as few men, I am persuaded, have been fated to experience. A new political organization was set on foot at the capital of the state, which was quickly ramified into every county and neighborhood in Mississippi, whose avowed aim it was to unite with the State of South Carolina in the extreme policy which she had avowed, and into this organization were invited all who concurred in opposing the measures of compromise, without regard to their former party ties or designation. It was most manifest that I had now naught upon which to rely save the protecting aid of a bounteous Providence, the good sense and sterling patriotism of the popular masses, my own zeal and activity, and the generous and manly aid of such friends of the cause of the Union, either in Mississippi or elsewhere, as might judge me worthy of their sympathy and countenance. Among these friends was the august chief of the Compromise* himself, whose voluntary and active zeal in my support at this crisis was as unexpected, and as unsolicited also, as it was profoundly gratifying. Without my knowledge, Mr. Clay addressed letters to his numerous political friends in Mississippi in my behalf, which I met wherever I went in the canvass I had afterward to perform, and which called around me every where en-

---

* Of course, I here allude to Mr. Clay. Before leaving this topic, I can not refrain from mentioning, in this unimposing form, a touching incident that had occurred a few weeks before the scene above described, which is worthy of preservation, as giving evidence of Mr. Clay's tenderness of heart and generously sympathizing nature. On reaching Washington City, after the contest between Messrs. Quitman and Davis, as the champions of disunion, and myself, I called on Mr. Clay, in company with Wm. R. King, of Alabama, and Daniel S. Dickinson, of New York. He entertained a high esteem and warm friendship for both these gentlemen, and met them, on this occasion, with the most graceful and impressive display of cordiality. After he had saluted them, I approached him, when, feeble as he was, he rushed toward me and seized me in his arms, manifesting every token of the deepest inward emotion, and uttered words of congratulation and gratitude commingled which I may not now recite. Suffice it to say, that the honor then bestowed on me by this great and good man has ever since been cherished as one of the proudest and most gratifying recollections of a life of suffering and vicissitudes, and has been often since a source of consolation when assailed by the low-minded, the envious, and the malignant; nor would I now exchange the remembered delights of that moment for all the dignities which the crowned monarchs of earth have it in their power to confer.

thusiastic and valuable supporters, without whose zealous aid it would have been altogether impossible for
me to weather the rude gales with which my frail political bark had now to contend. Nor was this conduct on
the part of Mr. Clay at all surprising, under all the circumstances which had been recently occurring. It was
true that I had opposed, in a temperate and courteous
manner, in the beginning of the session of 1849, '50, the
programme which Mr. Clay first laid before the Senate,
that programme containing, as all intelligent men know,
an *abstract* assertion of the power of Congress to prohibit
slavery in the territories, and to abolish it in the District of
Columbia; a declaration of opinion in regard to the right
of Texas to the disputed territory afterward conceded to
her, and a claim of *separate* admission in behalf of California—in regard to neither of which points could I agree
with him. But when he had, with true practical wisdom,
and with the most singular elevation of spirit, declined to
press either of the disputed points, and consented to become our leader in a scheme of general adjustment, I
hope that no one in Congress evinced for him a more
uniform and truly deferential respect than I did, or fought
under his command, according to the very limited measure of my abilities (and always, as I have ever confessed,
in a very *subordinate* position), than I did. Perhaps I
ought to have confidently anticipated this sympathy and ·
support from Mr. Clay, after having heard him declare in
the hall of the old Confederate Congress at Annapolis, in
the eventful summer of 1850, while standing precisely
upon that part of the floor of that hallowed edifice where
he learned that Washington had stood when, after the

war of the Revolution, he surrendered his sword to his re-
deemed country's representatives, that henceforward *that
party should be his party that showed itself to be most faithful
in defending and in maintaining the Union of our fathers.*

I shall leave it to some other to record (if any permanent recollection of it shall be deemed desirable) what
took place in Mississippi during the autumn of 1850 and
the summer and autumn of 1851, when, as candidate for
governor upon the Union ticket, I had first to encounter General John A. Quitman as an opponent, and subsequently, upon his withdrawal from the contest, the now
world-renowned Jefferson Davis.   I shall not in these
pages minutely tell how the Union cause became finally
triumphant; how the people of Mississippi, as the result
of a severe political contest, determined that I should
serve them in the office` of governor in preference to
either of my more popular military competitors, and be
again returned as their representative in the national
Senate, to the seat which I formerly occupied in that
body (having resigned it at the demand of the friends
of the Union, in order to test more fully the strength of
the compromise measures with which I was supposed to
be specially identified); how a majority of senators in
the state Legislature, Secessionists in creed, and holding
over from another election, refused to go into a joint
legislative convention in order to choose a United States
senator at the time provided for by law, *avowedly* for the
purpose of defeating my election, they knowing well that
in such joint convention I would have a majority of more
than thirty votes; how the Union organization was afterward unfortunately thrown into a state of partial dis-

solution in consequence of the coming on of the presidential election of 1852; how the same organization was fatally enfeebled by the direct intermeddling of the administration of Mr. Pierce, and by the corrupt employment of official patronage; how afterward the Secessionists of Mississippi, adroitly taking back the name of *Democrat*, which they had once solemnly and formally relinquished, suddenly recuperated their strength by the announcement of a new political issue involving the shameless and disgraceful *repudiation* of the Planters' Bank bonds, the validity of which stood explicitly and emphatically guaranteed by the state Constitution; how, in consequence of this last most opprobrious act, openly countenanced and undeniably participated in by Mr. Davis himself, I indignantly resigned the office of governor and migrated to the far-distant coast of California; how, even in California, I was afterward pursued by the remorseless vengeance of Mr. Davis and his cabinet allies, who, learning that I had been taken up by a large majority of the California Legislature as a candidate for the national Senate, mainly on the ground of my known devotion to the Union, and my openly-declared opposition to their corrupt use of the patronage of the government, again contrived, by employing exactly the same means which had been so successfully exerted for a similar purpose two years before in Mississippi, *to defeat a joint legislative Convention* by the vote of a bare majority in the state Senate, in each instance creating a vacancy in the senatorial representation of a sovereign state—all these things, thus runningly suggested, I now dismiss, and proceed to other matters of higher dignity.

After the result of the contests in Georgia and in Mississippi to which I have just referred, the good people of South Carolina, being summoned by the champions of extreme measures to assemble in convention for the purpose of adopting an ordinance of secession, and having the question fairly submitted to them whether they would *separately secede* or *await the co-operation* of other states, decided in favor of the latter proposition. So the "irrepressible conflict" was at least brought to a *pause;* an intermissive period of peace and good-will was allowed to have place, and the movements of sectional factionists on either side of the line of separation between the slaveholding and non-slaveholding portions of the Union were *suspended* for a season; and, indeed, until *similar causes* should beget *similar* consequences. Mr. Greeley, in his "American Conflict," is therefore fully justified in saying, as he does in the beginning of his sixteenth chapter, "But, whatever theoretic or practical objections may be justly made to the Compromise of 1850, there can be no doubt that it was accepted and ratified by a great majority of the American people, whether in the North or in the South. They were intent on business, then remarkably prosperous—on planting, building, trading, and getting gain, and they hailed with general joy the announcement that all the differences between the diverse 'sections' had been adjusted and settled. The terms of settlement were, to that majority, of quite subordinate consequence; they wanted peace and prosperity, and were nowise inclined to cut each others' throats and burn each others' houses in a quarrel concerning (as they regarded it) only the *status* of negroes. The compromise had taken

II 2

no money from their pockets; it had imposed upon them no pecuniary burdens; it had exposed them to no personal and palpable dangers; it had rather repelled the gaunt spectre of civil war and disunion, habitually conjured up when slavery had a point to carry, and increased the facilities for making money, while opening a boundless vista of national greatness, security, and internal harmony. Especially by the trading class and the great majority of the dwellers in sea-board cities was this view cherished with intense, intolerant vehemence."

Mr. Greeley in this chapter bestows a passing attention upon the gubernational contest in Mississippi, of which I have already said as much as is necessary to be here recorded, and does me the honor to state that I had "supported the compromise in Congress to the extent of my (his) ability," which is certainly all that I could possibly claim to have done, and for this frank acknowledgment by him of my supposed merits, I trust he will consider me as being truly grateful.

The quiet which the compromise had restored was not again seriously disturbed during the administration of Mr. Fillmore; and it is now most evident that, had this gentleman, with his wise and practical conservatism, been chosen President instead of Mr. Pierce in 1852, and had the principles which so honorably distinguished his administration been faithfully observed by succeeding presidents, the grim demon of disunion would not have been conjured into existence, and the permanent discredit which has fallen upon our country of having permitted the copious outpouring of the blood of brothers upon their own natal soil in unnatural domestic feud would have been, in all probability, avoided for centuries, if not for an indefinite period.

But such was not to be our good fortune. Mr. Pierce was put in nomination by the Democratic party for the presidency in 1852. He pledged himself most solemnly to recognize, in the high station to which he was about to be elected, the compromise measures of 1850, of which so much has been said in these pages already, as a "*final settlement*, in principle and in substance, of the distracting questions of slavery." He had been indebted for his nomination at Baltimore to the declarations which he was reported to have previously made of the duty of whomsoever might be constituted President so to distribute the official patronage in his gift as to encourage the purest nationality of sentiment, and to discourage every thing like sectionalism. And yet he had scarcely been elected to the presidency when he called into special conference Mr. Hunter, of Virginia, one of the most extreme men in his opinions that, outside of South Carolina, the whole South contained, and the noted Caleb Cushing, of Massachusetts, who had signalized himself very specially, many years before, by delivering the most furious and uncompromising abolition speech ever heard in Congress upon the occasion of Arkansas asking for admission into the Union, and who, although he had afterward yielded support to the administration of Mr. Tyler for a short period, for which his services had been rewarded with an Oriental commissionership, and had subsequently given his support to the Mexican War, and gone through certain romantic adventures beyond the Rio Grande without having a chance of staining his virgin sword with the hated blood of the foe, had really not a particle of claim to control the action of a Democratic administration entering upon its official career under such circumstances as those which now surrounded Mr. Pierce. These two sage advisers are understood to have counseled Mr. Pierce to call to his cabinet Mr. Jefferson Davis, of Mississippi, who was then in profound retirement after his unsuccessful experiment of secession in 1851, in which retirement it is quite certain he would have permanently remained but for Mr. Pierce being weak enough to act upon this advice. It is understood that this particular appointment was made with a view to conciliating the Secessionists of the South, who had yielded to Mr. Pierce but a cold and reluctant support; many of them, indeed, and especially in Mr. Davis's own state, having altogether declined voting in the election. Mr. Cushing, who was to be attorney general of the new *regime*, had reason to believe that, by force of early political affiliations, and by the skillful distribution of the spoils of office, he could bring into the fold all the aspirants to public station who then belonged to the abolition faction in the North, while Mr. Davis, by discriminating in appointments to office in favor of known disunionists, and against those who had battled so faithfully for the compromise measures throughout the South, it was confidently expected would work wonders in attracting to the support of his over-confiding chief the sectional factionists of that region. It was, fancifully enough, supposed that the friends of the Union every where would infallibly remain firm in the support of Mr. Pierce on the ground of his former professions, so that there was, upon the whole, as they opined, a capital prospect opening upon the country of an administration of four years which would be fortunate enough to encounter no enemies, and an equally flattering prospect that Mr. Pierce would himself be re-elected in 1856, or that the privilege would be accorded to him by a grateful country of nominating his own successor. How signally and cruelly all these fine-spun calculations were disappointed in the sequel, and how soon all these vapid and airy speculations were fated to pass away into the sombre region of *nothingness*, the world now knows. Mr. Pierce, who imagined himself to have, and was supposed by some of his friends to have quite a pretty talent for declamatory rhetoric, commenced, so soon as he had a chance to do so, discoursing, in his messages and otherwise, of the blessings of slavery; extolled the South, and her modes of thought and sentiment, in language of glowing exuberance; announced himself to all the world as the champion of her slave-holding rights and interests; and very soon managed to disgust most heartily every truly national man in the country; while his lavish outpouring of the sheaves of political patronage upon the Democratic free-soilers of the North enabled the Republican faction in the end to redeem itself most effectually from the discredit into which it had been plunged during the period of Mr. Fillmore's administration, building it up and strengthening it greatly for the expected presidential contest of 1856. Meanwhile Mr. Pierce and his cabinet assistants openly and unblushingly interfered in all the political elections in the states, employed patronage every where in order to control votes, and spread throughout the republic

such an abominable spirit of huckstering and corrupt
political bargaining as even Walpole, in his palmiest days
of official glory, had never been able to call into existence. In less than a twelve-month after Mr. Pierce's induction into the presidency, every man of solid understanding, both in Congress and elsewhere, who had aided
this ill-starred scion of the Granite State in reaching the
presidency, became satisfied that he was utterly incompetent for the performance of the high duties which had
devolved upon him, and honest men every where were
filled with mingled amazement and disgust at nearly all
that was from time to time reported to be occurring under his sinister auspices either at home or abroad. Such
men as Daniel S. Dickinson and the lamented Justice
Bronson, of New York, and many other Democrats of almost equal eminence elsewhere, were driven into opposition by such acts of official arrogance and folly as are
rarely known to mark the course of public events in a
free country; and innumerable official blunders, Ostend
manifestoes, and such like *vagaries* included, soon made
Mr. Pierce and his cabinet as sublimely ridiculous before
the world at large, as their domestic economy had rendered them alike powerful for mischief and impotent for
good within the confines of their own country.

Very unfortunately for that country, and, as I must
think, for Mr. Douglas's own well-earned fame, this gentleman was induced, under very strong solicitations from
various individuals of the extreme Southern school, and
by the persuasions likewise of at least one member of
Mr. Pierce's cabinet, connected with something like half
promises of future political support, to originate, or rath-

er to adopt from a Southern source, a new scheme of
action in regard to the then suppressed issue of slavery,
which, in its rapid development, was productive of renewed agitation both in the South and in the North, a
view of the consequences of which, had he been able at
that time to descry them in the future history of his
country, would have effectually deterred one of his patriotic impulses from running the fiery and troublous career
which was presently to open before him, and which was
in a few years to fill his bosom with poignant anguish,
to surround him with innumerable and irreconcilable
foes, to break down even his Herculean physical frame,
and to conduct him, amid the opening scenes of a fearful
civil war, to a premature grave. I am understood, of
course, as referring to the Kansas-Nebraska Bill, which
was made to contain a provision for repealing the Missouri Compromise, or, rather (which was virtually the
same thing), declaring the Missouri Compromise restrictive clause to be repugnant to the principle of *non-intervention*, which constituted the chief feature of the Compromise of 1850. I shall not now expatiate upon the Kansas-
Nebraska Bill. The world knows all its fatal provisions
by heart, and our country has freely bled over these same
provisions. I certainly never regarded any part of the
bill as unconstitutional, nor do I consider it to have made
war *directly* upon any principle embodied in the compromise measures of 1850; but I have ever been of opinion that this new arrangement was altogether repugnant
to the *spirit* in which the compromise measures of 1850
had been framed, and palpably violative of the principle
of *finality* upon which the peace of the country had been

expected to repose. I do personally know that it was not at all intended by Mr. Clay and those who co-operated with him in 1850, to interfere at all with the Missouri Compromise. It was contemplated that the question whether the restrictive clause in that compromise was or was not valid was to be left to the courts, and I will add, that some of us in 1850 acted in this matter upon the conviction which we had then clearly formed, and on several occasions had also expressed, that the Supreme Court of the United States, when that tribunal should be appealed to, would render just such a decision upon the constitutionality of the restrictive act of 1820 as has since been promulged. I confess that, notwithstanding my profound respect for Mr. Douglas, whose presidential aspirations in 1860 evoked my hearty support, I could not but be most painfully surprised when, away off upon the Pacific coast, I learned that he had consented, under any persuasions whatever, to be the chief actor in a proceeding which it seemed to me must inevitably renew slavery agitation; and especially was this the case, when I reflected upon the fact that he had objected even to the finality resolution introduced by me in the Senate in the winter of 1852, not at all upon the ground that he did not entirely approve its *object*, but *alone*, and most emphatically, upon the ground that it might by possibility renew sectional strife. It is really painful to look back upon the past, and observe that, even in the early part of the Thirty-third Congress, Mr. Douglas had himself brought in a well-written and most deliberate report, in which he had used the following clear and explicit language; referring to the restrictive provision in the Missouri Compromise, he says: "Under this section, as in the case of the Mexican law in New Mexico and Utah, it is a disputed point whether slavery is prohibited in the Nebraska country by *valid* enactment. The decision of this question involves the constitutional power of Congress to pass laws prescribing and regulating the domestic institutions of the various territories of the Union. In the opinion of those eminent statesmen who hold that Congress is invested with no rightful authority to legislate upon the subject of slavery in the territories, the 8th section of the act preparatory to the admission of Missouri is null and void; while the prevailing sentiment in large portions of the Union sustains the doctrine that the Constitution of the United States secures to every citizen an inalienable right to move into any of the territories with his property, of whatever kind and description, and to hold and enjoy the same under the sanction of law. Your committee do not feel themselves called upon to enter upon the discussion of these controverted questions. They involve the same grave issues which produced the agitation, the sectional strife, and the fearful struggle of 1850. As Congress deemed it wise and prudent to *refrain from deciding the matter in controversy then,* either by affirming or repealing the Mexican laws, or by an act declaratory of the true intent of the Constitution, and the extent of the protection afforded by it to slave property in the territories, so your committee are not prepared to recommend a departure from the course pursued on that memorable occasion, either by *affirming or repealing the 8th section of the Missouri act, or by any act declaratory of the meaning of the Constitution in respect to the legal points in dispute.*"

The two august chiefs of the compromise, Mr. Clay and Mr. Webster, were now, alas, in their graves. Had they continued to live, I am satisfied that no controversial dis-. cussion of this fearful question would have occurred of a nature calculated inevitably to sweep away in its *course*, as with the besom of destruction, slavery and all the existing legal regulations connected therewith. The verification of Mr. Clay's prophecy on this subject we are all now witnessing, some with feelings of tribulation, and some with those of rejoicing; the work of sectional agitation has been productive of its natural *consequences*, and in the presence of that startling social revolution which, under the providence of God, has been effected throughout that region once devoted to slavery, who, among those that have been so criminally unmindful of the dangers so often pointed out in language that would not have been unworthy of the most gifted of the Apostles, shall now presume to complain at the realization of a state of things which naught but a strict and faithful adherence to the solid guarantees of the Federal Constitution, and the doing nothing to undermine and enfeeble them, could possibly have averted?

And now, before taking final leave of Mr. Clay and Mr. Webster, let me offer one or two observations upon each of them.

Those who have heard Mr. Clay upon great occasions admit that he was, upon the whole, the most winning, electrical, and truly commanding speaker that has appeared in America during the present century. His conversational powers were almost equally remarkable, and there was an irresistible charm, both in his aspect, voice,

and manner, when he chose to exert his social powers
fully. He was the frankest of men, and was far too fearless of soul to seek safety in the concealment of his opinions on any subject, or in the profession of sentiments of
esteem and kindness for individuals which he did not
really feel. It is now well known that he could have
been president in 1844 had he chosen to yield the special
pledge as to his course upon the slavery question which
the Abolition supporters of Mr. Birney sought, in a *clan-
destine* manner, to obtain from him. There was no public measure of an important character in relation to which
the humblest of his fellow-citizens could not have obtained his opinions by making courteous application therefor. He was never suspected of unfairness or dishon-
est intrigue, except in connection with Mr. Adams's election in 1825; and I may be excused for here stating that
I was present, in the summer of 1850, on a convivial occasion of some note, when he adverted to this subject in
a pleasant and condescending manner, and gave utterance
to a very frank declaration which was exceedingly gratifying to all present. It was at the celebrated dinner-
party at the hospitable mansion of Mr. Sullivan, in Washington City, when the venerable Ritchie, his early friend
and associate in Richmond before he had commenced
his brilliant career in the West, and who, after long es-
trangement, had been recently reconciled to him, in a
manner half jocose, half serious, told him that if he carried through the compromise measures, and would promise never again to be a candidate for the presidency, he
would, if he should survive him, plant a sprig of laurel
upon his grave. Mr. Clay, kindly adverting to the long-

continued opposition of the Richmond Enquirer to his political advancement, and the grounds upon which that opposition had been based, said, that though his motives in voting for Mr. Adams, in the Congress of 1824–'5, were as pure as it was possible for them to have been, and though, were the election to come over again, he would have to vote precisely as he had done on that occasion, yet that, after the painful experience which he had had of the mischievous effects growing out of his acceptance under Mr. Adams of the Department of State, nothing could induce him to receive any official appointment at his hands. He confessed that this was a most serious official blunder, and had greatly impaired his public usefulness.

Linn Boyd, former speaker of the House of Representatives, called upon me one morning during the tempestuous session of 1850, and informed me that he had been for many years a bitter political adversary of Mr. Clay, and that he had, for a series of years, pressed with great earnestness the famous charge of *bargain and intrigue* against him connected with the election of Mr. Adams; declared that he had been greatly struck with Mr. Clay's patriotic course in the advocacy of the compromise measures, and asked that I would call upon that gentleman and request on his behalf a face to face interview, that he might have an opportunity of making the *amende honorable* as to past unkindnesses. I readily undertook the mission propounded, and very soon had the gratification of witnessing a thorough reconcilement between them. Several years after Mr. Clay's decease, I was called upon by Boyd, when very hotly pressed in a

political canvass in which he was then engaged in the
State of Kentucky, to bear written testimony to the transaction just related, which of course I could not *refuse to do.*

Of Mr. Webster I hesitate to speak. He was so much
superior in power of thought, in grandeur of conception,
in genuine logical power, in condensed vigor of expression, in brilliancy of fancy, in sprightly and amiable face-
tiousness, in the richest stores of well-digested knowledge,
whether scholastic, scientific, or practical, to any other
public man that I have had the fortune to know, or that
I have ever heard described, that I have no words in
which to express my admiration of him. I never heard
him talk at his own table, where, though the most modest
of men, at the instance of cherished friends, he sometimes
conversed freely, that I did not sigh for the presence of a
reporter to take down the golden words that came with
such a delightful impressiveness from his lips. I never
heard him speak in the Senate on any occasion whatever, when every sentence which he uttered was not fit to
be put in print. Who has ever read a paragraph of his
masterly composition and desired to change a syllable?
Then his heart was so kind, his manners were so cordial,
his aspect and demeanor so marked with touching sim-
plicity and unartificial dignity, that, had he not spoken a
word, he must yet have been loved and venerated. The
last time that I beheld this remarkable person was on an
occasion which no man that witnessed it can ever forget.
On the morning previous to my taking leave of the national Senate to return to my own home in Mississippi,
to buffet billows with which I was little able to contend,
I chanced to be present at a banqueting scene, to which,

having been long since depictured by others, I may now
for a moment recur. In a large room in the lower story
of Brown's Hotel, in Washington, a large convivial company was assembled. Most of the cabinet functionaries
of Mr. Fillmore were present, a considerable proportion of
the ministers from foreign countries in attendance upon
the government, and some six or eight of the members
of Congress then in session.

The dinner was capital, the wine was most select, the
banqueters apparently most happy. Having to leave
the city in the cars next morning, and not having yet
completed my preparations for the journey, I rose up
while my social companions were still absorbed in the
delightful interchange of thought and sentiment, and not
wishing to disturb the scene, made an effort to steal
away. I soon found this to be impossible. Whether
what follows was the result of previous arrangement I
know not, nor have I ever thought it needful to inquire;
but this is precisely what did in point of fact occur: Mr.
Webster, rising, and followed by the rest of the company, approached me as I was retiring, and presently addressed me, in the name of those present, an affectionate valedictory, such as he who hears can never forget.
He spoke for some five or ten minutes in prose, referring
to the various interesting public scenes which had recently occurred, and presently, without confusion or hesitation, he adopted the language of poetry, and poured forth
some twenty or thirty couplets, which either Pope or Dry-
den, Byron or Moore, might have envied, all perfectly
germain to the topics upon which he had been descant-
ing, and evidently *improvised* .at the moment, and con-

cluded by wishing me, in the name of all, an affectionate farewell. It has been published, years ago, that I was dumbfounded by this extraordinary address. I shall not say whether this is altogether true or not; but certainly, if I uttered any thing in response, it is all now lost to my memory in the overwhelming recollection of this most stupendous display of genius on the part of the wonderful personage of whom I have been speaking. "Daniel Webster still lives," and ever *will continue to live, in the admiration and affection of the wise, the patriotic, and the virtuous!!*

How surprised and indignant must the intelligent and magnanimous of other generations inevitably be on learning, as they will unfortunately do, that even such a man as this, compounded as he was of all the nobler and more gracious elements of our nature, was not permitted to escape the rough and heartless assaults of cold-blooded and mercenary calumniators when living, nor, even after death, suffered to remain quietly inurned, without being subjected to the objurgatory malevolence of some who knew him familiarly while still lingering in the realms of mortality, and whose most pleasant duty it should have been to keep his august and sacred name forever bright and untarnished, and continually to scatter laurels of unfading honor over and around that sequestered tomb which holds all that now remains of the most grandly and variously gifted man that has ever yet borne the proud name of *American!*

CHAPTER XI.

Excited Struggle in Congress over the Kansas-Nebraska Bill.—Manly but ineffectual Opposition to that Bill in Congress.—Regret expressed at the Disappearance from the public Scene of Mr. Clay, Mr. Webster, and Mr. Calhoun.—Confident Opinion expressed as to what would have been Mr. Calhoun's Course had he survived up to our Times.—Fearful awakening of sectional Excitement both in the South and in the North under the Influence of the Kansas-Nebraska Bill.—Multiplied Scenes of Blood and Violence in the Territory of Kansas.—Mr. Pierce and his Cabinet lose the Confidence of all Men of true Nationality of Sentiment. —Mr. Pierce defeated in the Cincinnati Democratic Convention by Mr. Buchanan, who is afterward elected to the Presidency by a plurality Vote over Fremont and Fillmore.—Mr. Buchanan delivers an Inaugural Address as President, replete with national Sentiment, which attracts to him the Support of the American Party, and his Administration grows overwhelmingly popular.—He afterward treacherously violates all his Promises to the Country under the Threats of Southern Secession Leaders, and his Administration suddenly becomes both odious and contemptible.—The Democratic Party of the North completely crushed and broken down by the fatal Lecompton Issue, and the way surely paved for the Election of a Republican President in 1860.—Review of the State of Parties at that Period.—Some Notice of the American Party and its particular Tenets.—Great Mistake of the Southern People in not yielding their Support to Mr. Fillmore in 1856.—Some Notice of the Republican Candidates for President and Vice-President in 1856, and of certain curious Scenes which took place during the short period of General Fremont's official Connection with that Body. —Sketch of General Baker, one of the earliest Victims of the War, and a recital of certain romantic Occurrences connected with his Residence in California and Oregon.—Signal Triumph of his extraordinary oratorical Powers over popular Excitement and Prejudice.

So was it with our country in the latter part of Mr.

Pierce's administration. Clay, Webster, and Calhoun
were no longer upon the arena of public action. Those
who had taken their places possessed but little of the
wisdom with which these great statesmen had showed
themselves to be endowed. General Cass, one of the
few men at that time in Congress that had either sufficient power as a parliamentary speaker, or sufficient
weight of character to render innocuous the elements of
mischief then at work, was, at this particular moment,
neither so active nor observant as usual, by reason of a
severe domestic misfortune which had just fallen upon
him, and which I personally know to have much de-
pressed his spirits and enfeebled his energies. Others
there were in the national councils from whom a far
wiser and more conservative course was to have been expected at this crisis, but who had, in the Kansas-Nebraska struggle, strangely disappointed the public hopes. Mr.
Badger, of North Carolina, honest, enlightened, and patriotic, a learned jurist, a calm and methodical debater,
who had been, during all his antecedent life, remarkable
for his moderation and forbearance, had for a moment
joined the extremists of the South in giving his high
sanction to a rupture of the *compact* of 1850; while Mr.
Bell, of Tennessee, always able, but most generally, from
a certain modesty of temperament, a little slow and inde-
cisive in his movements, had at this time been seen to
exert more than his habitual energy, had both zealously and manfully confronted all who showed themselves
to be inclined to measure swords with him, and had
fearlessly and vigorously essayed to throttle the monster

I

of sectionalism on the floor of the Senate, ere yet, like
Eolus, he should succeed in unchaining all the winds of
heaven once more, which had been now for nearly four
years quietly sleeping in their caves. But Mr. Toombs
was there, that Mirabeau of the South, fervid, impassioned, eloquent, bold, defiant, arrogant, high-souled, and
generous, but self-reliant, dogmatical, and reckless—better fitted than any man I have yet seen to conjure up a
sudden storm of popular excitement, but sadly deficient
in that calmness of soul so indispensable to the attainment of nearly all great public ends; and beside him
stood others, who, though perchance not possessed altogether of equal power in discussion or equal audacity of
spirit, were yet able to lend considerable aid in such a
confused struggle as was then going forward.

I have alluded to Mr. Calhoun as one of those whose
decease had deprived the public councils of a man who
would not at this conjuncture, had he been living, have
lent his great powers, and, if possible, still greater personal weight and influence, to the side of agitation and discord. I feel that I speak advisedly on this subject. A
few months subsequent to the death of this extraordinary
man in 1850, General James Hamilton, of South Carolina, one of his most trusted friends, and who had much
familiar conversation with Mr. Calhoun a few days only
before he ceased to live, published, about twelve months
thereafter, a long and interesting letter, in which he emphatically denied that Mr. Calhoun, had he continued
alive, would have yielded his sanction to that scheme of
rebellion against the national government which others

JOHN C. CALHOUN. 195

were at the very moment of the publication of this important letter so indiscreetly and causelessly attempting; and I can not but believe that Mr. Calhoun, who never claimed for the South aught but that she "*should be let alone*," who had even refused his assent to the proposition made by General Jackson, during his last official term, to interfere to some extent with the freedom of mail communications, avowedly with a view to preventing the circulation through the slaveholding regions of incendiary documents, would neither have given his sanction to the infamous Lecompton Constitution, fastened, or rather attempted to be fastened, upon the necks of a free people, without their consent and in undeniable opposition to their wishes; nor would so sober-minded and circumspect a man as Mr. Calhoun have been found, in 1861, co-operating with those inconsiderate and ill-judging Southern members of Congress who abandoned their seats merely because a presidential election had taken place, for the result of which they had made themselves chiefly responsible, before even any overt act violative of the rights of the South had been either perpetrated or been even distinctly menaced; when they knew that President Lincoln had been elected only by a *plurality of popular* votes; when they were also bound to know that they had it in their power, by acting faithfully and cordially with their Northern political allies, infallibly to defeat all hostile legislation which might be attempted against them or those whom they represented for the four years which were next to pass away ere another presidential election would occur; and that it was almost morally certain that in 1860 the reins of authority would be placed in the hands of a man elected conjointly by Southern votes and those of individuals friendly to Southern interests. And I will now announce my confident opinion that John C. Calhoun, had he survived until the eventful year of 1861, would have both seen and exposed the folly of going into so *unequal* and needless a war as that which has just closed, and especially without making some adequate preparation for all the terrible exigencies which were sure to arise therein; that he would never have sanctioned the conduct of the suddenly *improvised* Montgomery government in ordering so rashly the opening of the bloody tragedy which has since been so memorably connected with the spilling of fraternal blood at Charleston; that he would have been thoroughly nauseated with that compound of weakness, and corruption, and servility in the form of a cabinet which Mr. Davis so stupidly called around him, and retained, in spite of general public sentiment crying aloud against those who constituted it, until there was no longer any hope for the cause with which they stood officially associated; that he would have indignantly condemned the measures of confiscation, conscription, forcible impressment, the suspension of habeas corpus, the proclamation of *martial law*, and numerous enactments besides, adopted by a slavish congressional majority, in order to build up and arm with despotic power an over-ambitious and incompetent executive chief; that he would still more strongly have condemned the general spread of corruption into all the departments, both principal and subordinate, of Confederate trust; that he would not have hesitated, had he been destined to occupy a seat in either of the houses of the Confederate

Congress, to rebuke in a style of decorous courtesy, but yet with true Roman-like sternness and severity, the rank and ever-increasing abuses of power which he would have plainly seen to be going on—the obstinate retention in the highest official stations of men of depraved morals, and of the lowest and most profligate habitudes, the heartless persecution of the most meritorious military commanders, and the elevation over their heads of those whose single claim to promotion was a groveling and abject devotion to their executive chief; and lastly, that Mr. Calhoun, that honest and inflexible supporter of the rights of the states and of the essential muniments of freedom, would not have failed to denounce with all the power which a pure heart, a cultivated intellect, and a lordly spirit could confer, the wretched and fantastical scheme of setting on foot in the ancient and time-honored city of Richmond an irresponsible military despotism which, conjoined with the foul and bloody tyranny now essaying to establish itself upon the bosom of downtrodden Mexico, and the already organized and wide-sweeping imperial government of France, it was presumptuously and madly hoped would, after a while, prominently participate in dominating over the wide-spread affairs of both the eastern and western hemispheres.

But it is a little too early for me to descant upon these topics; let me offer a few additional *observations* upon the immediate *consequences* arising from the adoption of the Kansas-Nebraska Bill.

I shall decline the presentation of any detailed account of the multiplied efforts which were now made, both in certain states of New England and in several of the cot-

ton-growing states of the South, to obtain mastery upon
the new arena of contention which had been opened to
them, so unwisely, on the sunset side of the Father of
Waters. I have no taste for depicturing the schemes of
hot-headed and unreasoning sectionalists, whether located
in the famed land of the Pilgrims, or amid the fair savan-
nas of the South, or the teeming alluvial regions of the
far Southwest. A sober and thoughtful posterity will, I
fancy, feel but little interest in the operations of "New
England Emigrant Aid Societies," or in the silly and
lawless expeditions carried on in Kansas under the authority and auspices of the "Blue Lodges," the "Social
Bands," the "Sons of the South," or any other grim and
horrible form of "*Border Ruffianism.*" *Who* first unpardonably shed the blood of brothers upon the soil of
the disputed territory; *who* afterward became most renowned as the unnatural conflict proceeded, either in
slaying in open fight, in the perpetration of covert mur-
der, in the burning of infant towns and villages, in the
wholesale destruction of new-founded rural settlements;
whether ex-senator David R. Atchison, or the now world-
renowned Ossawatomie Brown, or perchance some other
of the numerous armed representatives of the "antagonistic elements" "of our *death-impregned* Federal Constitution, is to be transmitted to future generations as *the
chief hero* of this disgraceful "Kansas war," the accounts
which have reached us thus far are too vague and conflicting to enable any one not already overboiling with
partisan venom positively to determine. The successive
advents of territorial gubernatorial *missionaries of conciliation*, dispatched, one after another, by the perplexed

and vacillating Pierce (whose ominous comings and go-
ings seem now, to our organs of mental vision, more like
the changeful and flitting representations of a *phantasma-
goria* than the sober realities which the historic muse
would gladly garner up and preserve for the inspection
of future generations), it is best for us all should sink at
once into obscurity. The only fact which it is essential
now to notice is, that the scenes of contention in Kansas
which have been thus glancingly referred to continued
until the election and inauguration of Mr. Buchanan.
This gentleman had been nominated over Pierce by the
National Democratic Convention which assembled in the
city of Cincinnati in the month of June, 1856, in spite of
the most profuse and disgraceful use of official patronage, in order to secure the reign of the *intervention* policy
by a president solemnly pledged to *non-intervention*. I
believe it to be strictly true, as I heard directly from the
lips of Mr. Buchanan afterward, that the presidential
nomination on this occasion *sought him*, not *he it*. There
were now two other presidential candidates in the field,
Millard Fillmore and John C. Fremont. Mr. Buchanan
was chosen President, after a very fierce and excited
struggle, by a *plurality* of popular votes only, the following being the result of the canvass: Buchanan, 1,838,169
votes; Fremont, 1,341,264; and Mr. Fillmore, the American or Union candidate, 874,534.

I shall reserve the observations which I deem it proper to make upon Mr. Buchanan's eventful administration
to another chapter, and bring forward at present some
other matters needful to be considered in connection
with subsequent events.

It is now far too plain a proposition to be denied, that the South, in order to guard her slaveholding interests from immolation, should have thrown her whole presidential vote to Fillmore in the contest which had just terminated. This personage was well known to be a man of the utmost sobriety of spirit, of unsurpassed honesty of purpose, thoroughly loyal to the Constitution and all its well-known guarantees. Though conscientiously opposed to the *extension* of slavery into the vacant territories by congressional enactment, he was equally opposed to the *exclusion* of it therefrom by a similar instrumentality. In other words, he was a true non-interventionist of the Clay, Webster, and Cass school, and had given evidences during his former administration of his fearless devotion to principle, and his willingness to face all the dangers of anti-slavery opposition, which ought to have strongly commended him to the hearty support alike of the Southern slaveholding interest and of the true friends of national repose. Immediately on reaching the United States from a European tour, he delivered in the city of Albany the following noble harangue, which is, in my. judgment, in.tone and spirit, worthy of the best days of Athens and of Rome:

" We see a political party presenting candidates for the presidency and vice-presidency, selected for the first time from the free states alone, with the avowed purpose of electing these candidates by the suffrages of one part of the Union only, to rule over the whole United States. Can it be possible that those who are engaged in such a measure can have seriously reflected upon the consequences which must inevitably follow in case of success?

Can they have the madness or the folly to believe that our Southern brethren would submit to be governed by such a chief magistrate? Would he be required to follow the same rule prescribed by those who elected him in making his appointments? If a man living south of Mason and Dixon's line be not worthy to be president or vice-president, would it be proper to select one from the same quarter as one of his cabinet council, or to represent the nation in a foreign country, or, indeed, to collect the revenue, or administer the laws of the United States? If not, what new rule is the President to adopt in selecting men for office that the people themselves discard in selecting *him?* These are serious, but practical questions; and, in order to appreciate them fully, it is only necessary to turn the tables upon ourselves. Suppose that the South, having the majority of the electoral votes, should declare that they would only have *slave-holders* for president and vice-president, and should elect such by their exclusive suffrages to rule over us at the North, do you think we would submit to it? No, not for a moment. And do you believe that your Southern brethren are less sensitive on this subject than you are, or less jealous of their rights? If you do, let me tell you that you are mistaken. And, therefore, you must see that, if this sectional party succeeds, it leads inevitably to the destruction of this beautiful fabric, reared by our forefathers, cemented by their blood, and bequeathed to us as a priceless inheritance."

Doubtless these clear and manly declarations of principle by Mr. Fillmore did secure him, at the South, a large share of popular approval; and had the public men

I 2

of that section been in strict unison with the more moderate and conservative doctrines of Mr. Calhoun, who is known very uniformly indeed (with perhaps the exception of a portion of what was embodied by him in his last elaborate speech touching the admission of California) to have declared that all that we asked for the South was that *she should be let alone*, it seems certain that this worthy son of the Empire State must have been chosen president. If a consummation so desirable had been effected, a repetition of the golden era which has been already described might have been confidently anticipated, and, in all probability, the noxious weed of sectionalism, which had sprung up and attained such rank and luxuriant growth during the evil days of the administration then just closing, would never have been able to show its night-shade foliage above ground.

That sectionalism in the North had well-nigh lost its vitality when Mr. Pierce came into office, is unequivocally attested by no less a personage than Jefferson Davis himself, who, when taking a tour of observation through the New England States during the early part of his eccentrical and oppressive administration of the Department of War, sojourning, as he did, for weeks at several places on his route, in deliberate speeches, much commended by confiding Union men at the time, declared that *political abolition* was then nowhere visible; that the *virus* of anti-slavery had altogether ceased to permeate the veins and arteries of the body politic; and that the slaveholding population of the South might safely rely in future upon the organic shield provided in behalf of their peculiar property interests by the wise and far-seeing framers of the Federal Constitution. Nor were these mere fanciful conjectures of the late High-priest of Secession of the far Southwest, for I do myself well recollect that, at the period to which I am now referring, most of the leading Free-soil newspaper organs had altogether ceased to agitate the slavery question in their columns, and several United States senators from the North, who in 1850 had made fierce and rampant war upon the measures of compromise, and upon the Fugitive Slave Law in particular, had formally avowed their full acquiescence in all the wise and salutary enactments just mentioned. But, as before hinted, the pro-slavery champions of the South, since the adoption of the Kansas-Nebraska Bill, had located themselves upon an entirely new track in regard to slavery; they were by no means satisfied now with being left undisturbed by their Northern fellow-citizens on the subject of slavery, and they had determined to demand of Congress that their slaveholding rights should be given special *protection* by the legislation of that body, the boasted guaranties of the Constitution being no longer by them deemed sufficient.

I have said that it was a *new track* which these gentlemen had now taken. I must acknowledge that the absurd and impracticable idea of congressional protection for slavery in the territories was not absolutely of novel origin, since, as has been stated, Mr. Yancey had made his celebrated, but wholly unsuccessful experiment in this behalf, upon the National Democratic Convention of 1848, and Mr. Jefferson Davis had afterward gravely repeated this experiment in 1850, when the compromise measures were under discussion in the Senate, but with a similar want of success. That this was the grand object which the political leaders of the South held in view at this period in preferring Mr. Buchanan to Mr. Fillmore, was more or less indicated during the session of the Democratic Nominating Convention in Cincinnati, by the new-blown support of that gentleman's claims to be selected as the presidential candidate of the Democratic party, yielded by certain well-known supporters of secession in 1850; and this object became still more manifest in the imperious demands which these individuals set up in the sequel, to be allowed absolute control over Mr. Buchanan's action in regard to slavery in the territories, and to use the power which they boasted of having bestowed upon him as an effective instrument for their well-matured purpose to extend slavery by all the force of the national arm.

The American party, of which Mr. Fillmore was the chosen champion and exponent, was mainly a Union party, and avowed undying opposition to sectionalism in any form which it might assume. Unfortunately for this party and for the country, a few overheated zealots belonging to it had contrived, in several of the states, and especially in Virginia, to impart to it a *sectarian* cast. Wherever this occurred, of course this party had been signally defeated in the local elections which at that time took place, as it well deserved to have been. Every where, though, the members of this party insisted with *equal* zeal upon that particular feature of its creed from which its corporate name had been derived: they concurred in believing that the influx of persons of foreign birth and training had latterly become so enormous that

there was serious danger that all the distinctive character-
istics of our country would be lost. They still more painfully apprehended that, if full political rights and privileges should be accorded to all these new-comers, and
especially if laws should continue to be enacted by Congress which held out the most seductive rewards to all
the paupers of foreign lands to come to our shores, the
capacity of the American people for the task of self-government might become more or less impaired, and great
and radical mischiefs be seen to arise from the presence
and overmastering ascendency of so large a number of
persons in indigent circumstances, and of imperfect political education, in the large popular elections which must
always be expected to control, in a greater or less degree, the operations of our complex governmental machine. This may or may not have been an erroneous
notion. Its discussion would be wholly profitless at present, as this grave question has been already definitely
settled, and, in all probability, settled very wisely for our
country, in view of the great and radical social changes
which have lately taken place in the states of the South.
But I have one observation to make here, for which I
hope I shall be pardoned by the late vehement champions of slavery *extension:* it is obvious that nothing has
tended so fatally to weaken and undermine the slaveholding system recently existing in the South as this
very *foreign element,* the *over-rapid strengthening* of which,
the American party, with Mr. Fillmore at its head, struggled honestly to prevent; and so well satisfied had the
whole South become, three years ago, of the truth of this
affirmation, that it is a well-known fact that Mr. Clement

C. Clay, of Alabama, as a member of the Confederate
Congress, formerly a most unqualified antagonist of the
American cause, did not hesitate to bring forward a legislative proposition against the naturalization of foreign-
ers in the Confederate States 'far more stringent in its
terms than the platform of the American party was ever
by its bitterest opponents accused of being—which proposition, I am prepared to assert, upon the fullest knowledge of facts, did not evoke the smallest opposition in
either House of the legislative body referred to, or in
newspapers wheresoever printed, in any part of the South.
In looking back to the past, it is really not at all incuri-
ous to observe that the Hon. Henry A. Wise, one of the
most brilliant and electrical popular speakers that the
South, teeming in all generations with gifted orators, has
ever produced, at the close of his memorable canvass for
governor of the Ancient Dominion about this period,
standing upon the steps in front of some hotel in the city
of Washington, surrounded by a vast multitude of his
then admiring friends, poured forth an exultant oration
over the signal triumph which he had recently achieved .
upon the soil of his native state over that forlorn and
gloomy champion of *Know-nothingism*, who' he complained had kept his visor *down* over his hideous countenance on every occasion where he had met him in combat, and closing with a glowing peroration; in which he
declared that his election to the office of governor would
be "the death-knell of all Pacific Railroad schemes."
Now at that very moment, though perhaps he did not
know so *recondite* a circumstance, Mr. Buchanan had
pledged himself, in a letter printed only west of the

Rocky Mountains anterior to the presidential election, in which he had explicitly declared himself in favor of the early establishment of this great highway of nations over the American continent. Had this usually astute gentleman, Governor Wise, been able, at the moment that he uttered this oracular declaration, to descry the untold mysteries of the future, he would have seen that the very political result of which he was then boasting would, in a few years, by increasing the relative strength of the Northern sectional majority, fatally weaken the position of the Southern portion of the Union, and thus, whether through the instrumentalities of peace or war, impart an irresistible impetus to that grand scheme of internal improvement which, I venture to predict, will not hereafter encounter any serious opposition from enlightened men on either side of the renowned line of separation between the North and the South.

Truly man proposeth, and God disposeth!

Of the Republican standard-bearers and political platform of 1856 I shall on this occasion have but little to say. The newly-reorganized Free-soil party, which now for the first time appropriated to itself the designation which has been subsequently associated with so many signal political victories, as well as with other grand events which have attracted such profound attention throughout Christendom, had boldly placed itself upon unmistakable *intervention* ground, and had proclaimed to the world that "*the Constitution confers sovereign power over the territories of the United States for their government; and that, in the exercise of this power, it is both the right and the duty of Congress to prohibit in the territories those twin relics of barbarism, polygamy and slavery.*"

With Mr. Dayton, the nominee of the Republican party
for the vice-presidency, I became acquainted when I was
myself a member of the national Senate, and I am prepared to say of him that he ever impressed me most favorably, both in regard to his intellectual power and his
general temper and bearing, alike in social intercourse
and in debate; and it can not be doubted that, had he
been elevated in 1856 to the second office in the government, he would have shown himself altogether equal to
the duties of this high position.

I should, for certain reasons, be inclined to be absolutely silent concerning the gentleman who had become at
this period the Republican nominee for the presidency,
but that a passing notice of this personage can be hardly .
avoided in a work like the present, and but for the additional circumstance that he has since become a prominent
military character, whose career must be regarded as having more or less influence upon the general concerns of
the republic.

Colonel Fremont came into the United States Senate
from California in the eventful summer of 1850, as one
of the senators elected from the then newly-admitted
state of that name. He occupied a seat in that body
only some seventeen or eighteen days altogether, his colleague, Dr. William M. Gwin, having, with his accustomed good fortune, drawn the long senatorial term for the
State of California, while Colonel Fremont had drawn
the short one. The latter gentleman was not fortunate
enough to secure his own re-election to the elevated station of which he was in 1850 for a brief space the incumbent.

There were circumstances existing at the time, and especially my well-known variance with Colonel Benton, his father-in-law, which interposed insuperable impediments to our forming a personal acquaintance, at least in the usual way. General Fremont and myself have never yet been formally introduced to each other, and in all probability we never shall be hereafter. I certainly had no unkindness individually for this gentleman when we entered the Senate, nor have I a particle of personal ill-will toward him at the present moment. When the painful and protracted contest between this gentleman and Governor Mason, of New Mexico, was pending, and a meeting between these individuals upon the field of honor was confidently expected very soon to occur, at the earnest instance of a very worthy gentleman then in the Senate, and who is still surviving, I had ventured to interpose in this very delicate affair, with a view of preventing, if practicable, those tragical consequences which were so justly to be apprehended. I had never had the slightest reason to suspect that Colonel Fremont, as he was then called, cherished feelings of personal unkindness for myself, when, on the last night of the congressional session, the following very curious scene occurred. This gentleman had within a few days introduced several bills, the provisions of which involved, as I could not but believe, valuable mineral interests of the government, which bills, I was of opinion, should they become laws, would be infallibly productive of great public detriment. I had presented a firm and courteous opposition to them, as others had done, and they had been, by our joint efforts, defeated; when, coming to my seat, he accosted me politely and invited me to an interview outside of the Senate, which invitation I could not in reason refuse. After we had passed through the large central door of the Senate-chamber, which closed after us, he turned to me and said, "Colonel Benton is very much displeased at your conduct to-night." To which I responded, "I regret much to learn that such is the fact, as I have been laboring assiduously to conciliate *that* eminent personage for several years." To this he responded, "I do not at all like your conduct myself, nor will I allow you to interfere with my California concerns." I then said, "I do not understand how you can have any California concerns proper to become a subject of legislative action in the Senate in the consideration of which I may not legitimately participate. Besides," I continued, "Colonel, you must know that I intend in all matters to act with perfect independence in the Senate, without the least regard to whether you and Colonel Benton are offended or not;" and subjoined, "I opine that you have waked up the *wrong passenger.*" Upon which he exclaimed, "You are no gentleman!" On the utterance of this insulting language I struck him. He was evidently proceeding, with a sufficient display of spirit, to return the blow, when two senators coming out of the central door through which we had passed interfered between us and forcibly threw us apart. In about an hour I received a note of very significant import from Colonel Fremont, to which I wrote an assenting response. Before daylight several senatorial friends interfered in the affair, demanded the simultaneous withdrawal of both the hostile notes, and insisted that the dispute should be altogether dropped. This was mutually agreed to, and

I, regarding the altercation as terminated, proceeded the next day to my own distant home in the Southwest. In about two weeks thereafter I received several letters from eminent senatorial friends, informing me that, subsequent to my departure from Washington, Colonel Fremont had issued a hand-bill charging me with having instigated certain newspaper scribblers to ridicule his conduct in the transaction described, and denouncing me for this, my supposed conduct, in very unmeasured terms. These friends likewise advised me to let the matter pass by, as they did not consider that I was at all likely to suffer detriment from silence; and, in point of fact, this was the course pursued by me. - When, several years after, during the presidential contest of 1856, two or three of Colonel Fremont's Republican supporters in San Francisco called upon me one morning, and invited my attention to an editorial article which had just made its appearance in an Ohio paper, accusing their candidate of having made a violent personal assault upon me in the lobby of the Senate-chamber, I did not hesitate to deny the fact, and they being of opinion that the circulation of this charge would do him injury as a presidential candidate, I gave them a written certificate denying the accusation, which they published immediately.

There are some other facts of a different character connected with the presidential contest of 1856, so far as the same had its progress in the State of California, of far superior interest to the general reader than those which have just been narrated.

All America has long ago heard of the meritorious and splendid character of whom I have now to record some particulars of a nature to impart to sober reality much of the brightness and attractiveness of romance. General Edward C. Baker, who was recently an honored member of the United States Senate from one of the youngest and fairest daughters of this ocean-bound confederacy of states, and whose untimely death, in one of the earliest battles of our late unhappy civil war, all the admirers of genius, and all the sympathizers with true manliness of soul, must profoundly lament, was born in England, at a period not very remote from the commencement of the present century. He came to the United States, whether in company with his parents or under the care of some casual protector, when yet in tender years, and was domiciliated in the then rapidly growing State of Illinois, not far from the celebrated Ninian Edwards, who lent to his unprovided condition the tender care of a liberal patron and a sage admonitor. Where he obtained the rudiments of a plain English education, which was all he could ever boast, I have never been advised; but the faithful tutelage of Governor Edwards, and the access so liberally granted him to the large library of this eminent and learned person, left little to be lamented in regard to the want of regular academic instruction. Certain it is that at a very early age the subject of this notice was deemed qualified to practice the legal profession, and that in a very short time he attained such ascendency at the bar of his own immediate neighborhood that no one was supposed at all able to compete with him. He became, in due season, a representative in Congress, and successively represented two distinct congressional districts in the State of Illinois. When the Mexican War broke out, though condemning it in its commencement as an attack upon a feeble and neighboring republic, he eagerly enlisted therein so soon as he found that its prosecution had been positively resolved on by those in power. In the progress of the war he gained much eclat as a laborious and efficient officer, but, having only a limited opportunity of displaying his ability in this line of public service, he established no claims to that extraordinary renown which his own generous ambition prompted him most warmly to desire. At the close of the Mexican War he migrated to California, and located in the city of San Francisco, where, during the month of February, 1854, I first met with him, and where we contracted relations of reciprocal kindness and respect, which continued, as I have reason to believe, on both sides for some time after our personal separation by the accidents of war.

General Baker, when I encountered him first on the distant Pacific coast, was, as in a very few days I ascertained, universally recognized as altogether the most eloquent speaker at the California bar, and, on familiar acquaintance with him, I discovered that he was very far from being merely a brilliant and fanciful rhetorician, for I repeatedly heard him, both then and afterward, when engaged in the argument of legal causes of the greatest complexity and difficulty, and never did I find him at all unequal to the occasion. Whenever a difficult case was to be tried even in parts of California most distant from his own residence, he was sought for with the greatest eagerness, and oftentimes with a most unusual display of emulous contention.

During the last year of my four years' sojourn in Cali-

fornia the second organization of the celebrated Vigilance
Committee occurred, in regard to whose proceedings there
was at one time, both in California and elsewhere, much
contrariety of opinion. I might at present be trusted to
speak of the acts of this anomalous association, and might
reasonably expect my own *impartiality* to be confided in
by all who have any special feeling on this subject, as I
neither took part in the proceedings of the committee
while they were in progress, nor essayed in any way to
counteract them. I shall only say on this occasion,
though, that I am convinced that I had ample opportunity for scrutinizing the *motives* of the principal individuals who are given credit for setting the committee on
foot, and I am free to say that I never had reason to question their entire purity and disinterestedness. I am confident that the general action of the committee was productive of decidedly beneficial effects, though it would
be rather absurd to question that, in particular instances,
that action may have been both unjust and oppressive.
Early in the year 1856, a person called Corah, a French-
man or Italian by birth, a gambler by occupation, and an
individual of most debauched habits and degraded character, committed one of the most barefaced and wanton
murders ever perpetrated in a Christian country upon
General Richison, the United States marshal of the district in which San Francisco was situated. This flagitious
act, occurring in a city where crime of every sort was far
more frequent than agreeable to upright and orderly citizens, and where the administration of criminal justice had
for some years been notoriously lax and ineffective, was
naturally productive of intense and wide-spread excite-

ment. There was a general desire manifested, and by tokens most unmistakable, to have the alleged culprit subjected, as soon as possible, to exemplary punishment. It chanced that I personally knew General Baker to have been offered a large fee both to prosecute and to defend in this case. He appeared eventually on the side of the defense, and, after a most intensely interesting trial, the jury being unable to agree, Corah was sent back to prison. In a few days another appalling homicide was per- · petrated, and, in this instance, a man who had been once a penitentiary convict (Casey by name) had assassinated, in cold blood, a most popular newspaper editor, a gentleman of great worth, who had at one time been known as an eminently public-spirited and liberal banker. The people almost immediately arose in mass, assumed an organized character, took possession of the greater part of the arms and warlike munitions of the city, broke open the public prisons, and put to death several persons who were found in confinement, in addition to the two atrocious criminals already referred to. The city was *proclaimed* to be in a state of siege, and all municipal authority was declared suspended. Any ordinary man would have quailed before this terrible array. Not so General Baker. He immediately advertised a meeting of the citizens upon the public *Plaza* of the city, and announced his intention to address them. At the stated time and place, a considerable popular assemblage had convened according to notice. General Baker took upon himself the perilous task of addressing them. I never saw him calmer or more collected in my life. At first, those who were present listened to his gentle and soothing

strains in quiet, and apparently with attention. Presently the orator began to employ the language of complaint
and indignation in regard to the recent proceedings of the
Vigilance Committee. A low moaning sound was in a
few minutes heard in the very centre of the crowd, which
soon became a wild and multitudinous roar. Fierce menaces were distinctly uttered in various quarters. After
repeated efforts to gain attention, the audacious and gifted
orator, finding it impossible that a calm and undisturbed
hearing could be secured, retired from the stand. In an
hour or two he learned from his friends that his own
life was in danger, and he left the city of San Francisco
for Sacramento, the capital of the state, where he remained for several months without active occupation of
any kind. I chanced to visit Sacramento just as the
presidential contest was fairly commencing, and General
Baker came to see me. He told me that he designed entering into the canvass, but frankly disclosed several
causes of embarrassment which were at the time giving
him annoyance. He said that, being a *Whig*, he should
be pleased to support Mr. Fillmore, but he could not, as
a *foreigner born*, he thought, support a presidential candidate nominated by the *American* party; that he had been
contending with the Democratic party all his life, and,
therefore, he could not decently cast his suffrage for Mr.
Buchanan; that he had no special partiality for General
Fremont, and was by no means an approver of the extreme Free-soil creed; but that, upon the whole, having
resolved not to be idle at such a crisis, he thought he
should espouse the Republican cause, and exert himself
actively in its support. So indeed he did; for several

weeks thereafter, in traversing the state, I found at various points that General Baker had either preceded me, was expected to appear at the place which I had already reached in a few days, or, as once or twice happened, he was actually at the place of holding a public debate at the same time that I was. He spoke almost every day, and to immense crowds, in almost every part of the state, and with prodigious effect every where. Toward the close of his very brilliant campaign the fame of his wondrous achievements reached San Francisco, where a large majority of those whose hostility had driven him into banishment were ardent supporters of Fremont. Immediately such a revulsion in popular feeling occurred as I presume never took place before, save in the memorable case of Cicero, called back to Rome by the unanimous voice of the populace only a few months after Clodius had persuaded them to drive him into exile. The whole Republican party in San Francisco concurred in inviting the leading advocate of their cause, but whose life six months before would have been deemed but a just sacrifice to a furious popular resentment, to return to their midst, and deliver one of his soul-stirring harangues in their hearing. He came accordingly, and seldom has such an imposing ovation been tendered to any man. He ascended the stand prepared to be occupied by himself, and gave utterance to one of the most overwhelming popular harangues that has ever been any where listened to. A few months later, he was invited to the Territory of Oregon, to take part in the excited popular contest there then in progress. He complied with this invitation, went to Oregon, delivered

K

some twenty or thirty speeches, and was almost immediately thereafter chosen to represent the new Pacific state in the national Senate, where he soon took a prominent part in the proceedings of Congress; and then, in a few months more, the brilliant orator, the ardent patriot, the gallant soldier, disappeared forever from the view of men amid the smoke and toil of battle.

CHAPTER XII.

Some farther Notice of the "Irrepressible Conflict" Theory.—Analysis
of the Condition of Parties at the Time of Mr. Buchanan's Inauguration.—Statement of the Election Results during the first Year of his
Administration. — Historic Recital of some important Facts which
occurred during the Summer of 1857, anterior to Mr. Buchanan's suc-
cumbing to the Dictation of the Secession Leaders.—Efforts to reani-
mate his Courage made at that Period, all of which signally failed.—
Recital of Particulars connected with the Lecompton Struggle in Congress.—Some Scenes, both amusing and painful, which at that time had
their progress in Washington.—Remarkable banqueting Scene, in which
Mr. Seward bore the principal Part.—Last Interview between Mr. Buchanan and the Author, in which some startling Revelations were made.

THE fancied "irrepressible conflict of antagonistic elements imbedded in our complex frame of government,"
if such a necessary and inevitable conflict ever had an
existence, must be recognized as having displayed itself
first to the public view, in a distinct and menacing form,
about the year 1835, when the first abolition associations
were formed in England, and in the Northern States of
the American Union, for the eradication of African Slavery wheresoever it had gained footing, and especially in
the Southern States of the Union, where, wisely or unwisely, our fathers had yielded to it, *in all the states at
least*, as no one denied until recently, *organic guarantees
of protection;* which conflict must be supposed to have
farther developed itself during the eventful thirteen
years which intervened between 1835 and 1848, when

non-intervention became a fundamental principle of the
National Democratic creed; which would seem to have
been held for a few years in a state of feeble and harmless *suppression* under the firm and sage administration
of Millard Fillmore; and to have enjoyed another season
of temporary and feverish vigor in consequence of the impolitic introduction in Congress of the Kansas-Nebraska
Bill, and the maniacal administration of Mr. Pierce, which
daringly aimed to consolidate, extend, and perpetuate
African slavery by incessant agitation, and by the corrupt distribution of official patronage among the avowed
champions of free soil in the North, whose opposition it
was vainly hoped to buy up and terminate. And now
a second opportunity was presented of suppressing the
outbreaking lawlessness of sectional faction, both in the
North and in the South, by returning to the constitutional pathways so plainly marked out by the compromise
leaders of 1850, and the grand conservative principles of
mutual forbearance and reciprocal justice embodied in
the Federal Constitution. Mr. Buchanan had triumphed
in the presidential election of 1856. The united vote of
the Democratic and American parties in that election
constituted a decided majority of the whole popular vote
of the nation. It was evident that the great body of
voters who had supported Fillmore in that contest would
be ready to co-operate heartily with the new administration, if that administration should show itself true to the
principles of *finality and non-intervention* upon which Mr.
Buchanan himself had professed to accept the high executive station into which he was in a few days to be inducted. Between the period of his being chosen presi-

dent and the day of his official inauguration, the public
mind was filled with intense curiosity as to the course of
policy which the new president might ultimately adopt.
There was much speculation afloat also in reference to
the persons whom he might call around him as members
of his cabinet. Sound, practical statesmen earnestly
hoped that he would be more wise in the selection of his
cabinet advisers than Mr. Pierce had been, and that there
would be neither sectionalist, nor local demagogue, nor
political changeling, nor concealed abolitionist, hypocritically professing to be a genuine States-right Democrat,
to be found in close official alliance with the newly-made
president. A letter appeared about this time in the
newspapers over the signature of A. G. Brown, of Mississippi, a gentleman of very extreme views upon the slavery question, and who had been an ardent advocate of
disunion in 1851, which described an interview which he
had just held with Mr. Buchanan at his own residence in
Pennsylvania; which letter was not a little startling in
some of its statements, considering Mr. Brown's own political antecedents, his known eager desire for the *forcible
extension of slavery* into the territories by congressional
instrumentality, and the interpretation which he was understood to have affixed to Mr. Calhoun's political teachings. This letter concluded with the following statement
in reference to Mr. Buchanan: "*In my judgment, he is as
worthy of Southern confidence and Southern votes as ever Mr.
Calhoun was.*"

The inauguration scene occurred upon the 4th day of
March, 1857, and James Buchanan, of Pennsylvania, was
proclaimed President, and John C. Breckenridge Vice-

President of the United States of America. Mr. Buchanan's inaugural address, with very slight exceptions,
was a highly unexceptionable document. It embodied
sound national views in clear and forcible diction, and
was admirably received by the country. Scarcely a
whisper of disapproval or of distrust was any where
breathed. The Southern slaveholding class, ever more
conservative in their views and feelings than the noisy
and shallow demagogues in the two houses of Congress
and elsewhere, who have for twenty years past put themselves forward as its special and exclusive champions,
was entirely satisfied with Mr. Buchanan's solemn assurance that no unconstitutional infraction of their rights
would receive his sanction. The Free-soil faction, so recently and so signally defeated, seemed well-nigh crushed
out of existence, and its leaders appeared to be every
where meditating its formal disbandment. The American party were prepared enthusiastically to rally to the
support of an administration which stood pledged to pursue a course of policy which they did not doubt would
renew that delightful era of repose and general fraternal
feeling in which they had so much rejoiced while Mr.
Fillmore had occupied the presidential chair. The fierce
sectional leaders of the South saw plainly that this was
not altogether a favorable moment to originate the disorganizing movements which some of them had long medi-
tated, and confidently hoped in the end, either by adroit
persuasion or by thundering menaces of opposition, or by
both of these combined, they might be yet able to mould
Mr. Buchanan to their purposes, whom they took care to
remind very early that he had owed his election to the

presidency mainly to their management and support. The general condition of popular feeling in the country, as well as the relative state of political parties, was very soon made manifest in certain important state elections which took place during the very year in which Mr. Buchanan's administration began. These election results are well worthy of attention, as showing that the American people were really devoted to the principles of true constitutional conservatism, and only desired the government at Washington to be administered in the conciliatory and fraternal spirit so solemnly inculcated by the wise and patriotic statesmen of the Washington era. Fremont and Dayton had obtained in the whole North, in the autumn of 1856, 1,341,812 votes. The elections which took place in 1859 show a falling off in the aggregate strength of the Republican party of nearly 200,000 votes. The Republican majority was greatly diminished in every New England state. In the State of Connecticut especially, the majority of that party was reduced from 7715 votes to 546. In Ohio, Governor Chase, whose local popularity was known to be very great, was re-elected only by the slender majority of 1481 votes, though the Republicans had carried the state in the immediately preceding year by a majority of 16,623. In Iowa, where the Republicans had in 1856 carried the state by a majority of 7784 votes, Governor Lowe, the popular Republican candidate for governor, could only command the meagre majority of 2151. In Wisconsin, which had been carried by the Republicans in 1856 by the sweeping majority of 13,247 votes, their respectable gubernational candidate barely evaded defeat, his majority being 118 only. In the great State of New York a complete civic revolution was effected such as the history of the republic has rarely exhibited. In this vast and enlightened commonwealth, where the spirit of the people has been ever conservative, and among whom an intense and abiding love of the Federal Union has been always a distinguishing characteristic, Fremont's plurality of 80,000 was changed to a *Democratic majority of 18,000. "It appeared," says Mr. Greeley, in his "American Conflict," "in this (New York), as in the other free states, that the decline or dissolution of the American or Fillmore party inured mainly to the benefit of the triumphant Democracy, though Pennsylvania, and possibly Rhode Island, were exceptions. To swell the resistless tide, Minnesota and Oregon, both in the extreme north, each framed a state Constitution this year, and took position in line with the dominant party, Minnesota by a small, Oregon by an overwhelming majority—the two swelling, by four senators and four representatives, the already invincible strength of the Democracy." One of the most remarkable elections of this period remains yet to be specified. California, which had been carried by a majority of some 5000 votes by the American party (where, as I chance personally to know, it was a *Union Reform* party, and nothing more nor less), in the election of governor and other officers, in the year 1855, was carried for the Democratic party, just two years thereafter, by a plurality of more than thirty thousand votes. In the summer of 1857, Mr. Buchanan, in the high national attitude which he occupied, could look abroad over the land and find himself sustained by greatly more than two thirds of the whole body of the American vot-

ing population. It is melancholy to reflect how a shameless violation of the pledges with which this individual
came into office, a gross and almost unprecedented want
of statesmanship, and a timid and disgraceful subservi- ·
ency to certain daring and dogmatizing sectional leaders
of the South, in less than six months from this moment
of palmy prosperity for the whole republic, as well as for
the administration of Mr. Buchanan and the now thoroughly blended Democratic and American parties, had completely reversed this gratifying picture. The leaders just
spoken of managed in a few months thereafter to inveigle
this most unfortunate man in such a predicament of folly
and self-contradiction before the country as had never
been known before in American annals, and brought such
a crushing weight of odium upon the Northern portion
of the Democratic party, in connection with the *fraud-
conceived* and *knavery-generated* Lecompton Constitution,
as almost literally sunk that party into non-existence,
and paved the way for the grand and fatal misarrange-
· ment of 1860, whereby the strength of the Democratic
party was so causelessly divided, a Republican president
elected by a plurality of popular votes, and a scheme of
disunion, long before secretly prepared, in due season
carried into effect, civil war generated, and innumerable
mischiefs besides turned loose to prey upon the land,
the blasting and wide-spread consequences of which, it is
to be greatly feared, our children and our children's children may be compelled to experience and to deplore.
Well may the sagacious author of the ".American Conflict," while speaking of the extraordinary conduct of

K 2

Mr. Buchanan at this crisis, with mocking exultation, use the following emphatic language:

"The opposition was utterly powerless against this surge; but what they dared hardly undertake, Mr. Buchanan was able to effect. By his utterly indefensible attempt to enforce the Lecompton Constitution upon Kansas, in glaring contradiction to his smooth and voluble professions regarding 'popular sovereignty,' 'the will of the majority,' etc., etc., he enabled the Republicans in 1858 to hold, by majorities almost uniformly increased, all the states they had carried the preceding year, and reverse the last year's majority against them in New York; carry Pennsylvania, for the first time, by over 26,000 majority, triumph even in New Jersey under an equivocal organization, bring over Minnesota by a close vote, and swell their majority in Ohio to fully 20,000. They were beaten in Indiana, on the state ticket, by a very slender majority, but carried seven of the eleven representatives in Congress, besides helping elect an anti-Lecompton Democrat in another district; while Michigan, Iowa, and Wisconsin chose Republican tickets—as of late had been usual with them—by respectable majorities, and the last named by one increased to nearly 6,000."

In order to ascertain clearly what was the precise character of the admonitory suggestions made to Mr. Buchanan by the popular elections that occurred in the early part of the year 1857, and which he so strangely disregarded in the manner already specified, it will be proper to glance for a moment to what was going on in Kansas and elsewhere at that period. I contemplate entering into no tedious specification of particulars touching the matters alluded to, and shall confine my observations to leading and important FACTS.

The civil disturbances in Kansas still continued. The pro-slavery champions in that territory and the anti-slavery propagandists were yet fiercely controverting with each other in that remote region, and each of the contending factions which were there represented was aiming to

"Prove its doctrine orthodox
By apostolic blows and knocks."

Sharp revolvers, and other weapons of carnal warfare, were still being freely used on both sides, and the whole territory was fast becoming, under the unpardonable ministration of the government, an earthly Pandemonium. This precious legacy of anarchy and "confusion worse confounded" was meekly handed over by the retiring Pierce, and his now home-returning cabinet officials, to Mr. Buchanan, who had awakened such extraordinary hopes on all sides that, under his judicious direction, order would be speedily restored in Kansas, the dignity of the laws maintained, and the honor of the republic vindicated. There was plainly but one wise and honest course to pursue, and that was evidently, too, the only course that in the least degree promised to be successful. It was clear that there were enough people in Kansas, and that there was enough of intelligence and moral worth also, to justify the territory being immediately organized into a state. If these people should be allowed to form a state Constitution without any unauthorized foreign intervention, and in the absence of fraud and violence of any kind, it seemed certain that quiet would soon be re-

stored, a solid, prosperous commonwealth be formed, and
the republic be itself freed from any farther disquietude
in regard to its concerns.   Honesty and plain dealing on
the part of the government in Washington, with a proper display of firmness and respect for his avowed principles on the part of Mr. Buchanan, were now the things
most demanded.   Governor Geary, the third or fourth
of the territorial governors who had been dispatched
from Washington City to this far-off region, had just resigned in a very abrupt manner, and retired in disgust
from the territory.   It was necessary to lose no time in
appointing his successor.   Mr. Buchanan at once turned
his eyes toward two of the most suitable men, in all respects, that the country contained, for the office of governor and secretary of state of the new territory, Robert
J. Walker and Frederick P. Stanton.   Mr. Walker is understood to have accepted the place now tendered to him
with great reluctance, and, in point of fact, he sternly refused to take upon himself the painful responsibilities
which were now courting his assumption, unless he could
have a solemn assurance beforehand that he would be
faithfully sustained· by the government in the efforts
which he contemplated making to secure to the people
among whom he was going all the well-known rights
and immunities of American citizens, and especially their
rights, as a sovereign community, to dispose of the moot- ·
ed question of slavery precisely as they might judge
most wise and proper.   These assurances having been re-·
ceived, Mr. Walker and Mr. Stanton proceeded at once to
the Territory of Kansas, and entered upon the field of
duty assigned them.   I have already said that I should

not undertake to go into detail upon this oft-discussed theme. I may be allowed here to observe, though, that the whole conduct of Governor Walker and Secretary Stanton was in full accordance with the instructions which Mr. Buchanan had given to them when they departed from Washington; that their official acts were such as did them the highest honor; that both of them faithfully struggled to secure to the unhappy people of Kansas all the benefits which Mr. Buchanan was most sacredly pledged to guarantee to them; and that, had Mr. Buchanan, with true fidelity and manliness, performed his duty as first magistrate of the republic, Kansas would have been inevitably admitted into the Union at the very next session of Congress, and the conduct of the new administration would have been in the end approved by nine tenths of the whole American people. But such, I regret to say, was not by any means the conduct of Mr. Buchanan at this painful conjuncture in his country's affairs, and, by pursuing a course precisely the opposite of this, he has made himself most criminally responsible for a large proportion of the evils which have since befallen the republic.

I left the State of California in the summer of 1857, and arrived in the city of New York only a day or two antecedent to the assemblage of a large popular meeting, which was addressed by several very prominent public men, in support of Mr. Buchanan's administration, and especially in vindication of the truly national policy which he was known to have adopted for the settlement of the Kansas difficulties. Having been invited, also, to harangue the multitude, I did so in a very brief manner,

giving some account of the political victory which had ·
been then recently achieved in the State of California,
and of the utter prostration there of the Republican faction by the coalesced forces of the Democratic and American parties, and urging my brother Americans of New
York, so far as I judged it allowable for a stranger to do
so, to yield a hearty support to Mr. Buchanan's administration, then, as I thought, honestly exerting itself to do
all in its power toward the general pacification of the
country.

Just about this time certain leading Southern politicians in Georgia, Mississippi, and South Carolina commenced a course of open and unmeasured denunciation
of Mr. Buchanan on account of his having sent Governor
Walker to Kansas, and on account of the acts of this latter personage as governor of the territory, charging the
President with the basest ingratitude to the Southern
States and people, to whose support they asserted him to
have chiefly owed his elevation, and menacing him, in addition, with such opposition in Congress and elsewhere as
would speedily subject him to punishment for the gross
infidelity which they accused him of having exhibited
toward his political benefactors. Fearing very seriously
the effect of these movements upon Mr. Buchanan, who
I knew to be morbidly sensitive to public reproach, and
anxious beyond the wise sedateness of true statesmanship to please every body, I resolved to visit Washington without delay, hoping to find out there whether there
was any likelihood of the administration's recoiling from
the attitude which it then occupied. On arriving in that
city, where I remained only a single day, I learned from

the lips of Mr. Thompson, then Secretary of the Interior,
that though Mr. Buchanan had been much galled and
mortified by the course pursued toward him in the Southern States, he was resolved firmly to stand by Governor
Walker and non-intervention in Kansas, whatever might
be the consequences of his doing so to himself personally, or to the future prosperity of his administration. Mr.
Thompson having expressed in that interview strong fears
that in the Southwest, particularly in Mississippi and the
adjoining states, Senators Davis and Brown, with others,
might succeed, if not promptly counteracted, in mislead-
ing their fellow-citizens in regard to the Kansas *imbroglio*,
I volunteered to go in that direction myself, for the purpose of employing such influence as might still remain
to me, after a four years' absence, in furthering a cause
which I had so much at heart. I set out accordingly,
and journeyed at once to the city of Memphis, where,
being invited to address my fellow-citizens, I attended a
large popular assemblage convoked under the auspices
of the most influential public persons in that vicinage,
over which the eminently patriotic ex-Governor Jones
presided, and, in a harangue of several hours' duration,
called the attention of those present to the then existing
condition of public affairs, and labored to show them that
it was the true policy of the South, as of the whole country besides, to yield to Mr. Buchanan the most zealous
support at that perilous conjuncture. The address which
I delivered on this occasion, with the evidences of popular approval which the advice embodied therein had elic-
ited, in manner and form as the same were set forth in
the newspapers of the vicinage, I took occasion to trans-

mit directly to Washington for Mr. Buchanan's encouragement, after which I proceeded at once to the city of
Jackson, in Mississippi, where the Legislature of that
state was then in session. On arriving at this place, and
learning that the two Mississippi senators, Messrs. Davis
and Brown, had both addressed a large meeting at the
Capitol on the evening before my arrival, when each of
these gentlemen had denounced Mr. Buchanan's Kansas
policy in unmeasured terms, I accepted an invitation tendered to me to speak to a similar assemblage at the same
place on the very evening ensuing my arrival; having
done which, I again sent to Dr. William M. Gwin, then in
Washington City, to be handed over to Mr. Buchanan,
the newspapers of Jackson, containing an account of
these proceedings. It was unfortunately of no avail that
these efforts to *reassure* Mr. Buchanan were essayed by
myself and others; he had already become *panic-strick-
en;* the howlings of the bull-dog of secession had fairly
frightened him out of his wits, and he resolved to yield,
without farther resistance, to the decrial and villification
to which he had been so thunderingly subjected. In
point of fact, a week or two thereafter, the Hon. Glancy
Jones, of Pennsylvania, a well-known and confidential
friend of Mr. Buchanan, published in the newspapers a
letter, in which the first foreshadowing appeared of Mr.
Buchanan's determination completely to *revolutionize* his
course in the Kansas affair.

Having become, in common with thousands of others,
deeply alarmed at the condition of public affairs, I visited
Washington City early in the session of Congress next
ensuing, not without some faint hope, I confess, that even

my presence and efforts at the capital of the republic would not be altogether useless. I there encountered Mr. Buchanan's message recommending the admission of Kansas into the Union under the infamous *Lecompton Constitution*, and found a state of political excitement such as it was indeed most painful to behold. I was quite sensible that, as a mere private citizen, I could do but little to avert the rising storm, but I did, notwithstanding, all that I was capable of doing for that purpose.

Let us now look for a moment, and for a moment only, to the occurrences which had recently had their progress in Kansas. Two opposing Conventions had been held there. The Pro-slavery Convention had assembled at Lecompton on the first Monday of September. A pro-slavery Constitution was speedily framed. This Constitution was promulgated, and the people of Kansas were invited to vote, in regard to its ratification, in a mode which, I venture to say, was at the time altogether unprecedented, and, indeed, was consummately disgraceful. The formula prescribed by the Convention required that every citizen desiring to participate in the act of ratification should either vote "for the Constitution *with* slavery," or "for the Constitution *without* slavery." None could vote who would not submit to going through this absurd and farcical process. The popular vote in this election was soon announced as 6266 votes "for the Constitution *with* slavery," and 567 only "for the Constitution *without* slavery." So what was called a Constitution was in this form ratified by less than 7000 votes. The provisions of this extraordinary instrument prohibited any interference "with the rights of property in slaves"

for the present, and likewise prohibited any amendment
of its own clauses until the year 1864. The subject is
far too disgusting to be farther expatiated on at this moment. A more corrupt and fraudulent transaction had
never taken place in Christendom than the pretended
adoption and ratification of this pseudo-Constitution; a
more heartless and unprecedented attempt to *enslave* more
than ten thousand free American citizens could not possibly be imagined. And yet the abominable frauds
which no one could deny had been perpetrated in Kansas, had been done in the *name of the Southern States* and
people, whose escutcheon had, until this melancholy conjuncture, been ever kept pure and unstained, and in the
name of the Democratic party also, the members of which
were expected to stand up in their places in the halls of
the national Legislature, and proclaim that honester and
more legitimate proceedings had never been known to
occur in any territory seeking to frame a state Constitution preparatory to entering the Federal Union, and that
no man had better deserved the thanks and commendation of his countrymen than James Buchanan, who had
so nobly, as it was said, risked his darling popularity in
this wise and heroic effort to serve that country which
he loved so well, and to maintain those sacred institutions
of freedom which he professed to hold in such profound
reverence!

   *The death-blow to slavery had now been struck by its own
professed friends*, and the Northern members of the Democratic party in Congress, upon whose brawny shoulders
this intolerable burden had been imposed, were expected
to hold themselves erect notwithstanding, and to go back

to their own homes in a month or two arduously to battle with the fierce foes whom they had now armed for
their own destruction, and, if possible, uphold that firm
wall of defense against abolition hostility which the Northern Democracy had ever, up to that unfortunate moment,
constituted.

After Mr. Buchanan had sent into Congress two several messages earnestly recommending to that body to
ratify the Lecompton *swindle*, he began to grow very restless and uneasy, and I conversed with more than a dozen
members of Congress, who informed me that they had
just come from the White House, where the anxious
President had urged them, in language almost of impre-
cation, for God's sake, not to forsake him and the true
Democratic cause at this crisis. I heard from the lips of
Mr. Toombs, about this period, a rather amusing anecdote, alike illustrative of the uneasiness of Mr. Buchanan
as to the fate of his pet scheme in Congress, and his ingenuity in devising new expedients for the strengthening
of his political position. Mr. Toombs related that a few
days before he had been at the presidential mansion,
when the conversation turning upon the troubles then
existing in Congress, Mr. Buchanan said: "Mr. Toombs,
when I was a member of Congress some years ago, whenever the Democratic party was hard pressed, they always
went into *caucus*, where it was found quite easy to reconcile discordances, and secure a union of party energies.
Why do you not call a Democratic caucus now in Congress? I am sure it would be attended with exceedingly
beneficial effects." "Oh," responded the ever-facetious
and ready Toombs, "Mr. President, you have forgotten

my political history a little; when I came into Congress as a senator, a few years ago, I did so as a *Union Whig*. I could not, therefore, you know, with any show of decent consistency, go into a *Democratic* caucus until my present senatorial term shall have expired. Wait patiently, I pray you, Mr. President, a few weeks; my present senatorial term will expire on the coming 4th of March, and, having been recently elected to a second term, as a *Democrat*, whenever that shall commence its course, I shall be prepared for all the duties of my new position, and I promise you to be as good a caucus Democrat as ever you heard of."

During my stay in Washington City, while the Kansas Bill was yet the subject of contention, I received one day a very neat card inviting me to dine with a select party of gentlemen at a well-known *restaurateur* in that city. Of course, I·did not refuse the kindly summons, and proceeded at the time appointed to the place specified. Before I had arrived there, some special information was communicated to me which I will now impart. General Nelson, the personage who figured so prominently in Kentucky and Tennessee during the late war, and who was killed so unhappily in private combat at Louisville, had been on his way to the Capitol that morning, and had accidentally encountered a well-dressed Englishman, of rather eccentric appearance and manners, who inquired, in a sort of *Cockneyish* style, as was described to me, for the room of the Supreme Court of the United States. After supplying the desired information, a miscellaneous conversation sprang up between the general and this supposed Cockney acquaintance. He determined to attend him to the Supreme Court room, that he might see more of him. While there, it struck him that a very funny banqueting scene might be gotten up, if he should draw up a card of invitation to the aforesaid son of the "fast-anchored isle," asking him, in the name of several distinguished members of Congress easy to be obtained, to accept that very afternoon of a social repast, to be given in honor of Queen Victoria and the British people, at the *restaurateur* already referred to. The invitation had been very courteously accepted; and when I arrived at the designated place of social *rendezvous*, I found as gay and splendid a company assembled as it has been my lot at any time to behold. The English guest was occupying the seat of honor, and on different sides of him, and opposite to him, were seated the following gentlemen, with others whose names I have really now forgotten: the Vice-President of the United States, Mr. Breckenridge; William H. Seward, of New York; Colonel Orr, the then Speaker of the House of Representatives, since a distinguished Confederate military officer, and a still more distinguished Confederate senator in Richmond; Hon. Mr. Campbell, of Ohio; the celebrated Humphrey Marshall, of Kentucky; Albert Pike, the erudite lawyer, the brilliant colloquialist, and late prominent military officer in the Confederate service of Arkansas; General Nelson himself, and the writer of this notice. Dinner had already commenced when I reached the arena of action, and the first glass of wine was about to be drunk. A sentiment preceded it, which, being in honor of her gracious majesty Queen Victoria, called our English friend to his feet, when, without the

least embarrassment, and in as easy, dignified, and graceful a manner as either Lord Palmerston or Lord Ches-
terfield, when these polished worthies were alive, could
have exhibited, he poured forth an impromptu response,
which was, in every respect, a perfect masterpiece of its
kind. The whole company was manifestly *thrown aback*
for a time, the oratorical exhibition had been so unexpected, and alike imposing and appropriate. After a while
the wine commenced once more circulating, and glass after glass was drunk with hearty good-will; while choice
anecdote, brilliant repartee, and songs both merry and
pathetic, served to enliven the occasion. Just as the
company was rising from the table, Mr. Seward, who had
already contributed at least his share to the entertainment, rose, and, with more than usual gravity, asked to
be permitted to offer a sentiment, to which all the company assenting in a genuine *convivial* manner, he addressed the company pretty much as follows:

"Gentlemen, it has been my fortune to occupy a seat
in Congress, as you all very well know, for some years,
during which period I have made one of many genial
meetings like the present. I lament to say, gentlemen,
that it has uniformly happened heretofore on such occasions that the concord and agreeable hilarity of the dinner scene have been more or less marred by the unhappy
introduction of irritating sectional topics. To-day nothing of the sort has occurred, a circumstance to me exceedingly gratifying. I now give you, gentlemen, the
following sentiment: *May many such pleasant banquets as
the present hereafter occur among us, and may none of them
be interrupted or rendered less agreeable by the introduction
of sectional topics.*"

After this sentiment, or one in substance resembling it, had been duly honored, the company dispersed, in absolute good-humor with themselves and all the world. The very next day (being Sunday) I wandered down to the Rev. Mr. Pine's church, where, on entering, I beheld Mr. Seward again, and for the last time. He saw me enter, and, discovering that I had no pew at my command, he courteously stepped down the main aisle and asked me to take part of his own pew, which I did, and when the services of the day were over, took my leave of him, and walked toward my own lodgings on Pennsylvania Avenue. On the way I met President Buchanan. He accosted me kindly, inquired after my health, and told me he was just returning to the presidential mansion from the dwelling of Senator Bright, whither he had attended his charming daughter from church. Mr. Buchanan rebuked me kindly for not having visited him during my sojourn in Washington, and seemed to be somewhat inclined to converse for a moment upon the exciting topics of the day. The weather was far too cold for an extended conversation on the open street; so, after chatting with him for a minute or two, I said, " Mr. President, I shall be off to the Southwest to-morrow, and I wish I could return to my own home without carrying with me feelings of great uneasiness in regard to the condition of the country." I declared to him, in explicit but kindly language, my views as to the consequences likely to arise from the unfortunate *Lecompton experiment*, and closed by saying to him, "Mr. President, I know more of the schemes of the Southern secession leaders than you do. You have yielded much to them during the present session, and I fear that events have occurred, and are occurring, which will break down the strength of the Democratic party, increase that of the Republican party proportionately, secure the election of a Republican president in 1860, and then, *I warn you solemnly to look out for a secession movement to take place which will give the country and yourself great trouble.* I did not feel willing to leave Washington without uttering in your hearing these premonitory words." He responded, evidently with some embarrassment, pretty much as follows:

"Let me say to you, sir, in frankness, that if such dangers should arise as those to which you refer, I shall know how to do my duty. In 1852 I sought the presidential nomination at the hands of the Democratic party, and I did not obtain it. In 1856 the presidential nomination *sought me;* I did not make any effort to procure it. My attitude, therefore, is a very *independent* one; and if any body of men any where shall attempt to subvert the government, whose executive chief I am, I feel confident that I shall know how to deal with them, and the whole republic will find me not unfaithful to the great trust with which I have been invested." I replied, "I doubt not the goodness of your intentions; I trust that you will prove in all respects equal to the perilous conjuncture which I am sure is not far distant, but I fear much that you are confiding in the friendship and integrity of some who will fail you when the moment of danger shall arrive." So speaking, I took him by the hand *for the last time.*

It is certain that Northern and Southern members of Congress were made fully aware of all the dangerous consequences likely to arise from this fearful Lecompton movement. The certainty that the Northern Democracy would be almost virtually disbanded if this noxious measure should be generally supported by them, and that thus the republic would almost inevitably fall into the hands of the Free-soil party in 1860, was presented to them, not only in forcible and eloquent speeches in Congress, but in numerous conversational scenes, some of which I yet vividly remember. One of these I will here describe.

I had the honor to be invited to dine one day at the hospitable mansion of General Cass. A large company assembled at the table, among whom I well recollect Senator Evans, of South Carolina, Senator Bigler, of Pennsylvania, Senator Wilson, of Massachusetts, Glancy Jones, of Pennsylvania, and others. It was a mixed company, as might have been expected, composed alike of Northern and of Southern members of Congress. It chanced that Glancy Jones was seated near me on one side, and a well-known representative from Alabama on the other. The Kansas question presently fell under discussion, in a suppressed tone, between the member from Alabama, Mr. Jones, and myself. When we had run over the usual topics, I turned to Mr. Jones and said, "Now, sir, I desire to ask you a question or two, which I am sure you will answer frankly. If the Lecompton Bill shall be passed through Congress *by Democratic votes*, will not its passage be fatal to the Northern portion of the party, and secure success to the Republicans in the coming elections?" To this he answered "that he held this result to be certain; that it would be especially the

L

case in Pennsylvania, where it was not probable that a single Democratic representative would be returned to the next Congress; that he himself might possibly be elected, but, if so, it would be by the *skin of his teeth.*" Then I asked, "How is the South to be benefited by the adoption of a measure flagrantly unjust in itself, and violative of all the known principles of freedom, beneath which her friends and supporters in the North are to be broken down?" He answered that he could not but think that the South and the country would alike be benefited if the scheme of passing the obnoxious measure should be relinquished, in which event he held it to be certain that the Democratic party, which had been so signally successful in recent elections, would be able to sweep the whole North in 1860, and thus secure the slaveholding interests of the South from abolition assailment." "Then," said I, "my dear sir, if such be your views, why do you not enforce them on Mr. Buchanan?" "Because," said he, "I could not do so without giving him serious offense." After dinner, I talked for a few minutes with Senator Bigler, of the same state, whose anticipations as to the probable fate of the Democratic party of the North under this poisoned Lecompton chalice seemed to be most gloomy.

The whole country remembers how nobly Mr. Douglas battled in Congress against this abominable measure; how much higher intellectual powers he displayed than he had ever before exhibited; with what cruel malevolence he was assaulted in debate by senators from the South, for the conciliation of whom, in the Kansas-Nebraska struggle, he had sacrificed so much of his well-earned

Northern popularity, only now to become the victim of a foul and malign *conspiracy*, organized specially for his destruction, by individuals anxious above all things to enfeeble him for the presidential struggle of 1860.

The triumph of Mr. Douglas over his numerous adversaries was complete, as all who listened to the stormy debates which then occurred, or who have read them in the Congressional Globe since, will have no hesitation in admitting. Mr. Crittenden and Mr. Bell, from the South, spoke with great power and effect also; but these gentlemen did not come to the rescue in the contest quite early enough to achieve as much as they might have attained had they spoken in the beginning of the session, as many of their admiring friends, including myself, urged them both to do. It is within my own private knowledge, that General Houston, of Texas, had prepared some excellent and manly resolutions, declarative of his views in opposition to the Lecompton fraud, and had drawn up the heads of a speech which he intended to deliver in support thereof, when the *instructions* from the Legislature of Texas reached him, and paralyzed his energies for the session.

The subsequent proceedings in Congress are yet fresh in the memories of us all—the transformation of the Lecompton Bill, which had pretty well done its work of mischief already, into what was afterward known as the English Bill; the passage of this latter, in part by Southern votes, with a clause submitting the question of the Lecompton Constitution anew, on certain terms and conditions, to the people of Kansas, followed by a scene of public rejoicing at the White House over what appeared to be deemed by those assembled as a magnificent *Southern victory*, when, in truth, it only opened to the people of Kansas an opportunity of voting down themselves the Constitution which, in an evil hour, an unpaternal president and his abettors had essayed to *force* upon them.

And now the *conflict*, so easy to be *repressed*, if a wise and honest statemanship had been put in exercise, was renewed under auspices eminently perilous to the country. Can any sober and unprejudiced mind, on considering these details, agree still with Mr. Seward in that noted declaration of his which has been so often referred to in these volumes, and which will now be given in a somewhat fuller manner? These are his words:

"These antagonistic systems are continually coming into closer contact, and collision results.

"Shall I tell you what this collision means? They who think it is accidental, unnecessary, the work of interested or fanatical agitators, and therefore ephemeral, mistake the case altogether. *It is an irrepressible conflict* between *opposing and enduring forces*, and it means that the United States must and will, sooner or later, become either entirely a slaveholding nation or entirely a free-labor nation. Either the cotton and rice fields of South Carolina, and the sugar plantations of Louisiana, will ultimately be tilled by free labor, and Charleston and New Orleans become marts for legitimate merchandise alone, or else the rye-fields and wheat-fields of Massachusetts and New York must again be surrendered by their farmers to slave culture and to the production of slaves, and Boston and New York become once more markets for trade in the bodies and souls of men. It is the failure to apprehend this great truth that induces so many unsuccessful attempts at final compromise between the slave and free states; and it is the existence of this great fact that renders all such pretended compromises, when made, vain and ephemeral."

CHAPTER XIII.

Conspiracy of certain Senators to defeat the "Little Giant of the West" in his supposed presidential Aspirations.—Signal Triumph of this Gentleman as a Debater over all Opposition.—Opening of the senatorial Contest between Mr. Douglas and Mr. Lincoln, of Illinois.—Extraordinary Efforts of Mr. Buchanan and other Individuals of the Democratic Party to effect Mr. Douglas's Defeat and secure the Election of his Opponent.—Eventual Triumph of Mr. Douglas, who returns to the Senate to undergo *Ostracism* at the Hands of senatorial Democrats in Caucus under the direction of Mr. Buchanan.—Deep Injury done to the Southern Cause by the unjust Course pursued toward Mr. Douglas, which caused many of this Gentleman's political Supporters in the North to grow lukewarm in the support of Southern Rights.—Special Causes which now operated to produce sectional Excitement.—Indecent and ruffianly Assault upon Mr. Sumner.—Dred Scott Decision.—The South indiscreetly exultant over it, and the North indignant.—Attempt by certain Persons in the South to bring about the reopening of the African Slave-trade.—Important judicial Contest in Ohio touching the validity of the Fugitive Slave Law.—Ossawatomie Brown upon a Rampage in the Bosom of Virginia as a radical, political, and moral Reformer, ready to shed Oceans of Blood in defense of universal Freedom.—Interesting Debate in the United States Senate on this Subject. —Impolitic Execution of Brown, by which he was unnecessarily made a Martyr.

THE excited struggle in Congress was now over. All impartial men acknowledged that "the Little Giant of the West," as he was now popularly entitled, had prostrated all who had opposed the great eternal truths which he had labored to establish in the fierce and obstinately contested battles of principle which had been going on in

the Senate. All who had presumed to measure strength
with him in this body had been covered with disgrace,
and Mr. Buchanan, who, it was well known, had now conceived a hatred for this fearless champion of intervention
and popular sovereignty, proportionate to the humilia-
ting consciousness which he could not but feel of *baffled
management* and *counteracted trickery*, prepared, as a solace
for his wounded pride, to aid, as far as he might be able,
in having Mr. Douglas defeated in the approaching contest for senatorial honors in Illinois; in which contest all
the true friends of popular freedom, and all the sympathizers with harassed and persecuted merit, were in feeling enlisted on the side of one who had thus far shown
himself so far superior, both in moral and intellectual
power, to all who had ventured into combat with him.
It is a fact which has not heretofore awakened the consideration which is due to such conduct, that Mr. Buchanan and those of the Democratic party who concurred with
him in feeling, made the most strenuous, but, for the most
part, covert and illicit efforts to secure the defeat of Mr.
Douglas for re-election to the national Senate in Illinois.
If Douglas could be now beaten (these men argued), the
national Senate would be henceforth enfranchised from
the potential influence which he had been for several years
exerting in furtherance of doctrines which were altogether repugnant to the theory that *the power of the government might be properly used for the propagation of African
slavery, and for the purpose of extending its domain even into
regions not especially adapted to it.* On the other hand,
there were, and for reasons not wholly dissimilar, persons
in public life of exorbitant ambition, of capacities wholly

unfit to contest with the illustrious champion of popular sovereignty in the field of parliamentary debate, who
intensely sighed for his absence from that arena where he
had been recently acquiring such a surpassing and peculiar renown, in order to multiply the chances of their own
future advancement, and at the same time facilitate the
employment of Federal power as an efficient agent not
only for the exclusion of slavery from the regions where
it did not now subsist, but for its complete extinction
where it had heretofore stood protected by the most sacred constitutional guarantees. All who were any where
opposed to the grand conservative principle—alike valuable in politics, in religion, and in morals, *quieta non mo-
vere*—and who were still bent on the agitation of the question of slavery for any purpose, were alike opposed to the
clear-headed and magnanimous statesman who now plainly and painfully perceived the error which he had im-
pulsively committed in acquiescing in the attempt to re-
scind, by special legislative enactment, the Missouri Compromise, which had so long maintained the peace of the
country and held in suppression the factious restlessness
of sectional demagogues. Mr. Douglas felt an intense
scorn for the shallow, sophisticating dogmatists both of
the South and of the North, who noisily babbled forth
the ineffably nonsensical jargon, which is yet mistaken
for true political philosophy, that there must be an absolute *similitude* between the property interests and municipal arrangements of communities bound together by a
mere federative compact, in order to secure them against
collisions and misunderstandings. He had read the history of confederacies similar to ours, in other lands and

in other ages, and he had examined the profound exposi-
tions of political wisdom which had made at different
times their appearance in the world from the days of Aristotle and Cicero to those of Madison and Hamilton, Jay
and Marshall, Webster and Calhoun; and he would just
· as soon have supposed it impossible that two persons of
opposite sexes could live in nuptial harmony, as he would
have attached his faith to that essentially identical one
which asserts, "I believe this government can not permanently endure half slave and half free. I do not expect
the Union to be dissolved; I do not expect the house to
fall; but I *do* expect that it will cease to be divided. It
will become all one thing or all the other. Either the
opponents of slavery will arrest the farther spread of it,
and place it where the public mind shall rest in the belief that it is in a course of ultimate extinction, or its advocates will push it forward till it shall become alike lawful in all the states, old as well as new, North as well as
South." Mr. Douglas as little believed with the moon-
struck abstractionists of New England that freedom and
social happiness could not possibly subsist in a country
inhabited by races in several material respects distinguish-
able from each other, without the absolute blending of
all the members of them both in one homogeneous *misce-
genating* mass, as he did with the swelling and pompous
slaveholding rhetorician of the South that the republic
would never see perfect repose until he should have the
happiness of hearing "*read the muster-roll of his slaves at
the foot of Bunker Hill Monument.*"

The contest for the senatorial *toga* in Illinois, in the
year 1858, attracted far more attention than any similar

L 2

struggle has ever commanded. The Republican party,
some of the members of which had been on several occasions, during Mr. Douglas's conflicts on the floor of Congress with the pro-slavery champions, heard to express
more or less of sympathy for the fearless and indomita-
ble champion of non-intervention, could not forego the
tempting opportunity now presented of taking advantage
of the feud which existed in the Democratic party for the
purpose of securing an additional senator of their now
rapidly growing faction from the great Northwestern
state which Mr. Douglas had so long and so faithfully
represented. This party now brought forward, as its
champion in the contest just commencing, a man who
has since acquired much fame, and has left behind him
many claims to the enduring respect and kindness of his
countrymen. I shall hereafter have occasion to speak
much of this remarkable personage—sometimes in approval, sometimes in condemnation; but I am glad to
know that I shall be saved from the task of indulging in
language of harsh reprobation or of unkind decrial in
reference to one over whose recent untimely fate the
whole republic has profoundly grieved, and the foul and
barbarous manner of whose "taking off" has filled the
bosoms of all civilized people with sentiments of the
most lively horror and resentment. At present I shall
only notice one or two material facts connected with this
canvass, for which the worthy individual to whom I have ·
just alluded had not the smallest responsibility. The
first of these facts is, that a Democratic administration
openly and unblushingly employed its official patronage
in Illinois to defeat, if possible, the re-election to the na-

tional Senate of the ablest and most effective champion of the Democratic cause who was now any where on the public stage. The second fact to which I shall allude in passing is, that the exclusive pro-slavery champions every where in the South publicly avowed their earnest desire, and apparently, too, with general popular approval, that Mr. Lincoln should be chosen to the Senate instead of Mr. Douglas. How could the South reasonably expect to be defended hereafter by the Democratic statesmen of the North against abolition assailment, when she could be thus deluded into ungenerous, impolitic, and positively ungrateful conduct toward the most fearless and gifted of her Northern Democratic defenders? In spite of all the adverse circumstances brought into operation against him, Mr. Douglas was re-elected to the Senate by a small majority, and in a short time was able to show himself once more in that body, where very speedily he subjected to just responsibility several of the most leading of those senators who had enlisted in the unmanly and disreputable conspiracy for his overthrow.

And now do we not see a *cause* of future political weakness to the South, and her manifest exposure to multiplied future ills, which a provident sagacity might have averted, and the detrimental influence of which, attributable mainly to unprovoked injustice, and an almost unprecedented want of magnanimity and true manliness, might easily have been counteracted, if persistent folly and persecuting malice had in good season given way to returning equity and true heroism of spirit? As the Father of Poesy paints Achilles retiring indignantly to his tent, and his valiant myrmidonic legions withdrawn from the contest between the invading Grecian host and Troy, almost ready to succumb to her surrounding foes, in consequence of the arrogance and overbearing selfishness of Agamemnon and those subjected to his sway, so shall we perhaps see the all-indomitable Douglas and his multitudinous friends in the North driven, in the sequel, to the assumption of an attitude of cold and murky neutrality, or to the indignant abandonment of a cause which had lost, to their view, so much of its pristine dignity, together with its claims to sympathy and support.

But there were other causes besides which were now operating against the interests of peace and true brotherhood, the malign influence of which was in no respect ascribable to "antagonisms imbedded in the very nature of our heterogeneous institutions," to which I shall now give a passing notice.

All unprejudiced men will admit that the indecorous and ruffianly assault which had been made, several years anterior to the period we have now under review, upon a member of the United States Senate from Massachusetts, Mr. Sumner, by a heady and indiscreet member of the House of Representatives from the State of South Carolina, under circumstances of an extremely aggravated character, exerted, as was to be anticipated, a most potential influence in alienating the minds of humane and enlightened men in the free states of the Union from a cause which it was now plainly asserted sought, in its desperation, to sustain itself and perpetuate its existence by means which even the untutored savages of the forest would have disdained to employ; and though this unpardonable outrage was alike disapproved by all men

· of proper social refinement and of true manliness of sentiment alike in the South as in the North, yet was it plausibly attributed by excited orators and editors of sectional newspapers in the free states to the hated "institution" of slavery. Thus was the whole South made to suffer the penalties of an act of blood and violence for which nine tenths of her high-toned and chivalrous population would have disdained to assume the responsibility.

The celebrated judicial decision in the Dred Scott case, however sound may be both the conclusions to which a majority of the judges of the Supreme Court had, after full argument, arrived, as well as the reasoning by which those conclusions were supported, had been most deleterious in its influence upon the popular mind in both sections. Among the opponents of slavery in the North a suspicion had arisen that the case in which this important adjudication had been rendered had been adroitly gotten up *for the occasion*, and that the whole affair was, in fact, a mere political device of the pro-slavery zealots to bolster up a feeble and sinking system against the assaults which all Christendom was leveling at it. It must be confessed that this view of the matter, so well calculated to bring the highest judicial tribunal into contempt, and thus in some degree to discredit and subject to moral enfeeblement the whole frame of government of which the judiciary was so important an integral part, was strongly sustained by a portion of Mr. Buchanan's inaugural speech, which, though it did not attract any very special attention at the time of its delivery, yet, when the opinions of the judges had been given publicity, were supposed to indicate a secret understanding and arrange-

ment between the judges and the incoming executive, to
some extent justifying a fear that this "*more than Am-
phictyonic Council*" (to repeat the descriptive language
which Mr. Pinckney on a memorable occasion applied to
the Supreme Court of the Union) was about to become a
mere ministerial chamber in which to register executive
edicts. The words of the inaugural referred to were as
follows:

"A difference of opinion has arisen in regard to the
point of time when the people of a territory shall decide
this question for themselves.

"This is, happily, a matter of but little practical importance. Besides, it is a judicial question, which legitimately belongs to the Supreme Court of the United
States, before whom it is now pending, *and will, it is understood, be speedily and finally settled.* To this decision, in
common with all good citizens, I shall cheerfully submit."

While such was the state of feeling in the North in regard to the action of the Supreme Court of the United
States, a very opposite one was unfortunately awakened
among the pro-slavery devotees of the South, among
whom a strong sentiment of exultation was apparent, as
at the accomplishment of a signal triumph achieved over
their abolition foes. With all three of the departments
of government now apparently enlisted in the cause of
maintaining and diffusing African slavery, while numerous Southern presses and innumerable local orators were
rejoicing over this happy state of things, and anticipating
the rapid spread of slavery into every part of the American continent where climate and soil were at all adapted
to it, it is not at all surprising that certain enterprising

and over-excited persons should have judged that a favorable opportunity had arisen for reopening the African slave-trade. Some of the leading men of the South, in point of fact, about this period became the open advocates of the revival of this nefarious traffic. Many newspapers, edited by the unscrupulous agents of party, in several of the slaveholding states, earnestly advocated this accursed policy. The Commercial Convention, which assembled in the city of Vicksburg in the month of May, 1859, and which contained representatives from nearly all the cotton-growing states of the Union, after a long and heated debate, adopted resolutions denouncing the law which prohibited the carrying on of this traffic as piracy, as alike unconstitutional and impolitic, and declared the wish of that body that this infernal trade should be renewed by the South, in despite of the constitutional obstacles which had before that time been supposed to exist thereto. The discussions in the Convention on this important question were of a most heated and violent character. I heard these debates, and took some part in them also, in warm and indignant opposition to the policy proposed, which is all that I shall now say of my own action on this occasion. The leading advocate for the policy mentioned was Mr. Spratt, of Charleston, South Carolina, whose fervid and ingenious oration in support of this radical innovation upon the existing regulations of the government, containing the startling proposition that it had become necessary that slavery should assume an *aggressive attitude*, was, a few days after the close of the Convention, a second time fulminated in the capital of the State. Mississippi, in presence of an earnestly-approv-

ing audience, consisting, in part, of influential personages
who had held, as some of them were then doing, the highest official positions in the state. The timely and energetic efforts of Chief Justice Sharkey and others, who immediately convoked large public meetings, which they
addressed, in opposition to Mr. Spratt's seductive *commercial* theory, in a week or two roused so much indignation
among the slaveholding class in Central Mississippi (a
class, by-the-by, ever more discreet and moderate in spirit
and in action than the noisy and, in general, unscrupulous *non-slaveholding* champions who assumed to represent them) that the political managers of the Democratic
party deemed it wise to refuse the propounding of this
new political issue at the State Convention, which assembled in the city of Jackson a few weeks subsequent to
the proceedings which have just been recited. Of course,
though, the action of the Commercial Convention, and
the agitations in favor of reopening the slave-traffic, together with the fact that a considerable number of newly-
imported savages from the western coast of Africa were
being brought in at various Southern ports, and scattered
over the cotton and sugar growing region, were duly
made known in the North, and had a most unhappy influence in adding to and in inflaming sectional rancor in
that quarter of the Union.

Almost contemporaneously with these extraordinary
movements, the memorable *rescuing* occurrence took place
in the bosom of the State of Ohio, out of which, it will be
recollected, arose before the Supreme Court of that important commonwealth the important question of the *validity of the Fugitive Slave Law.* It was well known that

the present Chief Justice Chase, then governor of this intelligent and populous state, was taking all legitimate
steps to procure a decision of the highest appellate court
of Ohio against the constitutionality of that law, the passage of which he had strenuously opposed in Congress,
and doubtless under the most conscientious convictions ·
of public duty. For some time it was regarded as exceedingly doubtful in what manner this grave and momentous question might be decided—the more grave and
momentous by reason of the well-known fact that Governor Chase had announced his determination to *back up*
the action of the Supreme Court *by arms* against the whole
power of the general government, should the judges of
that high tribunal decide the law to be a nullity. The
present accomplished and able Justice Swayne (now also
a member of the Supreme Court of the United States)
argued the case, and with the most consummate ability,
before the court by which it was to be decided, and, a
good deal in opposition to the prevailing anticipation at
the period, the decision of the court was finally such as
to uphold the law and to preserve the public peace of the
country. It was my fortune to be journeying through
the State of Ohio at this period, and I can personally
avouch the verity of the preceding statement of facts, as
well as of the serious disturbance of the popular mind,
both North and South, at this crisis, by reason of the rapid diffusion of the reigning irritation through the various
and multiplied channels of intelligence afforded by the
newspaper press of the country.

But this was not all; for, in the month of October,
1859, one of the most extraordinary and astounding oc-

currences had taken place in the bosom of the "Ancient
Dominion," in the neighborhood of the lordly and classic
Potomac, and almost in sight of the Capitol of the republic, which has ever been recorded in history. The fearful movement of the celebrated Spartacus, who suddenly
called into existence a general servile insurrection in Italy, that at one time threatened to destroy Rome itself,
and which it cost many thousand valuable Roman lives
to suppress, scarcely smote upon the popular mind of
that region more powerfully than the intelligence which
one morning, only six years ago, was communicated to
the American people by fast-flying telegraphic dispatch-
es, that *Ossawatomie Brown*, with a furious band of abolition outlaws, had suddenly seized upon the government
arsenal at Harper's Ferry; had fired twice into the ex-
press-train passing through this town; had dispatched a
large number of rifles into Maryland; had cut the telegraphic wires, so as to preclude the distribution of intelligence touching the alarming scenes in progress; had
seized many white citizens, and impressed them into the
service of the conspirators, and a still larger number of
negroes; and had proclaimed the *universal freedom of the
blacks, and the general massacre of the white population of
Virginia, and of the whole South,* who should presume to
resist their hostile assaults. Brennus, in the Roman Fo-
rum; Alaric or Attila, swooping down with resistless force
upon the fair plains of France and Italy; Genseric, with
his Vandalic marauding soldiery, rapidly approaching the
piled-up treasures of the boasted metropolis of the European continent; Mahomet, and his fierce fanatical suc-
cessors, menacing the whole Christian world, had not

awakened a more lively feeling of consternation than now ensued.

The sanguinary scenes which soon had their progress at Harper's Ferry, or in the neighborhood of that town, are already graphically familiar to the public mind every where; and the grim hero who initiated this carnival of death has already found earnest biographers, and has even become the subject of encomiastic homage of late, both in slip-shod fustian prose, and doggerel lugubrious verse. I have no taste for such sickening details as have had currency, in regard either to the conflict of arms, which resulted ultimately in the capture of the wretched enthusiast Brown and several of his associates, or in relation to the execution of these persons which very soon after took place. I shall content myself with laying before my readers the *programme* of action adopted by the ill-fated Brown and his allies in crime, which has since been *authentically* published.

CONSTITUTION, ETC., ETC.

" PREAMBLE. — *Whereas* slavery, throughout its entire existence in the United States, is none other than the most barbarous, unprovoked, and unjustifiable war of one portion of its citizens against another portion, the only conditions of which are perpetual imprisonment and hopeless servitude, or absolute extermination, in utter disregard and violation of those eternal and self-evident truths set forth in our Declaration of Independence :

" *Therefore*, We, the citizens of the United States, and the oppressed people who, by a recent decision of the Supreme Court, are declared to have no rights which the white man is bound to respect, together with all the other people degraded by the laws thereof, do, for the time being, ordain and establish for ourselves the following provisional Constitution and ordinances, the better to protect our people, property, lives, and liberties, and to govern our actions.

"Art. I. *Qualifications of Membership.*—All persons of mature age, whether proscribed, oppressed, and enslaved citizens, or of proscribed and oppressed races of the United States, who shall agree to sustain and enforce the provisional Constitution and ordinances of organization, together with all minor children of such persons, shall be held to be fully entitled to protection under the same."

"Art. XXVIII. *Property.*—All captured or confiscated property, and all property the product of the labor of those belonging to this organization and of their families, shall be held as the property of the whole equally, without distinction, and may be used for the common benefit, or disposed of for the same object. And any person, officer or otherwise, who shall improperly retain, secrete, use, or needlessly destroy such property, or any property found, captured, or confiscated, belonging to the enemy, or shall willfully neglect to render a full and fair statement of such property by him so taken or held, shall be guilty of a misdemeanor, and, on conviction, shall be punished accordingly.

"Art. XXIX. *Safety or Intelligence Fund.*—All money, plate, watches, or jewelry captured by honorable warfare, found, taken, or confiscated, belonging to the enemy, shall be held sacred, to constitute a liberal safety or intelligence fund; and any person who shall improperly retain, dispose of, hide, use, or destroy such money or other articles above named, contrary to the provisions and spirit of this article, shall be deemed guilty of theft, and, on conviction thereof, shall be punished accordingly. The treasurer shall furnish the commander-in-chief at all times with a full statement of the condition of such fund and its nature." ·

Art. XXXIII. *Volunteers.*—All persons who may come forward, and shall voluntarily deliver up slaves, and have their names registered on the books of this organization, shall, so long as they continue at peace, be entitled to the fullest protection in person and property, though not connected with this organization, and shall be treated as friends, and not merely as persons neutral.

"Art. XXXIV. *Neutrals.*—The persons and property of all non-slaveholders, who shall remain absolutely neutral, shall be respected so far as circumstances will allow of it, but they shall not be entitled to any active protection."

"Art. XXXVI. *Property confiscated.*—The entire personal and real property of all persons known to be acting, either directly or indirectly, with or for the enemy, or found in arms with them, or found willfully holding slaves, shall be confiscated and taken, wherever and whenever it may be found, in either free or slave states."

"Art. XLVI. *These Articles not for the Overthrow of Government.*—The foregoing articles shall not be construed so as in any way to encourage the overthrow of any state government or of the general government of the United States, and look to no dissolution of the Union, but simply to amendment and repeal ; and our flag shall be the same that our fathers fought under in the Revolution."

It is exceedingly difficult to tell what would have been the wisest course for the government of Virginia to pursue at this conjuncture. Brown and his confederates had all unquestionably forfeited their lives, and neither the justice nor legality of putting them to death could be denied. Under the light of subsequent events, it seems to me at present that it would have been more politic to spare the lives of these guilty offenders, than by an exciting trial and public execution, under such circumstances as were connected with the occasion, to convert them, in the estimation of thousands of the ignorant and the fanatical, into *martyrs*. Certain it is that, anterior to the death of Brown, there were no striking indications of awakened sympathy to be found in any part of the North. I well remember being called to Cincinnati, Ohio, during the month of December, 1859 (in which month Brown suffered the penalties of the law), for the delivery of a *lecture on the value of the Federal Union*, and containing admonitory warnings of the dangers which seemed to my mind to be connected with the coming presidential election. This lecture was pronounced before the Mercantile Association of Cincinnati, on the night before Brown's mortal career was to be closed at Charlestown, Virginia. On the very day of his execution, I was journeying to Evansville for the purpose of there repeating the lecture referred to; on the next day I was on my way to Indianapolis for a similar purpose; and still, on the succeeding one, with a like duty before me, to be performed in the city of St. Louis. I had a most ample opportunity of testing the condition of the popular mind in regard to Brown and his attempted achievements, and I do now conscientiously aver that, in the whole course of my journeyings, I did not meet with one single man, one single woman, or one single child who appeared to have the least respect or sympathy for John Brown.

The actings of this fierce and bloody monster must, I suppose though, be *now* recognized as one of a series of events *predestined to occur from the foundation of the world*, as part and portion of an "irrepressible conflict between *opposing and enduring forces ;*" and we must be content to look back upon the same as matters which belong not to the ordinary concerns of earth, chargeable either to discretion and virtue, or to the want of these attributes, but to the mysterious ordinations of Divinity, entitled to challenge our unqualified respect and homage.   The storm of sectional hostility began by this time to rage most furiously all over the land ; for

> "Every mountain now had found a voice,
> And Jura answered from her misty shroud
> Back to the joyous Alps who called to her aloud !"

CHAPTER XIV.

Other Causes of sectional Excitement at this Period.—The Helper Book, and its unfortunate Discussion in Congress. — Resolutions forced through the Senate, mainly though the Agency of Mr. Davis, of Mississippi, having in View the double Object of destroying Mr. Douglas, and dragging the Democratic Party into an unnational and aggressive Attitude.—Movements of William L. Yancey in the Year 1859, and early in the Year 1860, having in View the breaking up of the Federal Union in the event of a Republican President being elected.—Efforts in the South to bring about the Election of Mr. Lincoln, in order to obtain the desired Object.—Democratic Conventions at Charleston and Baltimore reviewed.—Leading Incidents of the Presidential Canvass of 1860 and its Results.—Sketch of William L. Yancey.

WE now nearly approach the momentous presidential election of 1860, upon the result of which so much of the weal or woe of the republic was fated to depend. The session of Congress immediately preceding that contest was more than ordinarily marked with excitement. The fierce discussion of the merits of a foolish fanatical book (issued a short time before by an obscure and ignorant person in North Carolina) in the House of Representatives, so unwisely and unprofitably brought on at the instance of Mr. Clarke, of Missouri, and the debate upon the *Brown conspiracy*, allusions to which have already been made, were but preliminary to still more fervid controversies in the Democratic Presidential Convention, and before the people in their primary capacity. Several movements besides, having no great importance but as they throw more or less light upon the course of after events, will be now alluded to. In the Territory of New Mexico, where no reasonable being ever yet supposed that the system of African slavery, if it ever should be forcibly carried there, could long have a healthful and vigorous existence, by reason of the unpropitious character both of the soil and climate of that region, as Mr. Webster, before his decease, had so clearly demonstrated, legislative enactments, manifestly prompted from Washington City, and which could only be productive of increased sectional rancor, had been some months before adopted, *protective* of slaveholding rights in said territory. With a view of making the pro-slavery party in the Senate triumphant over Mr. Douglas and non-intervention, certain resolutions were dispatchfully forced through that body, the principal of which were as follows:

" *Resolved*, That neither Congress nor a territorial Legislature, whether by direct legislation or legislation of an indirect and unfriendly character, possesses power to annul or impair the constitutional right of any citizen of the United States to take his slave property into the common territories, and there hold and enjoy the same while the territorial condition remains.

" *Resolved*, That if experience should at any time prove that the judicial and executive authority do not possess means to insure adequate protection to constitutional rights in a territory, and if the territorial government should fail or refuse to provide the necessary remedies for that purpose, it will be the duty of Congress to supply such deficiency.

" *Resolved*, That the inhabitants of a territory of the

M

United States, when they rightfully form a Constitution to be admitted as a state into the Union, may then *for the first time*, like the people of a state when forming a new Constitution, decide for themselves whether slavery, as a domestic institution, shall be maintained or prohibited within their jurisdiction; and they shall be admitted into the Union with or without slavery as their Constitution may prescribe at the time of their admission."

These resolutions, with others, had been pressed to adoption mainly by the exertions of Mr. Jefferson Davis; and Mr. Douglas having been regularly voted in senatorial Democratic caucus to be no longer worthy of being recognized as a *Democratic* senator—a resolution for this purpose having been introduced by Mr. Slidell, of Louisiana (avowedly at the instance of Mr. Buchanan)—the scene of contention was shifted to Charleston, South Carolina, in which city it had been agreed that the next National Democratic Convention should assemble. Before the session of this body commenced, several other occurrences had taken place, which are necessary now to be noticed.

In the month of January, 1860, Mr. William L. Yancey, of Alabama, had delivered a speech, which had, as a printed pamphlet, been widely circulated, in which he had said:

"To obtain the aid of the Democracy in this contest, it is necessary to make a contest in its Charleston Convention. In that body, Douglas's adherents will press his doctrine to a decision. If the state-rights men keep out of that Convention, that decision must inevitably be against the South, and that either in direct favor of the

Douglas doctrine, or by the indorsement of the Cincinnati platform, under which Douglas claims shelter for his
principles. The state-rights men should present in that
Convention their demand for a decision, and they will
obtain an indorsement of their demands or a denial of
these demands. If indorsed, we shall have greater hope
of triumph within the Union. If denied, in my opinion,
the state-rights wing should secede from the Convention,
and appeal to the whole people of the South, without distinction of parties, and organize another Convention upon
the basis of their principles, and go into the election with
a candidate nominated by it as a grand constitutional
party. But in the presidential contest a Black Republican may be elected. If this dire event should happen,
in my opinion, the only hope of safety for the South is a
withdrawal from the Union before he shall be inaugurated—before the sword and the treasury of the Federal
government shall be placed in the keeping of that party.
I would suggest that the several state Legislatures should
by law require the governor, when it shall be made manifest that the Black Republican candidate for the presidency shall receive a majority of the electoral vote, to
call a Convention of the people of the state to assemble
in time to provide for their safety before the 4th of
March, 1860. If, however, a Black Republican should
not be elected, then, in pursuance of the policy of making
this contest within the Union, we should initiate measures in Congress which should lead to a repeal of all the
unconstitutional acts against slavery. If we should fail
to obtain so just a system of legislation, then the South
should seek her independence out of the Union." (Applause.)

In another speech, delivered at Columbia, South Carolina, in July, 1860, Mr. Yancey had said:

"But the true question is not, are we stronger than we have been, but are we as strong as our necessities require? Are we as strong as we rightfully ought to be? This question must be answered in the negative. Can we have any hope of righting ourselves and doing justice to ourselves in the Union? If there is such hope, it would be our duty to make the attempt. For one, I have no such hope, but I am determined to act with those who have such hope, as long, and only as long, as it may be reasonably indulged; not so much with any expectation that the South will obtain justice in the Union, as with the hope that by thus acting, within a reasonable time, there will be obtained unity among our people in going out of the Union." (Applause.) "If we remain in the Union, we must demand a repeal of every unconstitutional act against the institution of slavery. We must demand a repeal of the acts of 1807, 1819, 1851."

This same gentleman, who was presently to become the Magnus Apollo of the disorganizing portion of the Charleston Democratic Convention, had offered a resolution at a Commercial Convention which held its session in Montgomery, Alabama, in these words:

"Resolved, That the laws of Congress prohibiting the slave-trade ought to be repealed."

The same personage had published a letter in June, 1859, which contained the following declaration:

"For one, I am unwilling to see continued on our statute-books these semi-abolition acts, but desire to see the subject of slavery taken from the grasp of the Federal government, and that government only to be allowed to act upon it *to protect it.* Whether the African slave-trade will be carried on should not depend upon that government, but upon the will of each slaveholding state. To that tribunal alone should the question be submitted, and by the decision of that tribunal alone should the Southern people abide."

And now let us consider for a moment the conventional movements both in Charleston and Baltimore, in which Mr. Yancey was to participate so prominently. The Convention assembled on the 23d of April, 1860, and General Francis B. Flournoy, of Arkansas, was chosen as temporary chairman. The *inevitable* Caleb Cushing, of Massachusetts, was subsequently made permanent president of the body. This individual was well known to be confidently expecting at the time a position on the Supreme Bench of the Union, but perfectly well knew that he stood no chance of appointment unless his conduct in the Convention should be pleasing to the secession leaders, to whom Mr. Buchanan had virtually transferred himself, with all the official power and patronage which he possessed. It must be confessed that Mr. Cushing acted his part well as moderator, nor had those in whose services he had enlisted, *for a consideration,* any reasonable ground of complaint on the score of his failing to perform any part of the special duties which had been prescribed for his observance.

The various contests which arose upon the political platform, though sufficiently interesting at the time, are not needful here to be described. The great issue between the two wings of the Democratic party, the non-intervention and the intervention members thereof, has been already sufficiently explained. A non-intervention platform having been adopted by a decided majority of the Convention, the cloven foot of secession began at once to display itself. Mr. L. P. Walker, of Alabama, who was soon to become the Secretary of War of a new and distinct government, and, as such, was to have the doubtful honor of initiating the most unnecessary and profitless war that has ever yet been carried on, arose, and presented the written instructions which the Alabama delegates to the Convention had brought with them, received from the Democratic Convention of that state, to whom the delegates owed their appointment, and also a *protest* based upon said instructions; after the presentation and reading of which, the Alabama delegation, evidently in accordance with an arrangement long before agreed upon, withdrew, as the instructions under which they professed to be acting positively ordered them to do. Mr. Yancey was among the delegates of Alabama by whom this extraordinary part was enacted, and though, deeming it expedient to keep himself a little in reserve, he was evidently the ruling spirit in the proceeding. It was evident now that secession had put on its *cocked hat, had lashed its sword to its side, and was ready for combat to the death with all that might attempt to obstruct its long-cherished designs;* but Caleb Cushing remained still in his high and responsible position, and his neighbor and friend, Mr. B. F. Butler, of Lowell, Massachusetts, who was also fighting for official advancement, followed his illustrious example. Next in order, as was reasonably to be expected, was the withdrawal from the Convention of the Mississippi dele-

gation. Mr. Glen, of Mississippi, who had been, to my
personal knowledge, a flaming disunionist for more than
ten years, covered the retreat of himself and his co-dele-
gates with the following characteristic speech:

"Sir, at Cincinnati we adopted a platform on which
we all agreed. Now answer me, ye men of the North,
of the East, of the South, and of the West, what was the
construction placed upon that platform in different sections of the Union? You at the West said it meant one
thing, we of the South said it meant another. Either
we were right, or you were right; we were wrong, or you
were wrong. We came here to ask you which was right
and which was wrong. You have maintained your position. You say that you can not give us an acknowledgment of that right which, I tell you here now, in
coming time will be your only safety in your contests
with the Black Republicans of Ohio and of the North.
(Cheers.)

"Why, sir, turn back to the history of your own leading men. There sits a distinguished gentleman, Hon.
Charles E. Stuart, of Michigan, once a representative of
one of the sovereign states of the Union in the Senate,
who then voted that Congress had the constitutional
power to pass the Wilmot Proviso, and to exclude slavery from the territories; and now, when the Supreme
Court has said that it has not that power, he comes forward and tells Mississippians that that same Congress is
impotent to protect that same species of property! There
sits my distinguished friend, the senator from Ohio (Mr.
Pugh), who, but a few nights since, told us from that
stand that, if a territorial government totally misused

their powers or abused them, Congress could wipe out
that territorial government altogether. And yet, when
we come here and.ask him to give us *protection* in case
that territorial government robs us of our property and
strikes the star which answers to the name of Mississippi
from the flag of the Union, so far as the Constitution
gives her protection, he tells us, with his hand upon his
heart, as Governor Payne, of Ohio, had before done, that
they will part with their lives before they will acknowledge the principle which we contend for.

"Gentlemen, in such a situation of things in the Convention of our great party, it is right that we should part.
Go your way, and we will go ours. The South leaves
you — not like Hagar, driven into the wilderness, friend-
less and alone — but I tell Southern men here, and for
them I tell the North, that in less than sixty days you
will find a united South standing side by side with us."
(Prolonged and enthusiastic cheering.)

Next withdrew the delegation from Louisiana, except-
ing two of them, who chose to remain. Next the delegates from South Carolina made good their retreat.
Then Florida followed. Next went out the delegation
from Texas. Then three delegates from Arkansas. Now
the Georgia delegation asked leave to retire for the purpose of consultation; no one having objection to this,
they withdrew accordingly. Then two of the Delaware
delegates retired, and the third announced his willingness
to remain for a season. After a good deal of fiery and
fustian discussion of immaterial points mainly, the Convention commenced balloting for the nomination of president. Douglas received 145½ votes; R. M. T. Hunter, 42

votes; Andrew Johnson, 12; Daniel S. Dickinson, 7; Joseph Lane, 6; Isaac Toucey, 2½; Jefferson Davis, 1½; Franklin Pierce, 1. Several other ballots occurred; but no one having obtained a vote of two thirds, the Convention adjourned, to meet at Baltimore on Monday, the 18th day of June. The seceding delegates, having adopted an *intervention platform*, adjourned to meet at Richmond on the second Monday of June.

The majority of the Convention, who had agreed to assemble in Baltimore on the 18th of June, met accordingly; but it being soon ascertained that Douglas's strength had considerably increased since the adjournment, the most disreputable proceeding which had yet taken place occurred. Mr. Russell, of Virginia, one of the most expert political managers that Virginia has yet known, Mr. Lander, of North Carolina, Mr. Ewing, of Tennessee, Mr. Johnson, of Maryland, Mr. Smith, of California, Mr. Saulsbury, of Delaware, Mr. Caldwell, of Kentucky, and Mr. Clarke, of Missouri, announced the withdrawal of a whole or a part of their respective delegations. Mr. Cushing, uneasy about the judgeship for which he was ardently sighing, all hopes of which he must relinquish if he acquiesced in the support of Mr. Douglas, ingloriously *skedaddled**　from the chairmanship of the Convention, which then proceed-

* I trust this very classic personage, who I recollect was formerly accustomed to boast of his having been the university associate of Mr. Bancroft and other illustrious Cambridge graduates, will excuse my applying to him a term which is, I believe, not yet to be found in our English dictionaries. It being a strictly *military term*, though, which has recently crept into use, it is probable that one of Mr. Cushing's decided warlike tastes will, on reflection, perceive the manifest propriety of my using this very significant word as faithfully typical of his sudden *exodus* from the

M 2

ed to ballot for president, when, Douglas having received
173½ votes, the following resolution was adopted:

"*Resolved, unanimously,* That Stephen A. Douglas, of the
State of Illinois, having now received two thirds of all the
votes given in this Convention, is hereby declared, in accordance with the rules governing this body, and in accordance with the uniform customs and rules of former
Democratic National Conventions, the regular nominee
of the Democratic party of the United States for the office
of President of the United States."

Herschel V. Johnson was afterward nominated for the
vice-presidency.

The Convention of the seceders met at Richmond on
the 11th of June, adjourned to Baltimore, elected Caleb Cushing* their president, reaffirmed their intervention platform, nominated Breckenridge and Lane for the

august seat of moderator of the Baltimore Convention, which he had continued to occupy so long as he could be of service to his *employers.*

* This gentleman, who is never weary in well-doing, was luckily on
hand for this new directorial position, and his affection for his disorganizing secession friends proved itself to be absolutely exhaustless. Is it
not marvelous that Mr. Cushing should afterward have been among the
first to tender his *immaculate* sword to President Lincoln as a commander
of Union soldiery against those whom he had done so much to inveigle
into this same war? Luckily for his friend Jefferson Davis and those associated with him, this redoubtable champion was not given the throat-
cutting employment which he sought, else there is no knowing what wondrous deeds of valor he would have performed. It is perhaps fortunate for
the fame of Grant, Sherman, and others, that the field of glory was not
opened to this undeveloped Napoleon, since no one who knows him can
doubt that, had it been, he would have surpassed in heroic achievement all
that Cæsar, or Hannibal, or Alexander had done. The last time I talked
with Mr. Cushing, he was deliberating whether he should not enlist in a fil-
ibustering project on the Queen of the Antilles. How it happened that he

presidency and the vice-presidency, and then, after a speech from Mr. Yancey, adjourned.

¯ Thus was the ingenious scheme for the breaking up of the Democratic party as a national association, and rendering it utterly powerless for contesting in the North with its great Republican rival, most ingloriously consummated, and the way opened very conveniently for the execution thereafter, at a suitable time, of the long-cherished project of secession from the Union.

No fact is better known, and I can myself personally avouch it, that, had Douglas or any suitable man been nominated in 1860 upon a non-intervention or Union platform (for really at this period they meant the same thing), the American party, now assuming the name of "The Constitutional Union Party," would not have come into the field at all. Mr. Bell, always preferring the happiness of the republic to his personal advancement, would have sustained the Democratic ticket, and Douglas, or some other non-interventionist and true friend of the Federal Union, would have been easily elected. Nor do I make this statement as to Mr. Bell without full *authority;* for oftentimes have I heard from the lips of my venerated neighbor and friend declarations, both before he was nominated for the presidency and afterward, which fully justify me in what has been said upon this interesting point. Well do I recollect the friendly and almost fraternal interview which occurred between Mr. Douglas and Mr. Bell, at my own mansion in the city of Nashville,

concluded not to go in quest of immortal fame in that direction I have never been informed. Perhaps his future biographer may enlighten us.

on the evening of the day on which the former delivered his able speech in that city in the summer of 1860, as
well as the eminent magnanimity and patriotism which
breathed in every word uttered by either of them; and
I am well satisfied that at the moment when this meeting
took place, either of these personages would have rejoiced
to know that his generous and high-minded competitor
would be chosen president, assured, as he could not but
be, that the republic would be perfectly safe in such
hands, and that the mad war of sectionalism would be at
least held in *suppression* for the coming four years.

And now, at the hazard of being regarded by some as
a little egotistical, I find it convenient to insert a few
extracts from one of many popular addresses delivered
by me during the summer of 1860, all substantially similar—as similar in views and spirit, likewise, to various
political speeches delivered both in the North and in the
South, and alike by the supporters of Mr. Bell and those
of Mr. Douglas, during this eventful presidential campaign—which extracts are inserted here alone for the purpose of showing in a graphic and distinct manner how
earnestly solicitous many of those whom we shall, in less
than a year, see drawn into the vortex of rebellion, were,
five years ago, to avert those sad consequences which have
since ensued, by the seasonable utterance of frank and patriotic premonitions in reference to those dangers which
to all sagacious minds already began to be most easy of
descrial.

The political address referred to was delivered in the
city of Nashville, on Saturday, July 7th, 1860, at a meeting convened for the ratification of the conventional pro-

ceedings in Baltimore which had resulted in the nominations already mentioned. (This speech was printed at the time in the Nashville papers, and had more or less circulation.)

"*Mr. President and Fellow-citizens:*

"The present is truly a grave and momentous occasion, if, indeed, such an occasion can arise on this side that dread scene which is hereafter to bring to an end all the troublous and varied concerns of earth-born beings. The only people now existing in the world who can with propriety claim the full and unrestrained possession of civil and religious freedom, are in imminent danger of losing that freedom. We are now visibly trembling upon the very edge of that precipice down which so many republics of ancient and of modern times have tumbled into ruin. Institutions, the wisest and the best ever planned and put in prosperous exercise by the children of men, are even now tottering to their foundations, and, I seriously apprehend, are soon to be shaken and convulsed with a still more fearful and tempestuous commotion. The fierce, organized bands of fanatical abolitionists of the North are already girding on their armor and making ready their weapons of warfare for the most exciting and unsparing political conflict that our country has yet known. The rampant and furious secessionists of the South, inspired, energized, and led on by the Yanceys and the Davises of this sunny region, hypocritically claiming 'equality of rights,' and vociferously denying all treasonable projects, are aiming at this moment to rend the Union which we have so long loved and cherished, and,

by the skillful concealment of their real purposes, are enlisting thousands as proselytes and co-operators, who, if
they were apprised of the real objects of these insidious
and deceptious teachers, would start back with horror
and affright from the scenes in which they are expected
ultimately to bear part. The old fraternal ties, both of
church and state, which formerly constituted our surest
guarantee of national repose and happiness, have been
either rudely snapped asunder, or are at this very instant
violently strained to their utmost capacity of tension.
Corruption stalks abroad throughout the whole land, and
even the high places of civic trust are no longer free
from the taint of impurity. Demagogues of every stamp
and hue, numerous as the frogs of Egypt, are heard to
croak forth here, there, every where, their hollow sepul-
chral accents, dismally ominous of national confusion and
ruin. The wholesome conservative influence once possessed by the government itself has no longer any per-
ceptible existence, but has, indeed, been supplanted by a
malignant virus which is fast consuming the very vitals
of the body politic. Popular confidence in rulers is, for
a time, at an end. Anarchy, licentiousness, and lawless
violence are every where displaying themselves. The
Washingtons, the Jacksons, the Clays, the Websters, the
Polks, have passed away; a generation of babbling factionists, noisy declaimers, self-consequential, dreamy abstractionists, servile, sycophantic worshipers of ostenta-
tious false greatness has succeeded, who impudently claim
ascendency in our national councils. The high functionaries of government, with their innumerable subordinates
scattered and ramified all over the republic, in fearful

unison with that worse than Briarean monster, a corrupt
stipendiary press, instead of upholding and sustaining the
governmental system with which they stand affiliated,
with a strange and uprecedented blindness, are in close
alliance with those who have deliberately decreed that
system to destruction, and are urging that the dark fiends
of civic rebellion shall be invited to perform their infernal orgies in the very temple of freedom.   The whole
eighty millions of executive patronage is now being
wielded for the worst and most dangerous purposes of
faction.   The freedom of popular elections in the states
and territories is no longer regarded.   Since the reign of
Richard II., in England (that ill-fated monarch who was
dethroned and put to death for attempting, through the
sheriffs of the realm, to control the election of members
of the House of Commons), nothing so alarming has occurred on either side of the Atlantic as the efforts openly
and unblushingly made by Mr. Buchanan and those associated with him to influence the result of the election
of members of both houses of Congress by means of Federal official patronage.   It is evident that a few years
more of such vicious, tyrannic intermeddling, if unhappily successful, will fill the national Legislature with the
mere slaves and servitors of the executive will, prepared
to obey all his commands, and obediently to register his
edicts.   Whenever this state of things shall be brought
about, it is plain that popular freedom will exist no longer, nor independent legislation, nor any possibility, even,
of escaping the gulf of executive despotism.   All power
will be virtually concentrated in a single executive chief,
who, by whatever name called, will be, in fact, nothing

more nor less than an imperial autocrat. But it is scarcely possible that even so favorable a result will be realized. The overthrow of the Union, and the division and
subdivision of the republic into a half dozen or even a
dozen warring confederacies, all of them necessarily maintaining a standing army, and sooner or later destined to
become severe and bloody tyrannies, is the natural and
necessary result of the monstrous and undeniable alliance which has been lately formed between our present
Federal chief magistrate and the open enemies of the
Union. Washington firmly but resolutely drew the
sword against the whisky insurrectionists of Pennsylvania; Jefferson employed all his giant energies for the
suppression of the Burr conspiracy; Madison exploded
the Hartford Convention project; Jackson fulminated
his sublime overawing proclamation against the nulli-
fiers and secessionists of South Carolina; Fillmore, with
a quiet, serene wisdom, steered the ship of state for three
years successfully and peacefully, all the while observing
faithfully the prescriptions which Clay and his associates
placed in his hands, known as the Compromise of 1850;
Buchanan—oh, most shameful example!—has deliberately joined the ranks of the Southern disunionists. Meanwhile the true and reliable friends of the Union, the upholders of the Constitution and the laws, the advocates
of social peace and order, are, to a most serious and alarming extent, separated from each other, fighting in opposing party ranks, wasting in profitless and unfraternal
strife energies which, blended, united, inspirited with the
fervid glow of patriotism, and valiantly and persistently
wielded against the common foe, might rescue Liberty

from peril, save the Union from wreck, and reclaim, renovate, and preserve this great nation.

"Under these trying circumstances a presidential election is in a few months to occur, in connection with which it really seems to me that there are only two questions worth a moment's consideration. These are:

"1. *Is the government of our fathers to be preserved?*

"2. *Is corruption to be suppressed—the Augean stable to be thoroughly cleansed?*

"He who honestly labors for the attainment of these two public ends may possibly err in the selection of the means which he employs, but is worthy of the respect and love of all patriots for the goodness of his intentions; he who is opposed to either of these meritorious objects is unworthy to be called a freeman.

"Five presidential tickets are in the field. In relation to two of them I have nothing to say, either in support or in opposition. Were I to bestow upon them language of commendation, I should but disparage and discredit them; I should cease to respect myself were I tempted, at such a trying and perilous moment in our national history, to apply to them terms either of decrial or of ridicule. My fight is with Republicanism in the North, and secession in the South; and for the purpose of uprooting and destroying both these dangerous factions, I deem it my duty to yield a hearty support to the National Democratic presidential ticket, upon which are enrolled the names of Stephen A. Douglas, of Illinois, and Herschel V. Johnson, of Georgia.

"Every man whom I now address well knows that the Republican presidential candidate stands pledged, if elected to the station which he seeks, to labor for the exclusion, by congressional enactment, of African slavery from our vacant territories; for the abolition of slavery in the District of Columbia; and for the modification, in several vital respects, of what is known as the Fugitive Slave Law. The adoption of either of these measures will inevitably destroy the Union. Every Southern state, or rather a majority of them, have long been formally pledged to secession, as a *necessary remedy* against this, which they would deem *intolerable oppression*. Indeed, the Union men of the South, in order to procure a quiet and peaceable acquiescence in the compromise measures of 1850, had to pledge themselves to their excited countrymen that, in the event of the passage of such laws as those enumerated, or any one of them, they would themselves take the *initiative* in the work of disunion. Now I wish to deal fairly with this matter, and must therefore declare that, in my judgment, either Bell, Houston, or Douglas, in the event of election to the presidency, would promptly exercise the veto power for the defeat of any of these measures, which action on the part of the executive would in all probability effectually defeat such congressional enactments, for want of a two thirds vote in support of them in the two houses of the national Legislature. The veto power, in this view, must be regarded by all reasonable men as the very sheet-anchor of the public safety, calculated to afford more solid and substantial *protection* to Southern institutions than all the silly abstractions that ever entered the moonstruck and ill-balanced craniums of all the political metaphysicians that ever cursed the councils of the country with their baleful presence.

"But, again: certain sectional demagogues of the South, quite easy to be named, in several of the Southern and Southwestern states, have taken most foul and un-manly advantage of the peculiar sensitiveness and in-flammability of the popular mind of our mercurial region touching slavery, and have some time since contrived to inveigle their over-confiding countrymen in a solemn and formal pledge (either by legislative or conventional reso-lutions) to go out of the Union in the event of the elec-tion of a Republican president in November next. Hav-ing thus adroitly obtained this *perilous committal*, these same artful and unscrupulous managers immediately set themselves to work to get the Southern mind excited and infuriated by new questions connected with the institu-tion of slavery, intending, after a while, if they could suf-ficiently madden the feelings of those to whom they thus addressed themselves, to get the South, or at least what are known as the *cotton states* of this region, united fierce-ly in some new demand of congressional legislation, which being refused, as was confidently expected would be the case, they hoped to be able to '*precipitate these same cotton states into disunion.*' Especially did they expect this ter-rible result to arise from the election of a Republican president, an event which they confidently believed would be brought about by the continued agitation of the slav-ery question. Hence the Lecompton controversy. Hence the demand, last summer, by the Southern Commercial Convention which assembled in the city of Vicksburg, for the reopening of the African slave-trade, advocated openly and earnestly in that body by ex-Governor Mc-Rae, and to some extent abetted also by Senators Davis and Brown. Hence the almost unanimous adoption of a resolution by that Convention in favor of the renewal of that accursed policy. Hence the formal sanction by the same body of that most treasonable and disgraceful speech of Mr. Spratt, of South Carolina, in which he openly declared, in express terms, that the 'time had come for the South to take an aggressive attitude,' and unblushingly boasted that Southern juries would never convict any violator of the law, however manifestly proved to be guilty before them. Hence the furious advocacy of this damnable policy by some twenty or thirty Southern Democratic presses, mainly in the State of Mississippi. Hence the correspondent action of Yancey and others in Alabama, and their secession comrades in Georgia, South Carolina, Florida, and Texas. So soon as it was ascertained that the Southern States could not be brought into hearty co-operation in support of this extravagant demand, and that, on the contrary, Virginia, Kentucky, Tennessee, Missouri, North Carolina, and Maryland would prove as hostile to it as any of the free states even, then a new device was fallen upon, which it was hoped might be more successful. Mr. Davis had urged the measure of congressional protection, as a member of the United States Senate, as an amendment to the compromise enactments of 1850. It had been repeatedly voted down, and some, including him who is now addressing you, had denounced it warmly as '*the Wilmot Proviso South.*' Upon this very issue, with others, submitted to the people of the State of Mississippi in 1851, Mr. Davis had been defeated for governor of that gallant state, all the strong cotton-growing counties therein, and especially all those located

upon the bank of the Mississippi River, from the southern boundary of Tennessee to the northern boundary of
Louisiana, including the county of his own residence,
voting against him. Notwithstanding all this, it was resolved to bring forward this protective proposition again.
Nobody, of course, expected to obtain the protection
claimed at the hands of Congress. There could not have
been a human being in the Union mad enough to expect
it. But the bringing it forward in Southern Legislatures
and Conventions, and urging it fiercely in Congress, it
was hoped, would infallibly have one of two effects, and
perhaps produce both of them : Mr. Douglas, known to
be an inflexible non-interventionist, would be killed off,
and the Democratic party would be, in all probability, so
distracted and divided that the darling scheme of secession would at last be accomplished. The movements of
the secessionists in the United States Senate, and their
comrades in four or five of the Southern States, are thus
easily solved. Meanwhile, Mr. Douglas was to be mar-
tyred in advance, if possible, by a more compendious
process. The Lecompton issue was to be forced upon
him; he was to be simultaneously denounced by the administration presses throughout the South; an alliance
even with Republicanism was to be set on foot in Illinois, and Mr. Lincoln, the present Republican candidate
for the presidency, was to be aided by Mr. Buchanan as
strongly as possible in his struggle to supplant him. In
despite of all this, Mr. Douglas was able to triumph.
What then ? It was resolved to ostracize him in a Democratic caucus of United States senators. Mr. Slidell, the
President's *alter ego* and conscience-keeper, just after the

result of the Illinois election was ascertained, when he passed through the city of Memphis, publicly boasted that he intended to bring about the decapitation of Mr. Douglas by the very expedient afterward put in exercise. He had, just a month before, very publicly, in a conversation with me, avowed the interference of the President in the Illinois election, and justified it. Well, the *bowstring* was applied in caucus on the application of Mr. Slidell, as he had threatened, this gentleman being reported as declaring at the time that he did so on the advice and at the solicitation of the President himself. Then came the struggle for congressional protection in the Senate. Then was displayed to view the monstrous scene of some eight or ten presidential aspirants uniting their powers for the destruction of one man, merely because his superior merits had given him a larger share of public confidence than any of them. Then succeeded the most magnificent parliamentary triumph of modern times, the signal and disgraceful overthrow of all these conspirators in the open field of debate. Next came the struggle in Charleston; the corrupt and unscrupulous use of official patronage for the defeat of the noble champion of non-intervention; the schemings of secession leaders; the disgraceful treachery of Caleb Cushing, and others from the North, in wicked alliance with Southern disunionists, and under the seductive influence of promised official reward. Then came the disgusting scenes in Charleston, the still more disgraceful scenes in Baltimore, the ultimate triumph of Douglas and non-intervention, and the subsequent nomination of Breckenridge and Lane by a strange, anomalous assemblage, presumptuously calling itself a National Democratic Convention, in number but little exceeding one third of the whole Convention, composed mainly and almost exclusively of corrupt office-holding slaves to executive will, notorious and rabid secessionists of the Yancey and Jeff Davis school, and a small number of worthy delegates from Tennessee and other states, egregiously duped by the unscrupulous managers with whom they had to deal, and with whose noxious companionship I can not doubt they will, in a short time, become utterly nauseated.

"Now I take the ground, and propose to establish beyond doubt, that the nomination of Messrs. Breckenridge and Lane is a rank secession scheme; that they were nominated by most of those who voted for them with no earthly hope of electing them, but with a view to defeat-ing the regular nominees of the Democratic party, Messrs. Douglas and Johnson; that it was confidently expected by those who took the lead in this shameful disorganizing movement that the secession ticket would withdraw enough votes from Douglas to secure the election of Lincoln, and that Lincoln's election would inevitably bring about disunion. I charge distinctly that the platform adopted by the Yancey and Davis Convention looks, directly and palpably, to secession, as an object to be attained through the instrumentality of Mr. Lincoln's election, it being perfectly known and understood at the time this ticket was nominated that the claim of protection would infallibly defeat it in every free state, and it being also well known at the time that Mr. Yancey and his allies in the South already were solemnly pledged to unite in an act of secession immediately upon Lincoln's election, before even he could be inaugurated.

"Mr. President and fellow-citizens, friends and lovers of the Union, whether born upon a foreign soil and seek-ing the enjoyment of freedom in the natal land of Washington, and Jefferson, and Jackson, or drawing your first breath in some part of this noble continent, now perchance the last refuge of liberty on earth, I address you all as friends and brethren, and compatriots — not in a spirit of soul-withering and disciplined partisanship, still less in the language of sectional jealousy and strife. It has been my hope to speak to you in a tone of ardent and elevated patriotism worthy of the noble cause of which I am a zealous though feeble champion, worthy of this great assemblage of law-abiding, Union-loving, treason-hating patriots now assembled in the metropolis of that noble state where quietly repose the sacred ashes of a Jackson and a Polk. May I breathe no sentiment, utter no word, employ no argument, which the venerated patriarch of our proud city, whose severe physical indisposition alone prevents his presiding over our present deliberations (the bosom friend and trusted counselor of the immortal hero of the Hermitage for more than sixty years), could not conscientiously sanction and approve. We come hither to ratify the nominations of Douglas and Johnson for the presidency and vice-presidency of the Union, two men of approved integrity, of unquestioned patriotism, of high abilities, of ample attainments, of enlarged experience in public life, who have been deliberately recommended to us by more than two thirds of the grand national Convention which recently assembled in Baltimore. Let me, in the most concise manner, specify a few of the chief reasons which, in my judgment, should secure to these

gentlemen our undivided, hearty, and persistent support:

"1. They were nominated according to the established
usages of the great party of which they have long been
distinguished and trusted leaders.

"2. They were nominated honestly and fairly, without
trickery or illicit contrivance of any kind, by more than
two hundred delegates, unequivocally entitled to represent the great mass of Democratic sentiment of this broad
Union.

"3. They were nominated as known opponents of *sectionalism*, either in the South or in the North, enemies
alike of secession and of Black Republicanism.

"4. They were nominated in opposition to the whole
mass of executive patronage, openly wielded by a corrupt
and unscrupulous President, and that profligate band of
official janissaries whom he holds in his pay, and who,
with more than serf-like servility, stand ready to receive
his commands and execute his behests.

"5. They were nominated alone by national men and
men of the highest independence of spirit, there being
not one secessionist among them, nor one slavish tool of
power; a few honest and firm-minded men, incumbents
of Federal office, preferring their country to the enjoyment of executive favor, having dared to do their duty as
patriots at the hazard of immediate official decapitation.

"6. Because the Douglas and Johnson ticket constitutes the only available Democratic ticket now in the
field, to abandon them is to abandon all hope of Democratic success in the present presidential contest; to withdraw votes from them is to strengthen Lincoln and in-

N

crease the probability of his election, with all the dire consequences which will be certain to wait upon that event.
No man of sense, any where, believes that Breckenridge
and Lane can carry a single free state. It is admitted, on
all hands, that the running of Douglas can alone prevent
Lincoln's carrying every free state in the confederacy.
Therefore to drive Douglas from the field, if the thing
were possible, or seriously to weaken him, is to strength-
en Lincoln, multiply the chances of his success, put Southern institutions in the most serious danger, and bring the
Union itself into the greatest jeopardy. It is obvious
that there is no man in the republic who is so strong with
the mass of the people as Douglas; no man who has so
large a share of the public confidence; no man whose elevation to the presidential station would awaken such intense and general satisfaction. Every man knows that
no Democratic presidential candidate identified with all
the manifest corruptions and multiplied abuses of power
perpetrated by this most unfortunate administration can
possibly be elected. No man identified with the schemes
of the Southern secessionists can or ought to be made
President. No man can possibly triumph over Lincoln
except some individual known to be unflinchingly opposed to the whole scheme of disunion, and equally opposed to a perpetuation of existing official corruptions.
The people of the United States know well that the destruction of our institutions is at this moment doubly
menaced—by violent disruption, and that certain death
which comes from interior corruption and decay. They
feel assured that the election of Douglas would save them
from the experience of both these evils; he would main-

tain and preserve the Union, and reform and purify the government. Democrats, convinced that reformation is imperiously necessary even to the continued existence of our present form of government, are anxious that the spirit of redemption should spring up in the bosom of their own loved and honored party; that whatever of reformation shall take place shall be carried forward and regulated by *Democratic principles.* They recognize Mr. Douglas as the Pulteney of America; and what the great British statesman just mentioned achieved for England a little more than a century ago, when, without abandoning his party, or calling in question its time-honored principles, he attacked the corrupt leader of that very party, even while holding the reins of executive power and ostentatiously asserting that *every man in England had his price,* drove him from the post of prime minister in disgrace, vindicated effectually the principles which he had so vilely abased, restored the ancient dignity of the Whig cause in England, and paved the way for the introduction of those grand measures of national policy which afterward encircled the names of Chatham, and Burke, and Fox, and Erskine with a halo of imperishable glory."

Before closing this chapter, I shall avail myself of the opportunity of doing justice to an eminent individual, now, alas! in the tomb, who is alluded to in the above extracts in language of most harsh and criminating reprehension. With the views which I entertained of William L. Yancey, his political schemes and movements in 1860 (which I now continue to entertain in 1865 in relation to those schemes and movements), I could not have done otherwise, as one anxious to preserve the Federal

Union, than exert myself to the utmost of my limited intellectual powers, and still more limited influence, in warding off the perils which I conscientiously thought he and
others in alliance with him were bringing upon the country. I feel bound in frankness to declare, though, that
I do not at all doubt that his conduct, however grossly
erroneous and pregnant with great and lasting mischief,
as I certainly deem it to have been, was in all respects
regulated by a high but perverted sense of duty to that
section of the Union where he chanced to be born and
reared, and with the safety and permanent prosperity of
which his feelings were intensely affiliated. I was a close
observer of his conduct while a member of the Confederate Congress, and I take pleasure in bearing testimony to
the fact that his course, while laboring to provide for the
exigencies of a civil war, in the bringing on of which he
had so prominently participated, was, with very slight
exceptions scarcely worthy of mention, in happy unison
with his antecedent professions of devotion to state-rights
and popular freedom. He resisted with manly and persistent firmness the insidious and untiring efforts of
others to concentrate in the hands of Mr. Davis powers,
the possession of which even for a year or two would infallibly have resulted in the establishment of a most appalling despotism; and just at the moment of Mr. Yancey's lamented decease, he was preparing, at the next ensuing session of the Confederate Congress, to institute
grave and searching investigations, which would have enforced a terrible responsibility in the high places of governmental rule, and have caused thousands of petty offenders all over the land to shudder with affright at the

prospect of being at last held to something like a just official responsibility. He had long since ceased to entertain respect for Mr. Davis's abilities, either as the manager of difficult civic concerns, or as the chief controller
and director of military movements; and he began, with
a multitude of others, to fear that, if even the Southern
struggle for independence should be eventually successful, a second, and perchance a far bloodier struggle would
become necessary, in order to drag from the hands of Mr.
Davis and those associated with him the injudiciously
vested powers which they were every day so shamefully
and so unpardonably abusing. It is with a melancholy
gratification that I now call to mind the last interview I
had with Mr. Yancey. It was in the hall of the Confederate House of Representatives, a month or two before
his demise. He had come in for the purpose of witnessing the *last successful* struggle made in that body to defeat the re-enactment of the law for the universal suspension of the great writ of Liberty, the *habeas corpus.* The
contest had just terminated, and the champions of despotic power had been prostrated on the field of controversy.
Mr. Yancey approached me with extended hand, congrat-
ulated me cordially upon the triumph just achieved, and
said, "Mr. Davis has at last *cuffed* the two houses of
Congress into *independence;*" and intimated that he should
hereafter have more hope for the Confederate cause than
he had entertained for some months previous.

William L. Yancey was undoubtedly no ordinary man.
He possessed an intellect of great native activity and vig-
or, and he had cultivated his rare natural gifts both with
assiduity and success. He had but little of imagination,

and still less of humor; but he was clear, methodical, and cogent in argument; always expressed himself in chaste and polished language; his readiness and dexterity in controversy were astonishing, and his powers of sarcasm such as few men besides have possessed. He lacked nothing save a happier *equipoise* of his faculties, a little more *quietude* and *sobriety* of *temper*, a little less of tenacity in his own opinions, and a little more of deference for the views of others, to have become one of the most effective and useful public men that the republic has at any time produced.

Requiescat in pace!

CHAPTER XV.

THE long-hoped-for opportunity of trying the experiment of secession was now at last presented. Abraham Lincoln had been elevated to the presidency by a strictly sectional vote; and though the fact could not be denied that he had been elected in a perfectly *constitutional* manner, though he had not received any thing like a majority of the whole popular vote, and though he was admitted on all hands to be a man of excellent practical intellect, of many amiable qualities in domestic and social life, who had never manifested the smallest portion of that rancorous sectional malignity which so many were now displaying so deplorably on both sides of Mason and Dixon's line, yet, no sooner was it ascertained that it was almost certain that he would receive a majority of the electoral votes of the whole Union, than steps began to be taken for carrying into effect a revolutionary project which had engrossed the thoughts and sensibilities of a small class of extreme Southern politicians, mainly confined to the State of South Carolina, for some thirty years preceding. The *modus operandi* of the secession policy, as has been already made sufficiently apparent, was "to precipitate the cotton states of the South" into disunion, and bring about an early collision with the Federal government, in the confident hope that whenever it should be known in the border states of the South that war had been actually commenced, Virginia, Kentucky, Missouri, Maryland, North Carolina, and Tennessee would be compelled to unite in the movement, however they might be inclined to disapprove it, as well as the motives which had prompted it. This supposition was, indeed, not at all an unreasonable one, for the states just mentioned were to a very large extent possessed of property in slaves; and though the opinion prevailed therein very widely that no such solid guarantee for their slaveholding interests as that afforded by the Federal Constitution was at all likely to be conferred by a sectional war, yet perceiving, as they would be sure to do, that the relative strength of the slaveholding states left in the Union after the withdrawal of those of the cotton-growing region would be so far lessened as to leave them thereafter an easy prey to abolition hostility, it was regarded as next to certain that they would in the end feel constrained to join any new confederacy which might be set on foot in the South having the least prospect of strength and stability.

It was strongly suspected by the friends of the Union in the South, and had been distinctly charged to be true, in various forms, while the presidential contest was pending, that the followers of the great secession leaders were desirous that the Republicans should be successful therein, as only in this way would they be supplied with the pretext so much desired by many for withdrawing from civil associations with the free states of the North; and it is yet well remembered that Mr. Yancey, with that extraordinary skill as a political manager which distinguished him, had performed a pilgrimage to the North early in the summer of 1860 to counteract this very charge of desiring Mr. Lincoln's election, so far as the same applied to himself, the effect of which he apprehended might be such as to incapacitate him for the ultimate consummation of his hopes on this subject, unless he could succeed in securing to himself an opportunity of showing to his confiding partisans that he had really exerted himself in the North against the Republican presidential ticket. With what remarkable adroitness he executed this device no one who was a close observer of the events of that extraordinary period could have failed to observe; and yet nothing is more certain than the fact that the extremists of the South did *indirectly* cooperate, to the full extent of their power, in bringing about the election of Mr. Lincoln, with the views and purposes just specified. No one need, therefore, to feel the smallest surprise at finding in the pages of Mr. Greeley's work the following very striking paragraph:

"From an early stage of the canvass, the Republicans could not help seeing that they had the potent aid in

N 2

their efforts of the *good wishes* for their success of at least a large proportion of the advocates of Breckenridge and Lane. The toasts drunk with most enthusiasm at the Fourth of July celebrations throughout South Carolina pointed to the probable election of Mr. Lincoln as the necessary prelude to movements whereon the hearts of all Carolinians were intent. Southern 'fire-eaters' canvassed the Northern States in behalf of Breckenridge and Lane, but very much to the satisfaction of the friends of Lincoln and Hamlin. The 'fusion' arrangements, whereby it was hoped, at all events, to defeat Lincoln, were not generally favored by the 'fire-eaters' who visited the North, whether intent on politics, business, or pleasure; and, in some instances, those who sought to commend themselves to the favor of their Southern patrons or customers by an exhibition of zeal in the 'fusion' cause, were quietly told: 'What you are doing looks not to the end *we* desire; we want *Lincoln* elected.' In no slave state did the supporters of Breckenridge unite in any 'fusion' movement whatever; and it was a very open secret that the friends of Breckenridge generally— at all events throughout the slave states—next to the all but impossible success of their own candidate, preferred that of the Republicans. In the Senate throughout the preceding session, at Charleston, at Baltimore, and ever since, they had acted precisely as they would have done had they pre-eminently desired Mr. Lincoln's success, and determined to do their best to secure it."

So thoroughly matured was the project of secession in the minds of Southern extremists in South Carolina, that they are known actually to have commenced movements looking to this desired end before even the presidential election had taken place, and when the result which soon ensued was yet but a strong probability. Accordingly we find Governor Gist, as early as the 5th of November, 1860, addressing a message to the South Carolina Legislature, embodying the following bold and explicit declarations :

"Under ordinary circumstances, your duty could be soon discharged by the election of electors representing the choice of the people of the state; but, in view of the threatening aspect of affairs, and the strong probability of the election to the presidency of a sectional candidate by a party committed to the support of measures which, if carried out, will inevitably destroy our equality in the Union, and ultimately reduce the Southern States to mere provinces of a consolidated despotism, to be governed by a fixed majority in Congress hostile to our institutions and fatally bent upon our ruin, I would respectfully suggest that the Legislature remain in session, and take such action as will prepare the state for any emergency that may arise.

"That an exposition of the will of the people may be obtained on a question involving such momentous consequences, I would earnestly recommend that, in the event of Abraham Lincoln's election to the presidency, a Convention of the people of this state be immediately called, to consider and determine for themselves the mode and measure of redress. My own opinions of what the Convention should do are of little moment; but, believing that the time has arrived when every one, however humble he may be, should express his opinions in unmistakable language, I am constrained to say that the only alternative left, in my judgment, is the secession of South Carolina from the Federal Union. The indications from many of the Southern States justify the conclusion that the secession of South Carolina will be immediately followed, if not adopted simultaneously by them, and ultimately by the entire South. The long-desired co-operation of the other states having similar institutions, for which so many of our citizens have been waiting, seems to be near at hand, and, if we are true to ourselves, will soon be realized. The state has, with great unanimity, declared that she has the right peaceably to secede, and no power on earth can rightfully prevent it.

"If, in the exercise of arbitrary power, and forgetful of the lessons of history, the government of the United States should attempt coercion, it will become our solemn duty to meet force by force; and whatever may be the decision of the Convention, representing the sovereignty of the state, and amenable to no earthly tribunal, it shall, during the remainder of my administration, be carried out to the letter, regardless of any hazard that may surround its execution.

"I would also respectfully recommend a thorough reorganization of the militia, so as to place the whole military force of the state in a position to be used at the shortest notice and with the greatest efficiency. Every man in the state between the ages of eighteen and forty-five should be well armed with the most efficient weapons of modern warfare, and all the available means of the state used for that purpose.

"In addition to this general preparation, I would recommend that the services of ten thousand volunteers be immediately accepted; that they be organized and drilled by officers chosen by themselves, and hold themselves in readiness to be called on upon the shortest notice. With this preparation for defense, and with all the hallowed memories of past achievements, with our love of liberty, and hatred of tyranny, and with the knowledge that we are contending for the safety of our homes and firesides, we can confidently appeal to the Disposer of all human events, and safely trust our cause in his keeping."

Mr. Chesnut, then a United States senator, and whom I well remember as an outspoken advocate of secession in 1850, being present at the opening of the Legislature, is reported to have used language even of a more fervid and menacing character. He brought to bear upon a large popular assemblage convened in Columbia for the purpose of listening to him a very animated harangue, in which he is represented to have said that, "for himself, he would unfurl the Palmetto flag, fling it to the breeze, and, with the spirit of a brave man, determined to live and die as became our glorious ancestors, ring the clarion notes of defiance in the ears of an insolent foe." He then spoke of the "undoubted right of South Carolina to with-draw the powers delegated to the Federal government," and said that it "would be its duty, in the event contem-plated, to withdraw them."

One of the most alarming symptoms then exhibited in South Carolina was the fact that several of her eminent public men, including Mr. Orr and Mr. Boyce, both of whom had in former days been set down among the con-servatives, were now as eager for revolution as any of those who had been working for it night and day for more than twenty years. I desire not to particularize on this painful subject to an extent which might now prove annoying, and therefore proceed briefly to state that the Legislature of South Carolina provided for the assemblage of a state Convention, the members of which were to be elected on the 6th of December, while the conventional body itself was to come together on the 19th of the same month; that the Convention did assemble on the last-mentioned day, and, after an excited debate of several days' continuance, adopted an Ordinance of Secession on the 20th of December. Commissioners were sent with a copy of the ordinance to each of the slave states, in order to quicken co-operative action, and notification was duly made as to these events to the Federal government in Washington City.

The next secession movement it was expected would come off in the State of Georgia. A Convention for this purpose had been already called. It was known that Alexander H. Stephens, Herschel V. Johnson, and other public men, of elevated standing and of extended influence, would be members of the Convention, and it was expected that they would exert themselves to the utmost to prevent the imitation by the State of Georgia of the rash example which had just been set by South Carolina; and it was likewise known that eminent personages from the State of South Carolina would attend the Convention of Georgia, in order to urge immediate co-operation. Under these circumstances, I took it upon myself to persuade the public men of most influence in the city of Nashville, where I was then residing, to send ten or fifteen delegates forthwith to Milledgeville, respectfully and earnestly to protest against extreme action on the part of Georgia, believing as I did that, if this great and vastly influential state should add the force of her example to that of South Carolina, all the cotton states would promptly follow in the same track, and that afterward it would not be possible to prevent Tennessee and the remaining Southern States from being driven into the movement. I urged these views for several days most zealously, but, I regret to say, without success; some supposing that there was no serious danger of the Convention of Georgia adopting an Ordinance of Secession, and others that there was reason to fear, if we should send delegates to Milledgeville, it might result in fatally compromising our own attitude. The manly opposition made by Mr. Stephens to the attempt to draw Georgia into the secession maelstrom is well known. This want of success is a circumstance which I shall ever deplore as the most unfortunate event of a public nature which has occurred within my recollection. Alabama, Florida, Mississippi, Louisiana, and Texas were now soon enrolled among the seceded states. Tennessee, North Carolina, Virginia, Arkansas, Kentucky, Maryland, Missouri, and Delaware still stood firm, despite all the efforts essayed to shake their constancy.

It is indeed true, as Mr. Greeley has deliberately recorded, that after the secession "conspiracy had held complete possession of the Southern mind for three months, with the Southern members of the cabinet, nearly all the Federal officers, most of the governors and other state functionaries, and seven eighths of the prominent and active politicians pushing it on, and no force exerted against no in any manner threatening to resist it, a majority of the slave states, with two thirds of the free population of the entire slaveholding region, was openly and positively adverse to it, either because they regarded the alleged grievances of the South as exaggerated if not unreal, or because they believed that those wrongs would rather be aggravated than cured by disunion."

The cotton states having seceded from the.Union in the manner described, great uneasiness became manifest among the true patriots of the republic every where, and prodigious efforts were made at various places, and in various modes, to arrest the coming storm.

In looking back to this tempestuous and critical period, it is eminently gratifying to observe how multiplied were the evidences of a desire to prevent those fearful scenes of domestic commotion and violence which seemed to be now almost at hand. In the city of Philadelphia, on the 13th of December, a large popular assemblage was called together at Independence Square, where speeches were delivered and resolutions adopted worthy even of the illustrious era of '76. The first of the resolutions referred to pledged "the people of Philadelphia to the citizens of the other states that the statute-books of Pennsylvania should be carefully searched at the approaching session of the Legislature, and that every statute, if any such there was, which in the slightest degree invaded the constitutional rights of the citizens of a sister state, should be at once repealed." The closing resolution of the meeting declared that "all denunciations of

slavery as existing in the United States, and of citizens
who held slaves under it, were inconsistent with the
spirit of brotherhood and kindness which ought to ani-
mate all who live under and support the Constitution of
the American Union." Nor was the newspaper press of
the North inactive in the work of *conciliation and compromise* at this very perilous moment. The gentleman
who had for so many years edited with signal ability
The Albany Evening Journal (Mr. Thurlow Weed), and
who was generally understood as presenting, to a considerable extent, the views of Mr. Seward, brought forward
at this period a plan of *concessions* to the South of a most
equitable and judicious character, which he subsequently
vindicated, upon its being assailed by the more rabid
portion of the Republican press, in the most conclusive
and triumphant manner. Mr. Weed did not hesitate, in
a bold and explicit manner, to declare, 1st, that there was
"imminent danger of the dissolution of the Union;" 2d,
that "this danger originated in the ambition and cupid-
ity of men who desired a Southern despotism, and in the
fanatic zeal of Northern abolitionists," who, he charged,
sought "the emancipation of slaves regardless of consequences." He asserted that the "danger could only be
averted by such moderation and forbearance as will draw
out, strengthen, and combine the Union sentiment of the
whole country." He declared, and most truly, that there
was undoubtedly "a Union sentiment in the South worth
cherishing;" and said, in a spirit of wise and statesmanlike liberality worthy even of Webster himself, in reference to this Union sentiment in the South, "It will develop and expand as fast as the darkness and delusion

in relation to the feelings of the North can be dispelled. This calls for moderation and forbearance. We do not, when our dwelling is in flames, stop to ascertain whether it was the work of an incendiary before we extinguish the fire. Hence our suggestions of a basis of adjustment, without the expectation that they would be accepted in terms by either section, but that they might possibly inaugurate a movement in that direction. The Union is worth preserving; and, if worth preserving, suggestions in its behalf, however crude, will not be contemned. A victorious party can afford to be tolerant — not, as our friends assume, in the abandonment or abasement of its principles or character, but in efforts to correct and disabuse the minds of those who misunderstand both.

"Before a final appeal, before a resort to the 'rough frown of war,' we should like to see a convention of the people, consisting of delegates appointed by the states. After more than seventy years of 'wear and tear,' of collision and abrasion, it should be no cause of wonder that the machinery of government is found weakened, or out of repair, or even defective. Nor would it be found unprofitable for the North and South, bringing their respective griefs, claims, and proposed reforms to a common arbitrament, to meet, discuss, and determine upon a future.

"It will be said that we have done nothing wrong, and have nothing to offer. This, supposing it true, is precisely the reason why we should both propose and offer whatever may by possibility avert the evils of civil war, and prevent the destruction of our hitherto unexampled blessings of union."

Whatever may have been heretofore asserted to the contrary, I am prepared to bear witness that these timely publications of Mr. Weed had an exceedingly mollifying effect upon the general popular mind of the South, and especially in the border states, as they were called, including the State of Tennessee, where strong hopes were now beginning to be entertained that some wise and mutually satisfactory scheme of pacification would soon be adopted.

I will here incidentally notice two remarkable announcements which were made at this period in two rival Northern papers, which *together* have such an extended circulation in the various parts of the republic as it is believed no other two journals have ever had. I will not undertake to estimate the combined force of such *co-operative* declarations among those who were now meditating disunion, but all sound-thinking men will readily admit that it must have been considerable. The New York Tribune said:

"If the cotton states consider the value of the Union debatable, we maintain their perfect right to discuss it; nay, we hold, with Jefferson, to the inalienable right of communities to alter or abolish forms of government that have become oppressive or injurious; and if the cotton states shall decide that they can do better out of the Union than in it, we insist on letting them go in peace. The right to secede may be a revolutionary one, but it exists nevertheless; and we do not see how one party has a right to do what another party has a right to prevent. We must even resist the asserted right of any state to remain in the Union and nullify or defy the laws thereof. To withdraw from the Union is quite another matter; and whenever a considerable section of our Union shall deliberately resolve to go out, we shall resist all coercive measures designed to keep them in. We hope never to live in a republic whereof one section is pinned to the residue with bayonets." The New York Herald had said, on the 11th of November,

" If, however, Northern fanaticism should triumph over us, and the Southern States should exercise their undeniable right to secede from the Union, then the city of New York, the river counties, the State of New Jersey, and very likely Connecticut, would separate from those New England and Western States, where the black man is put upon a pinnacle above the white. New York City is for the Union first, and the gallant and chivalrous South afterward."

Tennessee and the border states were calmly and thoughtfully awaiting the chapter of events, when Congress convened on the 3d of December, and received that extraordinary message of Mr. Buchanan, of which a few striking extracts will be here presented.

" Why is it, then, that discontent now so extensively prevails, and the union of the states, which is the source of all these blessings, is threatened with destruction? The long-continued and intemperate interference of the Northern people with the question of slavery in the Southern States has at length produced its natural effects. The different sections of the Union are now arrayed against each other; and the time has arrived, so much dreaded by the Father of his Country, when hostile geographical parties have been formed. I have long foreseen, and often forewarned my countrymen of the now impending danger. This does not proceed solely from the claims on the part of Congress or the territorial Legislatures to exclude slavery from the territories, nor from the efforts of different states to defeat the execution of the Fugitive Slave Law.

"All or any of these evils might have been endured by the South without danger to the Union (as others have been), in the hope that time and reflection might apply the remedy. The immediate peril arises not so much from these causes as from the fact that the incessant and violent agitation of the slavery question through-out the North for the last quarter of a century has at length produced its malign influence on the slaves, and inspired them with vague notions of freedom. Hence a sense of security no longer exists around the family altar. This feeling of peace at home has given place to apprehensions of servile insurrection. Many a matron throughout the South retires at night in dread of what may befall herself and her children before the morning. Should this apprehension of domestic danger, whether real or imaginary, extend and intensify itself until it shall pervade the masses of the Southern people, then disunion will become inevitable. Self-preservation is the first law of Nature, and has been implanted in the heart of man by his Creator for the wisest purpose; and no political union, however fraught with blessings and benefits in all other respects, can long continue, if the necessary consequence be to render the homes and the firesides of near-ly half the parties to it habitually and hopelessly insecure. Sooner or later the bonds of such a union must be severed. It is my conviction that this fatal period has not yet arrived, and my prayer to God is that He would preserve the Constitution and the Union throughout all generations.

" What, in the mean time, is the responsibility and true position of the executive? He is bound by solemn oath, before God and the country, 'to take care that the laws be faithfully executed,' and from this obligation he can not be absolved by any human power. But what if the performance of this duty, in whole or in part, has been rendered impracticable by events over which he could have exercised no control? Such, at the present moment, is the case throughout the State of South Carolina, so far as the laws of the United States to secure the administration of justice by means of the Federal judiciary are concerned. All the Federal officers within its limits, through whose agency alone these laws can be carried into execution, have already resigned. We no longer have a district judge, a district attorney, or a marshal in South Carolina. In fact, the whole machinery of the Federal government necessary for the distribution of remedial justice among the people has been demolished, and it would be difficult, if not impossible, to replace it.

" The only acts of Congress on the statute-book bearing upon this subject are those of the 28th of February, 1795, and 3d of March, 1807. These authorize the President, after he shall have ascertained that the marshal, with his *posse comitatus*, is unable to execute civil or criminal process in any particular case, to call out the militia, and employ the army and navy to aid him in performing this service, having first, by proclamation, commanded the insurgents to 'disperse, and retire peaceably to their respective abodes within a limited time.' This duty can not by possibility be performed in a state where no judicial authority exists to issue process, and where there is no marshal to execute it, and where, even if there were such an officer, the entire population would constitute one solid combination to resist him."

But the *questio questionum* is thus pointedly and clearly propounded by Mr. Buchanan in his message, thus:

"The question, fairly stated, is, Has the Constitution delegated to Congress the power to coerce into submission a state which is attempting to withdraw, or has actually withdrawn, from the confederacy? If answered in the affirmative, it .must be on the principle that the power has been conferred upon Congress to declare and to make war against a state. After much serious reflection, I have arrived at the conclusion that no such power has been delegated to Congress or to any other department of the Federal government. It is manifest, upon an inspection of the Constitution, that this is not among the specific and enumerated powers granted to Congress, and it is equally apparent that its exercise is not 'necessary and proper for carrying into execution' any one of these powers."

The message of the President was referred to a special committee in the House of Representatives on the motion of Mr. A. R. Boteler, of Virginia, at the head of which was placed Mr. Thomas Corwin, of Ohio; but even while these efforts at pacification were proceeding in the House of Representatives, a stormy debate was in progress in the Senate, of which the following extracts may

serve to show the wild and disorganizing spirit now prevalent in that body. Mr. Clingman, of North Carolina,
said:

"They want to get up a free debate, as the senator
from New York (Mr. Seward) expressed it in one of his
speeches. But a senator from Texas told me the other
day *that a great many of these free debaters were hanging
from the trees of that country* (Texas). I have no doubt
they would run off a great many slaves from the border
states, so as to make them free states; and then, sir,
when the overt act was struck, we should have a hard
struggle. I say, therefore, that our policy is not to let
this thing continue. That, I think, is the opinion of North
Carolina. I think the party for immediate secession is
gaining ground rapidly. It is idle for men to shut their
eyes to consequences like this, if any thing can be done
to avert the evil while we have power to do it."

Mr. Iverson, of Georgia, said:

"Gentlemen speak of concession—of the repeal of the
Personal Liberty Bills. Repeal them all to-morrow, and
you can not stop this revolution. It is not the liberty
laws, but the mob law, which the South fears. They do
not dread these overt acts; for, without the power of the
Federal government, by force, under Republican rule,
their institution would not last ten years, and they know
it. They intend to go out of this Union, and he believed
this. Before the 4th of March, five states will have declared their independence, and he was satisfied that three
other states would follow as soon as the action of their
people can be had. Arkansas will call her Convention,
and Louisiana will follow. And, though there is a clog

in the way in the 'lone star' of Texas in the person of her governor, who will not consent to call the Legislature, yet the public sentiment is so strong that even her governor may be overridden; and, if he will not yield to that public sentiment, *some Texan Brutus may arise to rid his country of this old, hoary-headed traitor.* (Great sensation.) There has been a good deal of vaporing and threatening, but they came from the last men who would carry out their threats. Men talk about their eighteen millions; but we hear a few days afterward of these same men being switched in the face, and they tremble like a sheep-stealing dog. There will be no war. The North, governed by such far-seeing statesmen as the senator from New York (Mr. Seward), will see the futility of this. In less than twelve months a Southern Confederacy will be formed, and it will be the most successful government on earth. The Southern States, thus banded together, will be able to resist any force in the world. We do not expect war, but we will be prepared for it; and we are not a feeble race of Mexicans either."

The venerable John J. Crittenden and others spoke earnestly in favor of conciliation and peace; while A. G. Brown, of Mississippi, and Mr. Wigfall, of Texas, and others from the South, poured forth most heated and violent harangues in favor of extreme measures.

I shall not undertake to describe all the various propositions in either house of Congress, emanating alike from Northern and Southern members, looking to the adjustment of the pending issues. More unamiable, more wordy and profitless discussions, have seldom occurred ' in any part of the world, nor will future generations be

O

very strongly tempted to do more than glance over them in the most cursory manner; though there were then undoubtedly a small number of individuals, both in the Senate and House of Representatives, of whose wise and noble conduct at this crisis the future historian will be pleased to make honorable mention.

There are one or two observations which I will here offer as the result of much meditation, and a most impartial examination of disputed facts and conflicting statements.

1. It would have been quite easy for the Southern members of the Thirty-fifth Congress, had they come to Washington in the true compromising and conciliatory spirit, to have obtained such an adjustment of all the sectional issues then pending as would have been altogether in keeping with Southern honor, and preservative of Southern slaveholding rights.

2. The Democratic party having by recent elections secured a majority of votes in both houses of Congress, there was not even a possibility of slaveholding rights being subjected to serious detriment, had Southern senators and representatives been alike wise in guarding and protecting the interests of their constituents, and anxious to perform their duty faithfully to the whole republic.

3. There were several distinct legislative propositions brought forward by Northern members either of one house or the other, the acceptance of any one of which by the South would at once have terminated all controversy.

4. Mr. Crittenden's resolutions of compromise could,

doubtless, have been obtained, but for the fact that certain Southern senators, five in number (evidently by preconcert), when the motion to substitute the two resolutions of Mr. Clarke in lieu of them was voted upon, *refused to vote at all;* when, had they voted, as they ought to have done, Mr. Clarke's resolutions would have been defeated by a vote of 28 to 25, and Mr. Crittenden's have been afterward adopted.

5. When the last test-vote upon Clarke's substitute was taken in the Senate just before the session terminated, Crittenden's resolutions of compromise were defeated only by a vote of 20 to 19, a number of the Southern senators having, meanwhile, with equal want of *true wisdom* and of *practical fidelity* to the South, resigned their seats in Congress and returned to their own homes, to aid in consummating the work of secession then in such active progress.

6. The following proposition offered by Mr. Seward in the senatorial committee of 13, had it been accepted in behalf of the South, and incorporated into the Federal Constitution, would have given substantial security to the slaveholding rights of the South: " No amendment shall be made to the Constitution which will authorize or give to Congress any power to abolish or interfere in any state with the domestic institutions thereof, including that of persons held to service or labor by the laws of said state." To this proposition, strange to say (as is now well known), Mr. Davis, of Mississippi, and Mr. Toombs, of Georgia, refused to yield their support in said committee.

7. The resolutions reported to the House of Represent-

atives by the grand committee of that body, and sustained in the house in which they originated, as they would
doubtless have been in the Senate, had Southern senators
been at their posts, and ready and willing to do their
duty, would have given as much security to the slaveholding rights of the South as could in reason have been
demanded.

, 8. The joint resolve reported by the grand committee
of the House for the amendment of the Federal Constitution, which passed both houses, and which, on its ratification by a sufficient number of states, would have become part of the supreme law of the land, and have pre-
cluded forever all interference with slaveholding interests in any state not consenting thereto, was indignantly
rejected by excited Southern senators, who preferred incurring all the perils of disunion to accepting any of the
new securities now tendered to them.

So Southern secession senators and representatives,
abandoning their seats in the two houses of Congress,
and thus leaving their Republican adversaries in control
of those bodies, and of all the resources and power of
this gigantic republic, hurried on toward Montgomery,
Alabama, where, in the course of a few weeks of deliberation, *with closed doors*, they agreed upon and promulgated to the world the most ill-digested, incongruous, and
utterly impracticable Constitution of government that
the "rash dexterity" of visionary theorists has ever been
able to eliminate, under the *nominal* guidance and control of which a new confederacy was to have its confused
and anomalous action; an unnatural and bloody civil
war was to be *commenced* and prosecuted; state-rights

and popular freedom were to be speedily overthrown; such gross mismanagement, both of civil and military affairs, was to be practiced by a vain, prejudiced, and incompetent executive chief as the world had never before witnessed; under the authority of which government free-born American citizens were to be cruelly hunted down, plunged into filthy prison-houses, and even deprived in some instances of life itself, for daring to entertain and express Union sentiments, and to maintain a quiet and peaceable, but a stubborn and inflexible loyalty to the government of their fathers; under which government all rights of person and property were to be set at naught and trampled under foot, and even the boasted right of *peaceable state secession* to be formally and deliberately *denied*; and the long-venerated slaveholding rights, for the defense and maintenance of which this unwise and wasting war had been projected, were, in the fourth year of that very war, to be, upon the ground of *military necessity*, declared by a dogmatical executive *rescript*, subject to be violated, and even abrogated, at the pleasure of the great central agency in Richmond, which no longer held itself responsible to either God or man for its official acts.

CHAPTER XVI.

Speculative Views as to the self-defensive Powers of all Governments, and of the Government of the United States in particular.—View of the Circumstances existing, so far as the State of Tennessee is concerned, in the Outset of the War, and Vindication of the Conduct of that State.—View of the Condition of Things existing in Washington in particular, and of the non-action Policy of Mr. Buchanan.—Notice of this Gentleman's late Defense of himself.—View of Mr. Lincoln's moderate and patriotic Conduct after his Election, and Notice of Speeches made by him at Indianapolis, Pittsburg, and Philadelphia.— Mr. Lincoln's Inaugural Speech, and commendatory Remarks thereupon.—Admirably patriotic Speech of Mr. Alexander H. Stephens, of Georgia, demonstrating the gross Impolicy of Secession.—Some Allusions to the early Movements of the War, and a short Discussion of the Monroe Doctrine.—Enforcement of that Doctrine the true Means of restoring the national Unity and Concord.

IT would seem almost impossible to state a proposition more *axiomatic* in its character than the following one: Every government, being framed with a view to perpetuity, must needs possess the power of defending its own existence and all its essential rights, as well against dangers from *without* as from perils which disclose themselves in the bosom of the body politic. And this self-evident proposition would seem to include, by necessary implication, another, viz.: That self-preservation, being the general law of Nature, and applicable alike to all conventional associations as to all living creatures in their original character, whenever it shall happen, amid the complex and critical emergencies which it is in the power of a long-continuing war to engender, to have become plainly necessary to resort to the use of expedients the need of which the most long-sighted and clear-visioned lawgiver could scarcely be supposed to have specially anticipated, all such expedients must be regarded as rightfully subject to be employed. The quality which chiefly distinguished the Constitution framed by our fathers in 1788 from the Articles of Confederation which it superseded, is, that whereas the power of the latter could only operate on *states*, as integral members of the confederative association, that of the former was intended, on the contrary, to act on individual citizens of those states. These states, after the essential change in their character and attributes which had been then wrought, were no longer entitled to recognize themselves as the sovereign members of a *league*, but as existing, though still retaining their corporate capacity, in a condition in which they were bound to do fealty and exercise true homage, in many interesting respects, to that which, by solemn conventional arrangement, had been entitled to claim respect and obedience as a *government* of supereminent authority.

The power to constrain individual citizens, whether few or many, who, enjoying the protection of the government, are bound to exercise toward this grand representative of the whole nation such a loyal and effective obedience as the organic law itself contemplates, is by no means inconsistent with the continued existence of the reserved rights of the states and people thereof, the due preservation and maintenance of which is, indeed, one of the most sacred duties of the government established by *all, for the safety and liberty of all.* Those who persist in

recognizing the old confederative compact as continuing
to survive, and who hold on, in spite of all the lights of
history and all the force of argument, to the monstrous
doctrine of secession, may well feel justified in denying
to the government at present in operation authority to
enforce the duty of *obedience* within the confines of the
individual states, in opposition to acts of the local governments adopted for the express purpose of *nullifying* the
ties of allegiance existing at the time of the framing of
such acts between those very citizens and the government whose various forms of legislative action have been
alone declared, by the solemn organic instrument to
which all owe the most profound respect, to constitute
"*the supreme law of the land.*"   Since Mr. Webster's celebrated replies to Mr. Hayne and Mr. Calhoun, more than
thirty years ago, and the emanation of General Jackson's
world-famous proclamation, few, if any, except the open
supporters of the absurd and untenable theory of absolute state sovereignty, have undertaken to dispute the
right of the Federal government to *compel* all within the
.scope of its authority to bow in unresisting submission
to its lawful behests.

It does not, by any means, follow necessarily, from
this view of the subject, that it was the *duty* of Mr. Buchanan, and of the Congress to whom his last annual
message was addressed, to wage war upon the seceding
states so soon as any one or more of them had proclaimed
their connection with the Federal government at an end.
Happily for the comfort and happiness of the inhabitants
of earth, the illimitable power of the Deity is not always
inclined to reveal itself, for the punishment of the *err-*

ing, untempered with the gentler attributes which belong to his beneficent nature; and, at the period in American history which we are now reviewing, there were most weighty considerations which, in my judgment, most fully justified those then in power in the exercise of a moderation and forbearance which President Lincoln and his newly-appointed cabinet were, in the spring of 1861, extremely desirous of effectively employing.

The personage now occupying the high position of President of the United States, and whose commendable efforts to restore harmony and kindly feeling among the thirty millions who constitute this great nation, have secured for him already the gratitude of all who love freedom and abhor oppression, did, in my opinion, declare the true doctrine in regard to the relative powers belonging to the associated departments of our system of government on the memorable occasion when he exerted himself so nobly to check, in its early developments, the ambitious and lawless project of breaking up forever this sublime consociation of prosperous and happy commonwealths. I shall here take the liberty of suggesting that those who attach serious blame to the conduct of the good people of Tennessee at this period, where the doctrine of secession was in fact never ratified, and where all that was done, in the first instance, was simply to put the state in an attitude of *defense* against dangers supposed at the time to be imminent, would do well to take into consideration the theoretical notions at that time expounded by President Buchanan himself, and, still more elaborately, by his attorney general, Mr. Black. Nor should it be forgotten by those in whose hearts the dis-

O 2

position to practice *justice* is faithfully cherished, that the
people of this august commonwealth had voted down by
an overwhelming vote, in the month of February, 1861,
the proposition to call into existence a State Convention
for the simple purpose of peaceably *considering* existing
dangers and grievances; and that, while the proposition
to hold such a Convention at all was most decidedly
negatived, it is an ascertained fact that, had the proposed
Convention been even allowed to assemble, a very large
majority of its members would have utterly repudiated
all hostile movements against the Federal government.
It is but justice, too, to an intelligent, gallant, and truly
patriotic people, to bear in remembrance the fact that
Tennessee resisted all attempts to draw her into a disloy-
al and rebellious attitude until the various attempts at
compromise in Washington City had all signally failed;
until the exciting passage of arms at Fort Sumter had
taken place; until President Lincoln's proclamation calling out seventy-five thousand troops had emanated; until the *suggestive* and encouraging declarations of certain
Northern newspapers, and the still more encouraging
and persuasive declarations of certain influential public
men of the free states, had gained general circulation;
and until the time-honored and conservative States of
Virginia and North Carolina had both resolved upon
uniting their destiny with that of the original seceding
states; and that, at last, no formal act of secession was
committed, but a simple military and civil league entered
into.

For myself, while I willingly do homage to the superior firmness and constancy of others, and though I am

not at all confident of receiving much allowance at the
hands of the present excited generation for an error of
judgment in agreeing, under any circumstances, to take
part in a war so unnatural and impolitic, yet I am not
without a hope, however faintly entertained that hope
may be, that, in future ages, those of us who continued
to the last to exercise moderation and forbearance, and
who struggled in every practicable way to mollify the
unavoidable acerbities of a state of armed collision, may
not be regarded as altogether *unpardonable.*

Let us now take a calm and dispassionate retrospect of
the events which had occurred in Washington City between the day of Mr. Lincoln's inauguration and the opening scenes of the war.   President Buchanan had done
nothing to stay the march of rebellion, or to show that
he regarded the Federal Union as even *capable* of being
successfully defended.   In his recently published vindication he attempts to cast the discredit of his inefficiency
upon the two houses of Congress.   I have read with attention his elaborate essay prepared for this purpose, and
I have not neglected the reading of other publications on
the same vexed subject which have made their appearance of late.   I have, as I think, tolerably clear views as
to this whole affair, with which I shall not, on the present
occasion, disturb the public mind.   In reference to the co-
temporaneous action of President Lincoln, I confess that
I have a very different opinion from that which I entertained four years ago and very freely expressed.   I am
not at all ashamed to acknowledge that I regard his
whole conduct, after he had become the recipient of the
electoral vote which entitled him to claim the presidential

authority, as singularly marked with moderation, elevated patriotism, and true practical wisdom. In his speech at Indianapolis, the first of many which he delivered on his way to Washington City, he used language much misconstrued and denounced at the time; but who at present would seriously censure him for saying, "What, then, is *coercion?* what is *invasion?* Would the marching of an army into South Carolina, without the consent of her people and with hostile intent toward them, be invasion? I certainly think that it would be invasion, and coercion also, if South Carolinians were forced to submit. *But if the United States should merely hold and retake her own forts and other property, and collect the duties on foreign importations, or even withhold the mails from places where they were habitually violated, would any or all these things be invasion or coercion?"* Surely every man now whose reasoning faculties are not obscured either by passion or prejudice would be willing to confess that in this specification of acts Mr. Lincoln has only defined with great precision and clearness, but in kind and civil language, his own *sworn* duties as president under the Constitution. It is now pleasant, and even soothing to our sensibilities, to read a few of the characteristic sentences that he uttered at Pittsburg, where he said, "I repeat now, there is no crisis except such a one as may be gotten up at any time by turbulent men, aided by designing politicians. My advice to them, under the circumstances, is *to keep cool.* If the great American people keep their temper on both sides of the line, the trouble will come to an end, and the question which now distracts the country be settled, just as surely as all other difficulties of a like character which have originated in this government have been adjusted. Let the people on both sides keep their self-possession, and just as other clouds have cleared away in due time, so will this great nation continue to prosper as heretofore." At Philadelphia he concluded a modest and impressive harangue, at the raising of the United States flag over Independence Hall, thus touchingly: "Now, in my view of the present aspect of affairs, there need be no bloodshed or war. There is no necessity for it. I am not in favor of such a course; and I may say, and in advance, that there *will* be no bloodshed, unless it be forced upon the government, and then it will be forced to act in self-defense."

Those of the South who will now examine with a calm attention the inaugural address of President Lincoln, will not be much inclined to subject it to all the censures heretofore bestowed on it. Posterity will, I feel assured, recognize it as a most felicitous specimen of clear, unadorned, and idiomatic English, concise, nervous, and pointed, and breathing throughout a spirit of pure and disinterested patriotism, and a truly Christian moderation and forbearance toward his erring and excited fellow-countrymen of the slaveholding region, while indicating the most painful anticipations of those coming evils from which no one can doubt his anxiety to shield the republic, if it should be found possible to do so consistently with the high official duties which he was about to assume. Almost in the very commencement of his speech he said, "Apprehension seems to exist among the people of the Southern States that, by the accession of a Republican administration, their property, and their peace and personal security, will be endangered. There has never been any reasonable cause for such apprehension. Indeed, the most ample evidence to the contrary has all the while existed, and been open to their inspection. It is found in nearly all the published speeches of him who now addresses you. I do but quote from one of those speeches when I declare that '*I have no purpose, directly or indirectly, to interfere with the institution of slavery in the states where it exists.*' I believe I have no lawful right to do so, and I have no intention to do so. Those who nominated and elected me did so with this and many similar declarations, and had never recanted them. Moreover, they placed in the platform, for my acceptance, and as a law to themselves and to me, the clear and emphatic resolution which I now read: '*Resolved*, That the maintenance inviolate of the rights of the states, and especially the right of each state to order and control its own domestic institutions according to its judgment exclusively, is essential to that balance of power on which the perfection and endurance of our political fabric depend; and we denounce the lawless invasion by armed force of the soil of any state or Territory, no matter under what pretext, as the greatest of crimes.'

"I now reiterate these sentiments, and, in doing so, I only press upon the public attention the most conclusive evidence of which the case is susceptible, that the property, peace, and security of no section are to be in anywise endangered by the now incoming administration. I add, too, that all the protection which, consistently with the Constitution and the laws, can be given, will be cheerfully given to all the states, when lawfully demanded, for whatever cause, as cheerfully to one section as to another."

So much for non-interference with slavery in the states. Let us now see what he says in the inaugural touching fugitives from service. On this head he is indeed most emphatic. After citing the clause of the Federal Constitution relating to this matter, he comes squarely up and says, "It is scarcely questioned that this provision was intended by those who made it for the reclaiming of what we call *fugitive slaves*, and *the intention of the lawgiver is the law*. All members of Congress swear their support to the whole Constitution—to this as well as any other. To the proposition, then, that slaves, whose cases come within the terms of this clause, 'shall be delivered up,' their oaths are *unanimous*. Now, if they would make the effort in good temper, could they not, with a nearly equal unanimity, frame and pass a law by means of which to keep good that unanimous oath?" After kindly and respectfully suggesting some amendment in the existing law on this subject, so as to make its operation less rigorous, and thus to secure its more effective operation, he says:

"I take the official oath to-day with no mental reservations, and with no purpose to construe the Constitution or laws by any hypercritical rules; and, while I do not choose now to specify particular acts of Congress as proper to be enforced, I do suggest that it will be much safer for all, both in official and private stations, to conform to and abide by all those acts which stand unrepealed, than to *violate any of them*, trusting to final impunity in *having them held to be unconstitutional*."

After discussing in a very striking manner the mooted question of secession, and declaring, in firm but courteous language, his determination to maintain the constitutional powers of the government against all attempts to subvert them, he adds : " I trust this will not be regarded as a menace, but only as a declared purpose of the Union that it will constitutionally defend and maintain itself. In doing this, there need be no bloodshed or violence, and there shall be none, unless it is forced upon the national authority."

Again returning to the discussion of the right of a single state, or less than a constitutional majority, to disrupt the government or withdraw from the compact of union, and declaring his own preference for the conventional mode of amending the Constitution, he takes particular pains to state his assent to the constitutional amendment which had just passed Congress, in these words: " I understand that a proposed amendment to the Constitution (which amendment, however, I have not seen) has passed Congress, to the effect that the Federal government shall never interfere with the domestic institutions of the states, including that of persons held to service. To avoid misconstruction of what I have said, I depart from my purpose not to speak of particular amendments, so far as to say that, holding such a provision to be now *implied constitutional law, I have no objection to making it express and irrevocable.*"

The address closes in the following pathetic and solemn manner :

" My countrymen, one and all, think calmly and well upon this whole subject; nothing valuable can be lost by taking time.

"If there be an object to hurry any of you in hot haste to a step which you would never take deliberately, that object will be frustrated by taking time, but no good object can be frustrated by it.

"Such of you as are now dissatisfied still have the old Constitution unimpaired, and, on the sensitive point, the laws of your own framing under it, while the new administration will have no immediate power, if it would, to change either.

"If it were admitted that you who are dissatisfied hold the right side in the dispute, there is still no single reason for precipitate action. Intelligence, patriotism, Christianity, and a firm reliance on Him who has never yet forsaken this favored land, are still competent to adjust, in the best way, all our present difficulties.

"In your hands, my dissatisfied fellow-countrymen, and not in mine, is the momentous issue of civil war. The government will not assail you.

"You can have no conflict without being yourselves the aggressors. You can have no oath registered in heaven to destroy the government, while I shall have the most solemn one to 'preserve, protect, and defend' it.

"I am loth to close. We are not enemies, but friends. We must not be enemies. Though passion may have strained, it must not break our bonds of affection.

"The mystic chords of memory, stretching from every battle-field and patriot grave to every living heart and hearthstone all over this broad land, will yet swell the chorus of the Union, when again touched, as surely they will be, by the better angels of our nature."

How profoundly gratified will be all men in future

times, who may be capable of appreciating truth and reason, when they learn that this powerful appeal to the
hearts and understandings of Southern men was *backed*
and *fortified*, yea, even *anticipated*, by the following noble
utterances of Alexander H. Stephens.

"The first question that presents itself is, Shall the
people of the South secede from the Union in consequence of the election of Mr. Lincoln to the presidency
of the United States? My countrymen, I tell you frankly, candidly, and earnestly, that I do not think that they.
ought. In my judgment, the election of no man, constitutionally chosen to that high office, is sufficient cause for
any state to separate from the Union; it ought to stand
by and aid still in maintaining the Constitution of the
country. To make a point of resistance to the government, to withdraw from it because a man has been constitutionally elected, puts us in the wrong. We are
pledged to maintain the Constitution; many of us have
sworn to support it. Can we, therefore, for the mere
election of a man to the presidency, and that, too, in accordance with the prescribed forms of the Constitution,
make a point of resistance to the government, and, without becoming the breakers of that sacred instrument ourselves, withdraw ourselves from it? Would we not be
in the wrong? Whatever fate is to befall this country,
let it never be laid to the charge of the people of the
South, and especially of the people of Georgia, that we
were untrue to our national engagements. Let the fault
and the wrong rest upon others. If all our hopes are
to be blasted, if the republic is to go down, let us be
found to the last moment standing on the deck, with the

Constitution of the United States waving over our heads. (Applause.) Let the fanatics of the North break the Constitution, if such is their fell purpose; let the responsibility be upon them. I shall speak presently more of their acts. But let not the South, let us not be the ones to commit the aggression. We went into the election with this people; the result was different from what we wished, but the election has been constitutionally held. Were we to make a point of resistance to the government, and go out of the Union on that account, the record would be made up hereafter against us.

"But, it is said, Mr. Lincoln's policy and principles are against the Constitution, and that, if he carries them out, it will be destructive of our rights. Let us not anticipate a threatened evil. If he violates the Constitution, then will come our time to act. Do not let us break it, because, forsooth, *he* may. If he does, that is the time for us to strike. (Applause.) I think it would be injudicious and unwise to do this sooner. I do not anticipate that Mr. Lincoln will do any thing to jeopardize our safety or security, whatever may be his spirit to do it; for he is bound by the constitutional checks which are thrown around him, which at this time render him powerless to do any great mischief. This shows the wisdom of our system. The President of the United States is no emperor, no dictator; he is clothed with no absolute power. He can do nothing unless he is backed by power in Congress. The House of Representatives is largely in the majority against him. In the Senate he will also be powerless: there will be a majority of four against him—this, after the loss of Bigler, Fitch, and others, by the unfortunate dissensions of the Democratic party in their states. Mr. Lincoln can not appoint an officer without the consent of the Senate; he can not form a cabinet without the same consent. He will be in the condition of George III. (the embodiment of Toryism), who had to ask the Whigs to appoint his ministers, and was compelled to receive a cabinet utterly opposed to his views; and so Mr. Lincoln will be compelled to ask of the Senate to choose for him a cabinet, if the Democracy of that body choose to put him on such terms. He will be compelled to do this, or let the government stop, if the National Democratic men — for that is their name at the North—the conservative men in the Senate, should so determine. Then how can Mr. Lincoln obtain a cabinet which would aid him, or allow him, to violate the Constitution?

" Why, then, I say, should we disrupt the bonds of this Union, when his hands are tied—when he can do nothing against us?

" I believe in the power of the people to govern themselves, when wisdom prevails and passion is silent. Look at what has already been done by them for their advancement in all that ennobles man. There is nothing like it in the history of the world. Look abroad from one extent of the country to the other; contemplate our greatness; we are now among the first nations of the earth. Shall it, then, be said that our institutions, founded upon principles of self-government, are a failure?

" Thus far it is a noble example, worthy of imitation. The gentleman (Mr. Cobb), the other night, said it had proven a failure. A failure in what? In growth? Look at our expanse in national power! Look at our population and increase in all that makes a people great! A failure? Why, we are the admiration of the civilized world, and present the brightest hopes of mankind.

"Some of our public men have failed in their aspirations, that is true; and from that comes a great part of our troubles. (Prolonged applause.)

"No, there is no failure of this government yet. We have made great advancement under the Constitution, and I can not but hope that we shall advance still higher. Let us be true to our cause."

Occurrences were now soon to take place which all true-hearted American citizens must forever deplore, and which the friends and supporters of republican freedom can never cease most profoundly to lament. The opening scene of the war has imparted to Charleston, the boasted commercial emporium of South Carolina, a deathless claim to the mournful yet respectful sympathy of all who admire manliness, and valor, and skill in arms, and elevated patriotism, and wheresoever the honored names of Anderson and Beauregard, and of those who were associated with either of these renowned chieftains in the memorable affair of the siege and capture of Fort Sumter shall be printed or enunciated in any of the spoken languages of earth. It is not for me to record what was done and suffered on either side in the fratricidal contest which sectional strife had at last wrought up to the shedding of American blood upon American soil, and by American hands. I shall cheerfully leave to others, to whom this grim task may prove grateful, an account of the fighting of sanguinary and wasteful battles that never should have been fought, and the description of victories won or of defeats endured, the memory of which will ever be, in my judgment, a far fitter subject for painful remembrance and poignant lamentation, than for agreeable reminiscence and patriotic rejoicing. The rival merits of illustrious military commanders on either side whose unhappy fate it was to be drawn into sanguinary conflict— of Grant and of Lee, of Stonewall Jackson and Lyon, of Sherman and Joe Johnston, of Price and Thomas, of Sheridan and Ewell, and a host of bright names besides too numerous for recital, it is not probable that I shall ever undertake either to compare or portray. Should it happen hereafter that such personages as I have mentioned shall be associated upon fields of glory opened to them by our country's presiding genius upon a foreign soil, with commingled energies and blended sympathies, to maintain the venerated principles of our fathers; should it become needful that all the spotless chivalry of our whole vast country — of the North, the South, the East, and the West—should go forth to vindicate the honor of republican institutions in this hemisphere against the usurping violence of imperial despotism, and no fitter pen than mine can be found to record exploits which will at the same time redound to our own country's honor, and lend encouragement and inspiration to the oppressed strugglers for freedom contending in unequal contest against the efforts of earth's tyrants to enslave them, then shall I be prepared to render such aid as I can for the recounting of achievements, the fame of which will be as enduring as the mountains of our natal land, and as splendid as the unclouded rays of Heaven's grand luminary shining down on us from the central point of the firmament.

CHAPTER XVII.

Beginning of the War.—Its gross Impolicy.—Mr. Davis and his official Associates did not comprehend its true Dimensions.—Mr. Davis's several exultant Speeches after having been made President.—Striking Declaration made by the Confederate Secretary of War, Leroy Pope Walker, at Montgomery, Alabama. — Mr. Lincoln's View of the physical Impracticability of Secession.—Philosophic Views of the Effects of War in general, and of Civil War in particular.—View of the existing Condition of Things as the Result of the late War.—Responsible Attitude of President Johnson, and Duty of all good Citizens to sustain him.—Short Explanation of Author's own Attitude in the beginning of the War.—The Confederate Provisional Congress.—Its extraordinary Harmony and Unanimity, and the Causes thereof.—View of the permanent Confederate Congress.—Rapid Review of Mr. Davis's Conduct as Executive Chief.—Peace Efforts in the Confederate Congress. —Their signal Failure, and the Causes thereof.—Informal Efforts of Author, in Connection with many influential Persons of the South, to make Peace in Spite of Mr. Davis, and, if need be, by a Counter-revolution.—Failure of those Efforts, and probable Causes therefor.—Author asks Passport across the Ocean, which is granted him.—Close of the War, and Remarks thereupon.

WAR was now initiated by the firing upon Fort Sumter, under orders suddenly received from Mr. Davis's Secretary of War, Mr. Leroy Pope Walker, of Huntsville, Alabama, whose clear and sonorous tones had been heard, only a month or two before, in the goodly city of Nashville (up to that time still a Union-loving city), expounding the opening glories of secession. As some sprightly and vivacious urchin, who jocosely casts his lighted cracker at the heels of the way-side passenger,

whom he expects to see startled and affrighted with the
noise of the unlooked-for explosion, or, to speak a little
more classically, as the fabled son of Phœbus, who is reported as mounting the blazing chariot of the sun, auda-
ciously seizing the reins, and driving the celestial steeds
amain with furious celerity along the ethereal pathways,
until the whole heavens were set on fire, so Mr. Davis's
enterprising war secretary embraced with eagerness the
opportunity which his august chief had now so unwisely
afforded to him of plunging his native land, most causelessly and madly, into a war more wasting and bloody
than any which this western hemisphere had heretofore
experienced. Let us pause for a moment, and consider
the respective strength of the parties now suddenly "*pre-
cipitated*" into conflict. The Federal government in
Washington City represented at the time the power and
resources of nearly twenty-five millions of people. For
the cotton states could alone at that moment be confidently looked to for co-operative aid; and, making allowance for the strength of the Union element existing
in all the states of the South from the beginning to the
end of this unhappy contest, and for the African element
also, which all discerning men foresaw from the commencement, should the war endure long, would be infallibly wielded against the Southern claim to separate independence, no one can suppose that as many as five millions of people could at any time be found, during the
four years of terrible suffering through which it has been
the fate of the unhappy and deluded South to pass (including men, women, and children), whose hearts were
warmly enlisted in the attempt now making to subvert

the government of our fathers. Besides, the strong-willed and resolute men who had been left behind in Washington City by the rash and improvident Southern senators and representatives, henceforward to wield the thunders of state, without serious let or embarrassment from any quarter, against those who had resolved to organize wild, flaming rebellion in the South, were possessed of a considerable body of regular soldiers, a large navy, and abundant resources of every kind for the prosecution of warlike enterprises; while all the states of the Old World were open to them, and ready to send to them also such supplies as might be needed, and to transmit to them, if these should be desired, millions of willing soldiers, who only needed that a friendly invitation should be extended to them to fly across the deep, in order to aid in defending the venerated national emblem of our country against all who should dare to menace it with dishonor. Surely no historian has ever heretofore recited the incidents of a war in which between the conflicting parties there was greater disparity of strength. But Mr. Davis and his official associates had no correct conception of the true character and dimensions of the war into which they had so hastily plunged, as was afterward frankly confessed in many a lugubrious harangue, and in more than one solemn official document. They did not believe at first that the conflict would endure for a twelve-month, and were even weak enough to calculate most confidently upon strong *Northern aid*, which it is now well known there never was the least probability of their receiving; albeit ex-President Pierce and several others, whose letters to Mr. Davis have recently seen

P

the light, had plied this confiding personage with secret promises of support, upon which he built in part his hopes of one day wielding an imperial sceptre. As to the interposition of *foreign* powers in behalf of the now warring states of the South, though many deceitful assurances were received from abroad at different periods of the contest, no man of sound intellect any where now supposes that either the French or English governments ever seriously thought of embroiling itself in a transatlantic civic feud, the formal enlistment in which would, in all probability, bring upon itself swift and assured destruction. Mr. Davis evidently thought far otherwise when he said at Jackson, Mississippi, just before leaving his own home for the city of Montgomery, "England would not allow our great staple to be dammed up within our present limits; the starving thousands in their midst would not allow it. We have nothing to apprehend from blockade. But, if they attempt invasion by land, we must take the war *out of our territory*. If war must come, it must be upon Northern, and not upon Southern soil." Continuing to talk in this menacing strain along the road to Montgomery, when he reached Stevenson, an important railroad point, he said: "Your border states will gladly come into the Southern confederacy within sixty days, as *we will be their only* friends. England will recognize us, and a glorious future is before us. The grass will grow in the Northern cities, where the pavements have been worn off by the tread of commerce. We will carry war where it is easy to advance—where food for the *sword* and *torch* await our armies in the densely-populated cities; and though they (the enemy) may come and spoil our crops, we can raise them as before, while they can not rear the cities which took years of industry and millions of money to build." It was evidently, in part, under the inspiration of such speeches as these from his executive chief, that the war secretary, Mr. Walker, on the night after the storming of Fort Sumter, announced that " the Confederate flag would soon be seen flying from the top of the Capitol in Washington."

Far more to the point were the sober, practical words of Mr. Lincoln, when he had said, in his inaugural,

"Physically speaking, we can not separate; we can not remove our respective sections from each other, nor build an impassable wall between them. A husband and wife may be divorced, and go out of the presence and beyond the reach of each other, but the different parts of our country can not do this. They can not but remain face to face; and intercourse, either amiable or hostile, must continue between them. Is it possible, then, to make that intercourse more advantageous or more satisfactory after separation than before? Can aliens make treaties easier than friends can make laws? Can treaties be more faithfully enforced between aliens than laws can among friends? Suppose you go to war, you can not fight always; and when, after much loss on both sides, and no gain on either, you cease fighting, the identical questions as to terms of intercourse are again upon you."

It must ever appear to men at all given to philosophic meditation upon the concerns of government, and who have made themselves in the least degree familiar with great historic examples, exceedingly surprising that the

secession leaders at this perilous crisis (all of whom professed a profound regard alike for the corporate rights of
the states as for general popular freedom) should have
failed to discover the extreme dangers to both of these
which a continued state of war must engender. All professed writers on government, from Aristotle down to
Calhoun, have pointed out these dangers, and some of
them have expatiated with great force upon the inevitable tendency of belligerent measures to *centralize* all civil
power in a single hand. They have taught us that if the
state of war be continued too long, nothing but the greatest circumspection on the part of those interested in preserving freedom can prevent the building up of an irresponsible despotism. And this tendency to *centralization*
has, confessedly, always been more observable in such
wars as are waged by one portion of the citizens of a
free country against citizens of kindred blood, of the
same country and lineage, upon the natal soil common
to them both. It would be easy to specify the efficient causes of this, and quite as easy to illustrate and
support the stated proposition by numerous instances in
point. It is Mr. Webster, I think, who, in some one of
his majestic orations, likens the action of the governmental machine, in times of civil commotion, to the chariot-
wheels of antiquity, which are described as taking fire
from the celerity of their own motion. Two such ma-
chines, in close proximity, igniting from the same cause,
must each serve, by a natural reciprocation of power, to
increase the general combustion. It would have been
scarcely possible to preserve a well-balanced federative
system either in the North or in the South, while such a

war as that from which we have just so happily escaped,
was in fierce and ever-varying progress. Had peaceful
secession even turned out to be a practicable experiment,
the danger of constantly-recurring border wars would
have demanded the location of considerable bodies of defensive soldiery along the line of territorial separation
on the one side and on the other of that line, in order to
guard against hostile incursions, ever possible to occur.
These military bands would have soon grown into standing armies of great and constantly accumulating strength,
until each of them would, as so often has been the case
heretofore, have given to the country which should have
thus fallen under its control an imperial master, or would,
at least, have decreed the establishment of a government
far stronger in its frame than that of the republican form
has ever been heretofore adjudged to be. But a separation effected by the sword must have been fraught with
yet greater peril. A long and arduous struggle between two segments of the same republic, marked by
the copious shedding of the blood of valued citizens on
either side, would necessarily have engendered rancors
exceedingly difficult to be allayed, even after hostilities
should have ceased to be prosecuted. These rancors,
during the season of hostilities, would have been constantly multiplying and increasing in intensity. The ordinary expedients of war would have become, in the estimation of the parties struggling for superiority, far too
gentle and ineffective for the fierce and hellish purposes
of a wrathful and all-desolating vengeance. The infernal furies themselves would be called in by mutual and
trumpet-toned entreaties, to swell the thrice tragic scene

of general social ruin. *Sicilian vespers*, or *Feasts of St. Bartholomew*, would have ceased to awaken their accustomed horror, when confronting such scenes as those to which our own loved country was, only a month or two since, in danger of falling a prey. A state of things so appalling as that described would, of necessity, have demanded that large and latitudinous powers should be vested in the executive department of the government, wheresoever situated, in order to regulate and hold in some little restraint, if possible, all those potent elements of mischief. In order to prevent universal anarchy, universal butchery, and wide-sweeping crimes of every sort, the organization of a despotism would have become a fatal necessity. Such vast powers, once trusted in the hands of any man less virtuous than Washington himself, it would be absurd to expect would be *voluntarily* surrendered, and to tear them from so potential a depository by *force* might perchance be found impossible.

Is any man incredulous to these suggestions? Behold! are we not even now treading upon the cinders of a volcanic eruption, which is only just at this moment ceasing to emit smoke? Have we not seen, in the very war which has but the other day been brought to a close, that Mr. Lincoln, the most humane, moderate, and clement of men, was *compelled*, by circumstances which admitted of no discretion, to bring into exercise powers which he himself frankly and magnanimously acknowledged not to have been derived from the Constitution under which he had been called to his high station? Do we not now see his firm-nerved, sagacious, and energetic successor, a man as remarkable in his former life as any

American statesman, either dead or living, for his strict
and scrupulous regard for the great fundamental principles of our system of freedom, battling manfully and per-
severingly with a vast "sea of troubles," while, on the
right hand and on the left, blind and infuriated zealots,
extremists, and impracticables of every noxious creed
under heaven are, with emulous confusion, and with ever-
toiling malignity, striving to paralyze the arm which is
being stretched forth over the whole land—over the
North, the South, the East, and the West, for the purpose
of effecting a great and universal national deliverance?
Are not a few men far to the South presenting even yet
an unamiable and factious opposition to the reasonable
requisitions which their only protector on earth has made
upon them? And are there not others in the North denouncing that same personage for not carrying into effect
all their hell-born schemes of vengeance and spoliation?
And can any one doubt that all these are the natural
and inevitable products of such a war as that which was
brought to a close last spring?

I am aware that some might be inclined to ask why,
entertaining such views as have been just expressed, the
writer of these pages consented, four years ago, to occupy
a seat in the Confederate Congress? I wish it were in my
power to answer this most natural interrogatory in a
manner entirely satisfactory even to my own judgment
and sensibilities. It were but to display a vain and silly
egotism, to narrate all the influences to which my action
as a public man was subjected in the early part of this
most deplorable contest. I shall be content, for the present, to state that the motives which operated upon me

were of a nature most peculiar and pressing, a good deal
out of the ordinary routine of civic duty, anomalous and
eccentrical, if any one shall be pleased so to denominate
them; and I should greatly prefer to be burdened with
the largest amount of undeserved reproach to attempting
the difficult and perhaps impossible task of vindicating
my own political *consistency*, or proving to the excited
and prejudiced minds of a generation which is fast passing away, how, by pursuing the very course which, after
much and painful hesitation, and under the persuasions
of men of far higher intellect than my own, I finally consented to tread, I secured to myself the only chance, in
the event of certain exigencies which I then foresaw
most plainly were more than likely to arise, of aiding,
to some moderate extent at least, in warding off a portion
of the evils the whole integral mass of which it had already, in the rapid and tumultuous rush of revolutionary
events, become impossible to avert, and of participating,
according to the measure of my ability, also, in the prevention of *results* which, even at that period, I could not
but regard as most alarmingly *foreshadowed:*

Of the action of the Confederate Provisional Congress
I have but little to say. I have heard that there was a
good deal of ability in the body, and that there was much
harmony, also, in its proceedings. The revolutionary
machine, I should conjecture, had already been given
most decidedly the *centralizing* tendency which has been
already described, as it has been often stated in my hearing, by men who were bound to know all about the matter, that Mr. Davis vetoed more bills during the short
provisional *regime* than all the presidents of the United

States put together, from Washington to Lincoln inclusive, and that no attempt to pass a single bill over his head was ever made.

In reference to the proceedings of the Confederate government, after my unhappy and tempestuous connection with it was formed, I should have very much to say under different circumstances than those which now exist, all of which may be said hereafter, if it be apparent that the public mind is in a condition to profit by the painful revelations which it will be in my power to make. But President Davis and his cabinet are either in exile or in imprisonment; his multitudinous official servitors have retired to private life, or are gloomy wanderers in foreign lands. Those who, in despite of what a few independent and high-spirited men could do to prevent the passage of certain baleful measures, succeeded in enacting laws for the suspension of the great writ of liberty; for the confiscation of the estates of all who could not conscientiously range themselves in opposition to the flag of their fathers; for the forcible conscription of all male citizens capable of bearing arms, whether in friendly or hostile relations to the Confederate cause; for the forcible impressment of private property, wheresoever situated, at the discretion of men endowed temporarily with military authority; for the declaration and enforcement of martial law, and a number of acts besides of almost equal enormity; those who sustained Mr. Davis in the appointment of inefficient and mischievous officials, to the exclusion of the capable and the virtuous; who sanctioned the impolitic and ungenerous displacement of able and high-souled military commanders, in order to make way for

P 2

others whom the army despised, and the citizens at large
both distrusted and hated—these persons, the valueless
ephemera of an age over-fertile in *inanities*, have nearly
all disappeared from the jostling chaotic stage whereupon
they were enacting their parts, and,

> " Like the baseless fabric of a vision,
> Left not a wreck behind."

As to Mr. Davis, I must say that I regard him mainly
as the unfortunate victim of dark and dangerous political
heresies for which he is by no means primarily responsible; a victim, likewise, of the intriguing machinations of
cunning and unscrupulous managers, whose true character he had never penetrated; as the dupe of adulation
and of false promises from *abroad* which might perchance
have deceived men far more sagacious than himself; in
fine, as the almost *involuntary instrument* of dark and potential influences generated in the womb of *Revolution*,
which led him to claim and to exercise powers, the employment of which, though utterly subversive of freedom,
he believed to be indispensable to the successful execution of the grand scheme of secession, to which he had
for so many years devoted the best energies both of his
soul and his understanding.   Far be it from me to wish
evil to the late President of the Confederate States.   He
has been unfortunate, and I condole with him; he has
committed great and grievous errors, and I make all just
allowance for them.   He is unhappy, and I sympathize
with him.   He is in prison, and I pray night and day for
his enlargement.   Though he permitted his heartless Secretary of War, last winter, to deprive me of my own personal liberty, and to retain me in " durance vile" until

discharged on habeas corpus, alone on account of my presuming to attempt *pacification*, when I found both Congress and himself bent upon the farther prosecution of a war which they had already rendered utterly hopeless, yet, so far from feeling resentment or unkindness on this account, I can say with truth that, having myself thrice suffered the loss of personal liberty within the last twelve months, I can, in reference to Mr. Davis's present forlorn and suffering condition, painfully and sorrowfully exclaim (with a change of *gender* only), in the language of Queen Dido to Æneas, "*Non ignarus mali, miseros succurrere disco.*"

It will not, I trust, be transcending the limits which I have thus prescribed to myself to say that Mr. Davis must be inevitably held responsible by the future historian for the appointment to places of high civic trust, including the positions in his cabinet, of so large a proportion of incompetent public functionaries, as well as for his obstinate adherence to these individuals after their inability to perform the duties assigned to them had become manifest to all save himself; nor will he be easily excused for his unjust and illiberal treatment of some of the most meritorious Confederate military commanders, who had drawn their swords, and enlisted all they had of life, and fame, and fortune in behalf of Southern independence. The impolitic tenacity with which he continued to bolster up the reputations of such men as Bragg, and Pemberton, and Hindman, and a long list of others of the same stamp, in opposition to known public sentiment, both in the army and out of it, and to the utter sacrifice of all rational hopes of Confederate success, will

constitute a picture for the examination of an unprejudiced posterity alike unprecedented and indefensible.
Twenty years hence no one will be heard to deny that
to the *direct* and unwise interference in great military
movements on the part of Mr. Davis is to be attributed
nearly all the principal disasters of the war. In the gross
mismanagement of the War Department, under the su-
pervision and control of Mr. Davis himself, may safely be
charged the calamitous occurrences at Forts Donelson and
Henry, and at Roanoke Island. The withdrawal by his
own express order from the Army of Tennessee of nearly
ten thousand men for the purpose of being transferred to
the State of Mississippi, just before the battle of Murfreesboro', was undoubtedly the especial cause of the loss of
that sanguinary field. The order to fight that battle,
which emanated from Mr. Davis himself, while he was
yet in the neighborhood of Murfreesboro', and, in case of
defeat, to fall back at once to the line of the Tennessee,
was one of the most stupendous blunders of which the
annals of war have as yet borne testimony, and had the
effect of eventually losing the great and important State
of Tennessee to the Confederate cause. The rash order
afterward given by the same personage, that Longstreet
and some twenty thousand of the Confederate soldiery
should be detached from the already enfeebled Army of
Tennessee, and sent upon an unpromising and profitless
errand to Knoxville, Tennessee, brought on the disastrous
result at Missionary Ridge. Mr. Davis's antecedent displacement of Beauregard from the command of the Army
of Tennessee, and the substitution of Bragg in his place,
and the confiding to this last-mentioned officer the im-

portant invading movement into Kentucky, awakened at the time a strong feeling both of surprise and of regret in the minds of all men in the least degree capable of judging with discernment and accuracy touching the policy of such a proceeding; and when this *military favorite* of the President afterward allowed Buell and his feeble and somewhat demoralized forces to pass, almost in sight of his lines, on their way to Louisville, where it was known that the Federal army could be immediately strengthened by recruits to an almost indefinite extent, so palpable was this mistake, that there were not wanting men in the Confederate Congress, who were only *civilians*, to predict with confidence that Bragg, with the gallant army that he commanded, would be inevitably and speedily driven over the Cumberland Mountains and compelled to seek refuge once more in Tennessee. No reasonable man has ever doubted that the retention of Pemberton at Vicksburg; and the tardiness with which General Joseph E. Johnston was sent to aid in the defense of that city, brought about that memorable *Fourth of July scene*, which is really one of the most curious and romantic incidents of the war. The sudden displacement of General Joseph E. Johnston from the command of the army at Atlanta, the consequent fall of that city, and the absurd and unaccountable order issued by Mr. Davis that the Confederate army, then the only defense of Alabama, of Georgia, and of South Carolina, should be mysteriously dispatched upon a bootless errand to the city of Nashville, there to endure the most cruel disasters, while all the great cotton-growing region to the south was laid open to the strong invading force under Sherman, can scarcely be satisfactorily accounted for even on the score of judicial blindness.

By a somewhat singular coincidence, I had just writ- ten the preceding sentence, when the elaborate report of General Grant, which is at this moment commanding so much of the public attention, came to hand. I was natu- rally anxious to learn how far the views which I had expressed in my place in the Confederate Congress were in unison with those of one of the first military command- ers of the age. On glancing at that part of the report which refers to the conduct of Mr. Davis at this precise period, I find the following very striking remarks: "Gen- eral Sherman, immediately after the fall of Atlanta, put his armies in camp in and about the place, and made all preparation for refitting and supplying them for future service. The great length of road from Atlanta to Cum- berland River, however, which had to be guarded, allow- ed the troops but little rest. During this time Jefferson Davis made a speech in Macon, Georgia, which was re- ported in the papers in the South, and soon became known to the whole country, disclosing the plans of the enemy, thus enabling General Sherman fully to meet them. He exhibited the weakness of supposing that an army that had been beaten and fearfully decimated in a vain attempt at the defensive, could successfully under- take the offensive against the army that had so often de- feated it."

This same speech of Mr. Davis is one of the most re- markable on record in several other respects. In it he denounced, in very coarse language, the high-spirited and intelligent Governor of Georgia for having (as Mr. Davis,

it would seem, had been informed) charged him with intending to abandon Georgia to the mercy of the invading
force, when, at that precise moment, the very scheme of
abandonment, so emphatically denied, was in a course
of rapid execution. He assailed, at the same time, the
valiant Johnston, whom he had recently so unwisely dis-
placed from the command of the Army of Tennessee, in
language alike unjust and impolitic. I remember well
that, when the printed copy of this extraordinary harangue reached the city of Richmond, Mr. Davis's earnest
friends and admirers there were as much shocked by its
appearance as was the population of that city generally,
and it was openly declared by them to be a shameful *fab-
rication.* Upon Mr. Davis's return to Richmond, though,
he having duly acknowledged its genuineness, these same
friends and admirers, including the conductors of the
government organ (the Sentinel), fell into ecstasies over
it, declaring that it was a wise and paternal address of
the *pater patriæ* to his *erring children.*

When, in the month of February, 1862, I reached the
city of Richmond, the condition of Confederate affairs
was beginning to wear a most gloomy and discouraging
aspect. The disastrous affair at Fishing Creek had occurred; Forts Donelson and Henry had fallen into the
hands of the Federal forces; General Albert Sidney Johnson had been forced to abandon Bowling Green, and retreat before the overwhelming Federal force through
Tennessee, down to the neighborhood of the northern
portion of the State of Mississippi; Roanoke Island had
been also attacked and captured, and·New Orleans was
evidently in danger of undergoing the same fate. All

these calamities, and a number of other casualties not necessary to be now specified, had been directly traced to the
gross incompetency of the Secretary of War, Mr. Judah
P. Benjamin, who, by-the-by, though, had never been any
thing more than a *mere clerk* in the War Department, acting
uniformly under the direction of his executive chief, Mr.
Davis.   Under these circumstances was Mr. Davis inaugurated as permanent President of the Confederate States.
It was obvious to me, at a moment's glance, that the Confederate cause was then almost at its last gasp, and that
unless something was immediately done to buoy it up,
the hopes of Southern independence, a few months before
so confidently indulged by some, would be forever extinguished.   It is a most remarkable fact, the truth of which
is indisputable, that neither Mr. Davis nor his Secretary
of War had, even up to that time, become satisfied of the
importance of erecting defenses, either by land or water,
which might serve to save the city of Richmond from
being entered by the forces of the United States, known
then to be on their way to the Confederate capital.   Governor Letcher had endeavored to attract the attention of
Mr. Davis to this important matter, and had been treated
on the occasion in a manner most discourteous—Mr. Davis seeming to regard it as an act of supreme presumption on the part of this vigilant and discerning functionary to intermeddle with an affair which he, as Confederate president, recognized as exclusively within the scope
of his own jurisdiction.   It was obvious to me, as it was
to all men of discernment with whom I held intercourse
at the time, that it was utterly impossible for the claim to
Southern independence to be maintained by arms, unless

great and radical reforms in the administration of Confederate affairs could be affected without delay. No sensible man could for a moment doubt that an immediate and pretty general change of cabinet officers was indispensable. There were only two of these functionaries whose official qualifications were even respectable—the Attorney General, Mr. Watts, of Alabama, and the Postmaster General, Mr. Reagan, of Texas. The Secretary of War (Mr. Benjamin), besides his inability to meet the military exigencies which he had been encountering, as well as the more serious ones in prospect, was subject to other objections, as the incumbent of a high cabinet position, of the greatest and most vital character. His reputation for *integrity* had never been good, and of late years it had become deeply tarnished by his known participancy in schemes of notorious corruption both in the State of Louisiana and in Washington City. The offensive moral odor arising from the celebrated *Houmas fraud* (one of the most unblushing and profligate legislative transactions that had ever disgraced the annals of a free people) had affixed such a stigma upon the reputation both of Mr. Benjamin and his friend and patron, Mr. John A. Slidell, as it was not possible that any lapse of time could entirely efface. It was quite evident that it was not in the power of Mr. Davis, or of a thousand such persons, to reconcile the unsophisticated popular mind of the South to either of these personages; nor would it have been possible, even for Washington himself, to have preserved his own fame unsullied, while apparently yielding his unreserved confidence to such notorious dabblers in iniquity. At the moment of Mr. Davis's entering upon his official career as permanent president, it was plain that an excellent opportunity was presented to him of correcting the mistakes which, it was most manifest, he had committed in the beginning of his official career as the chief executive officer of the Confederate States; and it was confidently hoped by many that this opportunity would be promptly embraced by him of calling around him men of the highest abilities and of the most unquestioned moral worth that the Southern States contained. Besides, it had in some way happened that Mr. Davis, always too much of a mere *party man* in the former part of his career, had filled a very large number of all the official positions in his gift with persons who had voted with him in 1860 for Breckenridge and Lane; and as the whole population of the South (that is to say, all who had yielded their adhesion to the Confederate cause) had voted for him in the presidential election which had just terminated, it was regarded as both reasonable and proper that, in the distribution of official appointments, he should show himself altogether superior to ancient party prejudices. But such was far from being the case. The names of such men as William C. Rives, John Bell, William A. Graham, and others, when mentioned to him in connection with important offices in his gift, are well known only to have called forth from him the most scornful and derisive responses. Censures imposed upon his chosen cabinet advisers he was ever ready to treat as a direct insult to himself, and, in fact, as the perpetration of a sort of contempt for his own official dignity. The truth is, that it was very soon ascertained that his head had been completely turned by his sudden elevation to the place which he then occupied, and he had become the victim of "that weakest weakness, *vanity.*"

At this period nothing like a manly opposition to Mr. Davis's administration in either house of Congress had been displayed; and yet it was most plain that, unless some such opposition should soon manifest itself, all for which the Southern people were so valiantly struggling would be inevitably lost to them, together with all the freedom which they had claimed to possess before the commencement of the struggle then in progress. I know not what other men may suppose it was my duty, as a man originally averse to the war, and sincerely anxious for an honorable peace, to do under such circumstances as I have described; but I know what I did do. This has already been stated by a gentleman who has recently given to the public three volumes of a well written and interesting historic work, and in language strictly in unison with the truth, except that this accomplished writer has been far too complimentary to myself, and has, as I believe (doubtless unintentionally), failed to do full justice to others in the Confederate Congress well worthy of praise, both for personal independence and for very high ability.*

* "There was but little opposition in Congress to President Davis; but there was some which took a direction to his cabinet, and this opposition was represented by Mr. Foote, of Tennessee — a man of acknowledged ability and many virtues of character, who had re-entered upon the political stage after a public life which, however it lacked in the cheap merit of partisan consistency, had been adorned by displays of wonderful intellect and great political genius. Mr. Foote was not a man to be deterred from speaking the truth; his quickness to resentment, and his chivalry, which, though somewhat Quixotic, was founded in the most noble and

Just about the time that I was laboring most assiduously to relieve the Department of War of Mr. Benjamin,
by calling forth, as far as it might be in my power to do
so, co-operative responses from the people, an occurrence
took place in social life in Richmond which had much
effect, not only upon the fate of Mr. Benjamin, but which,
in the sequel, had much influence also upon the course
of public events. I chanced to be invited to a dinner-
party, where some twenty of the most prominent members of the two houses of the Confederate Congress were
congregated, including the Speaker of the House of Representatives, Mr. Orr, of South Carolina, and others of
equal rank. General Joseph E. Johnston was also an invited guest. While the banquet was proceeding, Mr.
Benjamin's gross acts of official misconduct becoming the
subject of conversation, one of the company turned to
General Johnston, and inquired whether he thought it
even *possible* that the Confederate cause could succeed
with Mr. Benjamin as war minister. To this inquiry,
General Johnston, after a little pause, emphatically responded in the *negative*. This high authority was immediately cited in both houses of Congress against Mr. Benjamin, and was in the end fatal to his hopes of remaining in the Department of War. Mr. Davis, after defer-
ring the sending in of his nominations for cabinet ap-

delicate sense of honor, made those who would have bullied or silenced a
weaker person stand in awe of him. A man of such temper was not
likely to stint words in assailing an opponent; and his sharp declama-
tions in Congress, his searching comments, and his great powers of sarcasm, used upon such men as Mallory, Benjamin, and Huger, were the
only relief of the dullness of the Congress, and the only historical features
of its debates."—POLLARD's *First Year of the War.*

pointments, under the permanent Constitution, for nearly four weeks, in order to have it in his power to persuade the Senate to confirm Mr. Benjamin as Secretary of War, in the event of his being renominated, ultimately relinquished this object in despair—that body, however accommodating it was in general to executive fancies, having been found unwilling to participate in the terrible responsibility of such an act. Mr. Benjamin was finally nominated for the Department of State, and was confirmed, by a very small majority, for that place, where he had it in his power, both abroad and at home, to perpetrate more barefaced acts of corruption and profligacy than any single individual has ever been known to commit in the same space of time in any part of Christendom. I will here remark, in passing, that this frank and manly declaration of General Johnston rendered both Mr. Davis and Mr. Benjamin alike hostile to him, and he was fated to experience the effect of their malevolence on more than one subsequent occasion previous to his ultimate deprivation of military command.

All the efforts which could be essayed by others as well as by myself to effect the removal of Mr. Mallory, the Confederate Secretary of the Navy, and of Mr. Memminger, the Secretary of the Treasury, were completely ineffectual, though these efforts continued to be made for several years. About six months before the fall of Richmond into the hands of the Federal forces, I succeeded in obtaining a vote upon a resolution declarative of want of legislative confidence in Mr. Memminger, which compelled the friends of that gentleman in the House to engage for him that he would resign immediately after the close of the session of Congress then in progress, if I would consent not to press my resolution to a final vote. This I cheerfully assented to, and in a few weeks thereafter Mr. Memminger gave place to Mr. Trenholm, of South Carolina, who proved himself to be a most competent and efficient officer, and a most meritorious and worthy gentleman.

Very great mischief notoriously resulted to the Confederate cause from the long retention in the office of commissary general of Colonel Northrop. This person is understood to be a native of South Carolina, and had spent some years in the city of Charleston anterior to the war as a practitioner of medicine upon the *vegetarian* system. Some mysterious circumstances, not heretofore explained, had in some way, many years previous to the commencement of the war, established relations of special amity and confidence between himself and Mr. Davis, in consideration of which he had been located in an official position for which he was in every way as utterly unfit as any human being could be well imagined to be. His appearance was most unprepossessing indeed; his manners were coarse, overbearing, and insulting; his temper was austere, crabbed, and irritating; he was utterly ignorant of the duties of the post assigned him, and was not at all solicitous to make himself acquainted with them. His self-esteem was the most inordinate that I have ever known any human being to possess, and no man at all capable of judging of such a matter would have regarded him as in all respects *compos mentis*. A general impression had long prevailed in Charleston that he was, in point of fact, more or less disordered in mind; and dur-

ing the three years that I occupied a seat in the Confederate Congress, I received numerous letters from citizens
of the highest respectability residing there, urging me, in
the warmest terms, to aid in displacing him from the position which he was so signally disgracing. I am not
prepared to assert any thing in regard to his pecuniary
honesty; but it is undoubtedly true that all over the
Confederate States he had men employed to purchase
supplies for his department of notoriously bad character,
not a small number of whom are known to have accu-
mulated large fortunes during the war, the names of some
of whom I could, were it necessary, quite easily specify,
having brought their iniquities heretofore to the view of
the Confederate Congress. The heartless tyranny practiced by this monster of iniquity in all the States of the
South, in connection with the system of forcible impressment established, has, I am persuaded, scarcely ever been
equaled. · His brutal indifference to the sufferings of the
Confederate soldiery, by all of whom he was most cordially detested; his indecent and habitual disregard of
the requisitions made upon his department, from time to
time, by the various military commanders with whom he
was necessarily thrown into contact; his open and notorious employment of disrespectful and contemptuous language in regard to those in official station to whom he
was legally subordinate, are matters upon which it would
be now superfluous to dwell. Yet he was retained in the
Commissary Department for four years, in utter contempt
of remonstrance, of complaint, and of direct and positive
accusations of delinquency. It is even true that Mr.
Northrop was not a *constitutional officer;* after the com-

mencement of the permanent Confederate government he
was never nominated to the Senate. But, though this
matter was brought to Mr. Davis's special notice by grave
proceedings in both houses of Congress, he still held on
to Northrop, nor did he ever deign to present his name to
the Senate for the sanction of that body up to the latest
moment of his own official existence.

When Mr. Benjamin was compelled to forego re-ap-
pointment to the secretaryship of war, Mr. Davis was persuaded to appoint to the vacant place a gentleman of rare
qualifications and of eminent moral worth—Mr. Randolph,
of Virginia, a grandson of Thomas Jefferson. During this
gentleman's occupancy of the department of war his conduct was eminently exemplary; his high ability was constantly displayed in the performance of his arduous official duties, his industry was most untiring, and he gave
the most indisputable evidence, every day and hour, of
his eminent virtues, and his disinterested devotion to the
cause which he had espoused. He was a man, though,
of singular independence of spirit; and, though sufficiently deferential toward those to whom he was officially responsible, yet he possessed too elevated a feeling of self-
respect, and too much regard for his own well-established
fame, to become the mere slave of a vain and arrogant
chief magistrate; so, in a short time, the public learned
with regret that General Randolph had resigned and gone
into private life, and that Mr. James A. Seddon, also a native of Virginia, had shown himself so indecently regardless of the honor of the "Ancient Dominion" as to consent to occupy the vacant post.

From a man who had been willingly inducted into office under such circumstances not much was to be reasonably expected, either of manly and efficient service or of official purity and disinterestedness. The career of Mr. Seddon, as Secretary of War, will long be remembered by all who ever entered the War Department while he sat enthroned therein with unmingled regret and indignation. It may be safely asserted that he did not possess one of the qualities needful to a creditable and useful performance of the duties which were now devolved on him. He was never able to learn even the ordinary routine of official business, and often scornfully declined attendance to matters of the most urgent importance. He was as arrogant and insulting to those who approached him in his official *sanctum*, as he was notoriously servile and fawning to his own executive chief. He evinced, from his very entrance into office, an utter disregard of all constitutional obligations; and in the exercise of the authority committed to him, he proved himself to be the most heartless and ruffianly tyrant whom I ever yet saw in the possession of official power. Though he had always been an ardent state-rights man *in profession*, up to the breaking out of the war, it soon became evident that he had never sincerely cherished the smallest regard for the principles embodied in the well-known state-rights creed; and he habitually trampled under foot, and without a blush upon his livid and atrabilious visage, all the anciently-recognized muniments of state sovereignty. I shall not waste time now by going into an elaborate specification of this man's multiplied offenses. It is perhaps sufficient to state that he enforced, with the most unfeeling rigor, all the most stringent and

Q

oppressive enactments of the Confederate Congress, in
connection with forcible impressment and conscription;*

* I seize the opportunity here presented of mentioning an instance of
the greatest atrocity, which I have not yet recorded, and which will be at
once seen to be curiously illustrative of the shameful disregard, now generally felt in official places, of all the recognized principles of civil liberty.
General Hindman, of Arkansas, who, when a very young man, had, in
the State of Mississippi, been a most noisy and unscrupulous advocate of
Jefferson Davis and secession at that time propounded—who had afterward gone to Arkansas, where he had led, for several years, a very turbulent and disreputable life, but, who, by force of party drill, had been sent for
a year or two to the Federal Congress—when the war broke out, was almost
immediately given a high military command, and was rapidly promoted,
until, as a major general, he was sent to the state of his own residence, for
the purpose of holding an important position there. This man, as his
own formal report to the War Department evidenced, finding, as he said,
that the very comprehensive provisions of the conscription law were not
quite comprehensive enough to suit his purposes, deliberately amplified
them by proclamation; declared martial law throughout Arkansas and
the northern portion of Texas, and demanded the services of all whom he
had thus illegally and tyrannically embraced in his own wide-sweeping
conscription list. All who refused to obey his mandate, as he expressly
confesses, were apprehended, subjected to trial by a military court appointed at the instant by Hindman himself, and when convicted, as a considerable number were, of an offense which he unblushingly acknowledges in
this same report were wholly unknown to the law of the land, he had
them executed, and, going even beyond the infernal Jeffreys himself in •
barbarity, he, as he also ostentatiously declares in that same report, took
care to be present to witness the dying agonies of his victims. This man
seized upon all the cotton and other property for which he had use (as he
boldly avows), burnt some, retained some, and appropriated a third portion to such purposes as he pleased. His cruelties were so enormous in
Arkansas that it became unsafe that he should remain there longer,
when he was brought across the Mississippi River, under the order of the
War Department, made president of a court of inquiry for the trial of
General Lovell, and, after having made such a report in that case as was
necessary to shield the officials in Richmond from blame in connection

that in many known instances he went very far beyond
the scope of these odious enactments, while in others he

with the capture of New Orleans, was immediately put in command of the
largest division in the Army of Tennessee, where he remained until, run-
·ning into collision with a more potential presidential favorite, *Bragg*, he
was relieved from command, and is reported to be now a wanderer in
some part of the Mexican republic. . I exposed all the enormities of this
wretch in open session in the Confederate Congress on more than one occasion, and took pains to have my exposition put in print, and yet could
I not persuade Mr. Davis or Mr. Seddon to take the slightest notice of
these fearful enormities.

I have incidentally alluded to General Bragg. This military commander first set the example of proclaiming martial law, which he did repeatedly, and upon the most unsatisfactory pretexts. I assert what I
know to be true—charged to be true on more than one occasion in the
Confederate Congress, and now stand prepared to establish, by the most
irrefutable proof, that he deliberately put to death, on repeated occasions,
without the least show of legal authority (even such authority as the legal
regulations existing under the Confederate government recognized), as
meritorious and valiant soldiers as he had under his command. He
evinced on all occasions, while he commanded the Army of Tennessee, an
utter disregard of all the established principles of constitutional freedom,
committed such excesses as a Sylla or a Marius would scarcely have ven- ·
tured upon, and yet, in spite of all that could be done, his removal from
command could not be effected until the Confederate cause had become
well-nigh utterly hopeless. On one occasion, in company with a majority of the Tennessee representatives and senators, I united in demanding the removal of General Bragg, and the substitution in his place of
General Joseph E. Johnston. A written communication had been addressed to the Confederate President requesting an interview, and desiring that it should be a *private one.* He had consented to see us at
a particular hour at his office (I could not have seen him elsewhere, as
I never once called at the presidential mansion while a member of the
Confederate Congress). We were received with sufficient politeness,
but we presently perceived that Mr. Hunter, of Virginia, and Mr. Barnwell, of South Carolina, were to be also present. I addressed these gentlemen, and suggested to them that as they seemed to have *precedence*

criminally relaxed the law in order to accommodate special friends or the members of his own family connection;
that he was an earnest advocate for the suspension of the
writ of habeas corpus, and that when this writ was suspended in a manner completely to uproot every thing
like civic jurisdiction in every part of the South, he eagerly took advantage of this condition of things to fill the
prison-houses every where with as good citizens as the
South contained, and to compel individuals to do military
duty, in violation of the most solemn governmental *com-
pacts.* This was especially true in regard to the six or
seven thousand volunteers from the State of Maryland,
who, after enlisting, without persuasion from any quarter,
in the Confederate service for *a specified period,* when this
period had expired were rudely seized upon by the myr-
midons of the War Department with a view to compelling
them to re-enlist, under the penalty, if they disobeyed the
mandate of the despot in whose hands they found themselves, of being tried and punished as for *desertion.* It is
even true, within my own knowledge, that when that

over us, we would withdraw until their business was dispatched. To this
they answered, "No, it is unnecessary," and took their seats between a
large table and the wall, near enough to hear all that might go on. Our
interview was very brief. Mr. Davis gave us to understand that the
change which we demanded should be made, and we withdrew. This,
by-the-by, was not done, and Bragg remained in command for many
months thereafter. I recollect that Major Henry, of Tennessee, inquired
of me, as we left the room, whether I thought that Mr. Hunter and Mr.
Barnwell had been requested by Mr. Davis to be present, in order to bear
witness to what might occur. To which I answered, that I would not undertake to decide; but, considering that we had been all treated most
disrespectfully, it was the last official visit that I should pay Mr. Davis, as
indeed it was. This surely needs no comment.

firm and upright judicial magistrate, Judge Haliburton, undertook in certain cases to grant writs of habeas corpus in behalf of some of those persecuted Marylanders, and manifested a disposition to do them simple justice as far, at least, as was in his power, Mr. Seddon evinced an open disregard even of the authority of the Confederate district judge, and that officer was even informed, in the columns of the recognized governmental organ (the Sentinel), which doubtless "spoke by the card," that the Secretary of War would pay no respect whatever to the most deliberate adjudications of the court in which he presided, touching the grave questions which had thus arisen before him for decision. And yet Mr. Davis retained this man in the office of secretary of war, amid continual indications of popular indignation and disgust, from month to month and from year to year; nor would he have been at last seen to vacate the official position which he had so long deeply dishonored, but for the undeniable fact that I had directly charged him, upon *recorded testimony*, that is to say, upon the evidences supplied by the books of his own department, of having caused to be paid to himself, by his own official subordinates, *forty dollars per bushel* for his whole crop of wheat for the year 1864, while he was, by the instrumentality of *forcible impressment*, compelling the farmers of North Carolina, Georgia, and other states, to yield up their wheat to the government officials at the inadequate price of from *seven to nine dollars in Confederate paper*. I made this exposition in the last speech which I delivered in the Confederate Congress. Mr. Seddon resigned the Department of War *the very next day*. As chairman of a special com-

mittee of the Confederate Congress, organized at my own instance, for the purpose of inquiring into cases of illegal imprisonment, I obtained from the superintendent of the prison-house in Richmond, under the official sanction of the Department of War itself, a grim and shocking cata-
logue of several hundred prisoners then in confinement therein, not one of whom was charged with any thing but *suspected political infidelity*, and this, too, not *upon oath* in a single instance. Before I could take proper steps to procure the discharge of these unhappy men, the second suspension of the writ of liberty occurred, and I presume that such of them as did not die in jail remained there until the fall of Richmond into the hands of the *Federal forces*.

It is a notorious and undeniable fact, that Mr. Seddon, as the incumbent of the War Department, did actually interfere, in the most rude and unfeeling manner, to prevent the passing beyond the Confederate lines of ladies of the highest respectability desirous only of carrying their infant female children to school in Maryland and other states, where the ordinary means of education yet existed, hoping in this way to save them from a portion of the worst consequences of the unfortunate war then in progress. This I assert upon my own personal knowledge of facts, and shall be content at present to state a single instance—that of Mrs. Ficklin, of Falmouth, in the State of Virginia—a lady of the highest social standing, and resident in the very neighborhood where Mr. Seddon had been himself born and reared to maturity.

Mr. Seddon had been, at one time, for several years a member of the Federal Congress, and in the tempestuous

period of 1850 I well remember him as a sectional factionist of the most extreme opinions. In the celebrated
Peace Conference of 1861, he signalized himself by going
beyond all other Southern members of that body in the
demand of new securities for slaveholding rights in the
South. He avowed himself to be wholly unsatisfied
with the provisions of the Crittenden Compromise, and
proposed several amendments to the Constitution in addition to the guarantee of slavery forever in all territories
south of 36° 30', one of which recognized the right of
peaceable state secession, and another, of which denied "the
elective franchise and the right to hold office, whether
federal, state, territorial, or municipal, to all persons who
were, in whole or in part, of the African race." Just before his appointment to the Department of War, he had
been very badly defeated for a seat in the Confederate
House of Representatives in the Petersburg district.

It is by no means just to the two houses of the Confederate Congress to suppose that there were no members
of that body who did not discern the fatal tendency of
affairs almost from the beginning of the contest, and
who did not strive energetically to arrest the march of
disastrous events. In both houses, I am glad to recollect that there were a considerable number of honest,
painstaking, and able legislators, whose public experience
had been considerable, whose literary attainments were
far from being contemptible, and whose oratorical powers would have commanded respect almost any where.
That there was too much inclination, both in the Confederate Senate and in the House of Representatives, to succumb to Mr. Davis's dictatorial will, may be admitted,

without attributing motives, at least to any very large
number of these individuals, of an unworthy and disreputable character; and however strange may have been
the action of the Confederate legislators toward the close
of their official career in Richmond, and however blinded they must be confessed to have shown themselves to
have been to occurrences which were then almost on the
eve of taking place—the *foreshadowings* of which, indeed,
were beginning to be most distinct and palpable in the
vista of the future—philosophy, tempered with generos-
ity and fraternal sympathy, must cheerfully exonerate
them from all harsh and ill-natured condemnation. Let
all these things now pass by forever; they *may* have
been, in the order of Providence, merely the means supplied by Divine Wisdom for the ultimate restoration of
that Union—of rights, of feelings, and of energies—established by the wisdom of the past, never more, as we must
hope, to be disturbed or endangered by the efforts of rebellious violence.*

---

* Before taking leave of the subject discussed above, I deem it proper
to offer, in this unimposing and somewhat unattractive form, a few miscellaneous observations, the presentation of which will at least serve to
gratify a reasonable curiosity apparently felt at this time in several quarters touching certain matters a good deal discussed of late.

1. The celebrated *Erlanger Loan*, the proposition to enlist in which
came to Richmond under the sinister auspices of Mr. John A. Slidell,
seemed to a considerable number of the members of the Confederate Congress to be a *speculative project*, adroitly set on foot chiefly for the benefit
of Messrs. Slidell, Benjamin, & Co., their aiders and abettors in the United
States and in foreign countries, and we therefore struggled most earnestly to defeat it by every expedient known to parliamentary tactics. By
the aid of the celebrated *ten-minutes rule* and the sitting with *closed doors*,
it was finally carried by a somewhat meagre majority in the House of

Early in the month of December, 1864, to all men of discernment and foresight in the city of Richmond, the

Representatives. The dissentient members filed an elaborate *protest* against this injudicious and unpardonable measure, which, it is hoped, will see the light one of these days. Those in Europe who are now complaining of severe pecuniary losses in consequence of having participated in this luckless scheme of finance will know whom to hold responsible.

2. The Confiscation Act was opposed from the first in the House of Representatives by a considerable number, including myself, alike upon the ground of its unconstitutionality, injustice, and impolicy.' This was carried also in *secret session*, under the abominable *ten-minutes* rule, which rule I labored in vain, session after session, to get repealed, but which was retained by the votes of individuals justly apprehensive of the censures of an outraged constituency, should all the dark machinations which had their origin in this disreputable *conclave* be ever made known through the public journals. The special supporters of Mr. Davis were always ready to go into secret session, a thing very easy to be effected, since a single member moving for it had it in his power to bring about the immediate closing of the doors.

At the very last session of the Confederate Congress the Confiscation Law was made still more cruel and onerous, at the instance of individuals who have since shown themselves more than willing to save their own beloved estates from the *forfeiture* to which they were formerly so ferociously inclined to subject others who chanced to differ from them conscientiously, both in reference to the *feasibility* and *propriety* of the scheme of revolution. I do not know when my feelings were more outraged than they were only a few weeks anterior to the vacation of my seat in the · Confederate Congress, by the heartless and unmanly attempt to confiscate the estates of all *absentees*, unless they *had* gone, or should thereafter go abroad with the consent of the government officials. This was intended mainly to operate upon Dr. Duncan, of New York, and others of that class, who had been sojourning for several years before the beginning of the war outside of the Confederate States, and who it was known had very large possessions in said states. It was confessedly designed, likewise, to reach the estates of certain ladies of considerable property who had thought proper to go to New York, to Philadelphia, or even beyond the ocean, for the purpose either of avoiding the horrors of internecine

Q 2

collapse of the Confederate cause appeared to be inevitable. There was only one possibility remaining that the

strife or for the suitable education of their infant children. In looking back to the past, I confess that I am yet full of surprise and indignation that persons professing to be civilized men and *Christians*, should have dared to attempt the perpetration of this double-damned iniquity.

3. It is well known that Mr. Davis and his cabinet were originally opposed to the Conscription Law. They were notoriously *dragooned* by a portion of the Confederate press into a recommendation of its adoption. But when this rank *centralizing* measure had been once put in operation, these gentlemen were not slow in perceiving how, by means of its rigid enforcement, and the general suspension of the writ of *habeas corpus*, they would be able to put down all opposition to their scheme of despotic domination. It is a remarkable fact that, even in the message of Mr. Davis, which first recommended to the Confederate Congress a resort to this anti-republican expedient, he declared that there had been no abatement whatever of the volunteering spirit, which still, he said, rather needed *repression* than *stimulation*. How strange must it not now seem to all reasonable men, that in a war *avowedly* commenced *by the people of the South for their own safety exclusively*, it should have been deemed allowable, even had the *volunteering spirit* then altogether disappeared, to *force* the same people, under the most harsh and dishonoring penalties, to continue the war after they should have themselves grown weary of its prosecution!

4. It is a fact worthy of notice, that nearly all the legislative enactments of the Confederate Congress most deleterious in their operation upon state-rights and popular freedom originated with ultra state-rights men, and ultra Democrats in profession. One of the most maniacal and astounding propositions brought forward in that unfortunate body was the one introduced about eighteen months ago by Mr. Barksdale, of Mississippi, which was a bill to establish *martial law generally* throughout the Confederate States. The peculiar relations existing between this individual and Mr. Davis fully justified the presumption that this latter personage had been duly consulted before the bringing into the legislative hall this worse than political *hydra*. Did the Mountain party in the French Revolution ever manifest more ferocity than was indicated in this movement? Posterity will hardly believe the statement, and yet is it absolute-

rushing tide of ruin could be staid even for a few weeks. It was thought by a few that the immediate restoration

ly true that the ultra secessionists, who professed to have brought on the war chiefly to *maintain the right of separate state secession*, were the first to deny the existence of any such right when certain movements were understood to be in progress in North Carolina looking to peaceful secession from the Confederate States themselves; and these persons urged most vehemently the putting the whole country under *military law*, in order to counteract all such attempts at withdrawal. I well remember that certain fiery zealots from the "Old North State" came to Richmond about two years ago, and openly urged the sending of a military force at once into that region, in order to suppress all efforts at counter-revolution. This course of proceeding was even urged upon me. What response I made to these *secession-anti-secession* worthies I shall leave to others to conjecture.

5. No one will doubt, ten years hence, that the only chance for the eventual success of the Confederate cause lay in the immediate purchase by the *newly-improvised government* of all the cotton and tobacco of the South in the beginning of the war, depositing it in safe and convenient localities, and dispatching certificates of deposit, properly authenticated, to Europe, for the raising of the requisite fiscal means for the prosecution of the war. Confederate paper had not yet depreciated; the Southern people had not yet become disgusted with the Confederate authorities at Richmond, and the Southern planters, it is known, were still generally willing to sell their cotton to the government for Confederate notes and bonds at from ten to twelve cents per pound. This policy was warmly urged upon Mr. Davis and Mr. Memminger, neither of whom could appreciate its wisdom; nor did Mr. Davis's Secretary of the Treasury cease to denounce and ridicule the project, denominating it "*soup-house legislation*," until cotton had risen to nearly one dollar a pound, and Confederate paper was circulating at the rate of four or five to one, and then this grand minister of finance commenced buying most lustily. Mr. Davis, it would seem, from certain published letters of his, did not cease to admire and extol Mr. Memminger's abilities as a financier up to the close of this remarkable struggle.

6. Mr. Pollard, in his "Third Year of the War," states that, after the celebrated Dahlgren raid occurred, "The Libby Prison was undermined,

of General Johnston to the command of the Army of
Tennessee, and the granting of authority to himself and

several tons of powder put under it, and the threat made that, if any dem-
onstration on Richmond such as Dahlgren's was ever again to occur,
the awful crime, the appalling barbarity would be committed of blowing
into eternity the helpless men confined in a Confederate prison." I had
before heard of this, but only as a vague and unauthorized rumor, and
I regret now to see this extraordinary fact asserted by one who is in
every way so well entitled to credence. I seize this opportunity of declaring my own oft-avowed condemnation of every branch of this worse than
Hunnic or Vandalic barbarity, including *raids* on defenseless cities, the
burning of them at midnight, poisoning in all its forms, and all other expedients not justified by the rules of civilized war. While on this subject,
I shall proceed to state some additional particulars alike in justice to the
dead and the living. I had known Colonel Dahlgren as a genteel and,
apparently, very amiable young man, several years before the breaking out
of the war. He was understood to have been in part brought up and educated at the house of his worthy and accomplished uncle, General Dahlgren, near the city of Natchez, in the State of Mississippi, and was repeatedly a visitant, in company with the latter, to the city of Nashville, and to
the celebrated Beersheba watering-place in that vicinage. I had the
pleasure of entertaining him, also, once or twice at my own residence in
Nashville. I will not undertake to say what changes the war may have
wrought in his heart and character, but I must be permitted to doubt
whether the genial and kind-mannered young man whom I knew so well
five years ago could, in so short a time, have become the horrible monster
that some over-excited persons have chosen to consider him. I have
never been willing to believe that the *raid* which he attempted on Richmond had for its object a tithe of the atrocities which have been charged,
nor have I ever regarded the evidence relied upon in support of this view
of the matter as entirely satisfactory. That he intended to deliver the
Union prisoners of war then held in Richmond, destroy, as far as he
should be able, all the warlike munitions and military supplies there ac-
cumulated, and seize and carry off Mr. Davis and his cabinet, can not be
doubted. That he designed a general massacre of the people of Richmond and the burning of that goodly city, or the summary execution of
Mr. Davis and his official associates, I must be permitted to doubt. The

General Forrest to raise, if practicable, a hundred thousand additional troops in the states of the South and

subject is of a very delicate nature, and I do not choose to state here all that I suspect in regard to the marvelous publications made at the time in regard to this extraordinary and startling affair. After several weeks had passed away, and the public mind seemed to be restored to its wonted repose, a letter was addressed to me by General Dahlgren (the gentleman above referred to), dated at Atlanta, Georgia, where, with his amiable family, he was then residing, calling my attention in a very touching manner to the recent decease of his nephew, and to the anxious wish of his brother, Admiral Dahlgren, that the dead body of his son should be restored to him by the Richmond authorities—the general presuming, as ho stated in his letter, that enmity toward his ill-fated nephew *must necessarily cease with his death.* This letter I immediately inclosed to Mr. Davis, not doubting that it would be at least accorded a respectful consideration by him, as the writer of it had, very early in the war, received a high military appointment at his hands. What action was taken upon the letter I never had the means of knowing. I must hope, though, for the honor of tho South, that Mr. Davis and his cabinet were not so shamefully unmindful of the principles of a high-toned humanity as to persist in keeping the dead body of this victim of an unnatural war long after the reception of this impressive epistle. If any one shall blame me for interposing on this occasion in behalf of the principles of civilized warfare, I shall submit to all that may be said in reproof quite as patiently as I did some two years ago to the harsh denunciations and ingenious falsifications to which I was then subjected for daring persistently to remonstrate against all needless maltreatment of Union prisoners of war. I am neither ashamed nor afraid to declare that I condemn all brutal treatment of military prisoners, by whomsoever ordered, countenanced, or executed ; and in a civil war, carried on between human beings of the same derivation and lineage, it is doubly atrocious, and I am confident that in this sentiment I am in perfect accord with ninety-nine hundredths of our whole national population. As to my conduct in endeavoring to secure the restoration of Ulric Dahlgren's mortal remains to his affectionate and grief-stricken father, he who disapproves it, I am sure, could hardly have made himself familiar with some of the most interesting examples which the page of history holds in preservation, nor even have read the thrilling account given by the Father

West, with which to face the advancing army of Sherman, might, at least for a short time, save Richmond
from falling into the hands of Grant. Should this city
be captured, nobody doubted that the struggle for Southern independence must immediately terminate. Prodigious efforts were made by night and by day to procure
the restoration of Johnston, but *Mr. Davis was inexorable;*
nor did he consent that this most able and gallant, but
deeply injured officer should return to that army of
which he was the idol until it was altogether too late for
any abilities whatever to retrieve the sinking cause.

Under these circumstances, I thought I saw that, unless
some early efforts to obtain peace should be made, a state
of things might arise which would be almost as calamitous as the permanent continuance of the war. I was satisfied that President Lincoln and his cabinet, if application should be made to them in season, would grant
terms of pacification to the South of a far more liberal
and beneficial character than were at all likely to be ob-

of Poetry himself of the visit of the aged Priam to the tent of the grim
Achilles, who, cruel and relentless as he is described to have been, did
not refuse the exanimate body of Hector to parental imprecations. Plu-
tarch tells us that it was Hercules, the renowned *slayer of monsters* and
remover of monstrosities, who first enforced the duty of humanity toward
the dead; and I trust that the day will never come when a disregard of
this duty will not be every where recognized as an unmistakable relic of
barbarism. This affair belongs to a class of matters which, in the present
inflamed state of the public mind, it is not prudent to dwell upon, but the
time is coming when it will be safe to disperse much of the mystery which
now veils the past. When that time shall have arrived, the curtain which
conceals certain transactions of enduring interest will be doubtless uplift-
ed by the hand of some man who will dare to speak *the truth, and the
whole truth, both as to men and their acts.*

tained, if nothing should be done in the way of procuring peace until Savannah, Charleston, Wilmington, and Richmond itself should have fallen, all of which, I felt assured, after conferring with some of the first military men on the continent, was both proximate and certain. I am not at all ashamed to confess that I gave my hearty consent to certain resolutions about this time introduced into the Confederate Congress by several gentlemen of great weight and intelligence, proposing to divide the responsibility of the movement tending to peace with the President. I will even acknowledge that each one of these peace propositions was shown to me before it was offered in the House of Representatives. When these had all signally failed, mainly in consequence of the overwhelming executive influence arrayed against them, I resolved still to do all in my power to stave off that general ruin which I could not but regard as imminent. I consulted freely with many of the most enlightened and influential men that the South then contained, including three of my own valued colleagues, Messrs. Atkins, Colyar, and Mcneese, and including also several military men of great eminence, and shaped my conduct accordingly. The fact was very well known to me that Mr. Davis and his friends were confidently looking for foreign aid, and from several quarters. It was stated in my hearing repeatedly, by several special friends of the Confederate President, that *one hundred thousand French soldiers* were expected to arrive within the limits of the Confederate States by way of Mexico; while it was more than rumored that a *secret compact*, wholly unauthorized by the Confederate Constitution, with certain Polish commissioners, who had

been lately on a visit to Richmond, had been effected,
by means of which Mr. Davis would soon be supplied
with some twenty or thirty thousand additional troops,
then refugees from Poland, and sojourning in several European states; which latter force, when it should arrive,
not being levied under congressional authority, would be
completely at the command of the President for any purpose whatever. I was perfectly satisfied that, should Mr.
Davis even consent to the sending of commissioners to
President Lincoln to treat for peace, he would so manacle
their hands by *instructions* as to render impossible all attempts at successful negotiation. It would be quite in
my power to show, did I choose to do so, that President
Lincoln had avowed himself willing to guarantee to his
fellow-citizens of the South peace on most liberal terms,
including *universal amnesty*, provided they would at once
relinquish their hostile attitude and return to their ancient allegiance.

The following copy of a pamphlet, addressed to my
own political constituents in Tennessee, and sent to them
in the month of March last from the city of London, is
here inserted, with a view of showing what were my objects, and the objects of those with whom I was acting at
this period in furtherance of peace.

"Golden Cross Hotel, The Strand,
London, February 24, 1865.

" To the Sovereign People of the State of Tennessee:
"When, fellow-citizens, a little less than two years ago,
you demanded that I should *continue* to represent you in
the Congress of the Confederate States, at a moment when
I had resolved, for various reasons of a most substantial

character, to repair once more to the walks of private life, I little thought that, in so brief a space, I should, in order to commune with you freely in regard to matters vitally associated with your honor and your happiness, be compelled to seek refuge in a foreign land, where, thanks to the wisdom and patriotism of the descendants of our noble Anglo-Saxon forefathers, freedom of speech and freedom of the press are yet inflexibly maintained, and where all valuable truth, connected either with politics, morals, science, or religion, may be boldly asserted and freely diffused. But such is the actual condition of things in both sections of my own dear native country at the present time, that I have found it necessary to pass to another hemisphere, that I might safely state to you facts, a knowledge of which is indispensable to your future welfare, and which, were I not to communicate to you in some form or other, you would doubtless regard me, and justly too, as a great official delinquent.

"Rumor has doubtless some time ago informed you, in her own vague and ambiguous manner, that I have for several months past altogether disconnected myself from the legislative councils of the Confederate States, and the reasons which have influenced me in thus (*voluntarily*) declining farther to represent a people whom I so much love and honor, and who have in various ways placed me under such profound obligations to them, it is more than probable have been, at least in some confused and distorted manner, already communicated to many of you. It is my purpose on this occasion to open to your view the whole truth of the matter, in order that I may be thus saved from the unmerited disapproval of those whose favorable and friendly judgment I prize far above the smiles and commendation of all the crowned monarchs of earth. "When you first deputed me to Richmond, nearly four years ago, you well knew the political principles by which my conduct as your representative would be guided, and were not at all ignorant of what my action had formerly been in connection with all the great public questions which had occupied the popular mind in the United States for more than twenty years past. You knew that in 1850, that most trying period in American history, I had proved in every possible way my entire devotion to the Federal Union, and my zealous and unbending opposition to every thing in the shape of *sectionalism*, whether making itself manifest either in the North or in the South. You knew that, in harmony with the examples of Virginia and North Carolina, Maryland, Kentucky, Missouri, and Arkansas, I had, as nearly the whole population of Tennessee besides had done, refused all connection with the perilous scheme of secession, projected by certain political zealots many years ago, which had been defeated (most signally) when an effort was made to carry it into practical execution in the year 1851, but which, notwithstanding, had been still secretly cherished in the bosoms of its hot-headed and visionary devotees, until, about six years since, these wildly adventurous personages came to the conclusion that the period had at last arrived when a few ingenious expedients, easy to be devised and put in effective execution by such skillful architects of mischief as they (very justly too) considered themselves to be, would be sufficient to bring about, in connection with the presidential election of 1860, the perfect fruition of all for which they had so long been struggling. When, without any earnest solicitation on my part, you sent me to Rich-mond as the representative of your opinions and the cham-pion and defender of your interests, you knew that I had as little in common with the boasted secession leaders as any other public 'man in the South; that I had earnestly opposed all the incipient steps which had led to the fear-ful state of things then existing; that I had openly de-nounced, in every part of the United States which I could reach, in 1860, the conduct and motives of nearly all the prominent actors in the gloomy yet ludicrous tragi-come-dy of national ruin then enacting; that I had on numer-ous occasions solemnly warned my Southern fellow-coun-trymen every where that the breaking up of the Federal Union would be followed by a bloody civil war, by the destruction of slavery, and the general devastation of the South; and, finally, that I had never fully acquiesced in the propriety of our entering into the contest now in progress, until the Southern senators and representatives in the Federal Congress had, with a want of wisdom and true moral courage unprecedented in the world's history, ingloriously vacated their seats in that body, and (doubt-less in accordance with a plan previously agreed upon among them) hastened to the city of Montgomery, framed a new Constitution of government, and taken all the need-ful steps for the bringing on of a war, without the im-mediate commencement of which they well knew their scheme of disunion would turn out to be altogether im-practicable.

"Under such circumstances, and with the fullest knowl-edge of them on your part, I repeat, I was dispatched to

Richmond, and entered the Confederate Congress in the month of February, 1862. Whether my course in that body since has been honest, independent, and capable, I shall leave you to judge. My general course as a legislative functionary is doubtless already familiar to most of you. My early and persistent attempts to effect a remodeling of the wretched cabinet by whom I found Mr. Davis surrounded, which attempts were crowned in the end with perhaps as much of success as could have been reasonably anticipated; the exposition of rank official corruption which from time to time I have felt constrained to make; the firm and unyielding opposition which I have uniformly presented to the shameful efforts of Mr. Davis and his servitors to undermine the public liberties and establish a despotism upon their ruins; the zeal with which I have labored to supply your suffering soldiers in the Confederate armies with every thing necessary to their comfort and efficiency; the earnest and seasonable vindication of certain of our most meritorious military commanders when heartlessly and wickedly assailed by Mr. Davis and his *employés*—the merits of which com- manders are now universally admitted; the untiring industry which I have displayed in the arraignment of incompetent generals with a view to their dismissal—the egregious demerits of whom no one now denies—all these things, I am sure, are already fully known to you, and upon them I need not now expatiate. At length (three months ago), owing mainly to the gross and undeniable mismanagement of the military and civil concerns of the Confederate States by Mr. Davis and his cabinet associates, abetted and sustained by an incompetent and servile

Congress, it became evident to every man of discernment
with whom I held intercourse that unless an early and
an honorable peace could be speedily effected, the South
would be inevitably ruined. Perceiving that Mr. Davis
was bent upon a farther prosecution of the war, for purposes which I knew to be of a character wholly selfish,
after freely consulting with the best and wisest men whom
I met, I resolved to lose no time in introducing resolutions
in the House of Representatives looking to immediate action on the part of Congress itself with a view to securing
a termination of the war. These resolutions receiving no
favor in a body notoriously, to some extent, under executive control, and other resolutions, having the same object
in view, brought forward upon consultation with me by
several worthy members of the House having met with
a similar fate, I deemed it necessary to make the somewhat unusual experiment which will be presently explained to you.

"Before I enter farther into this business, though, I
must be allowed to say, in justification of my subsequent
conduct, that the condition of Confederate affairs seemed
to me to be at the moment almost hopeless. The unwise
action of President Davis in removing General Joseph E.
Johnston from the command of the Army of Tennessee,
and sending General Hood upon an objectless errand to
the neighborhood of the city of Nashville, had evidently
compromised most thoroughly the only military force
which could be seasonably made available for the defense
of the whole country west of the Alleghany Mountains
and east of the Mississippi River, and had opened at the
same time the States of Georgia, Alabama, South Caro-

lina, and North Carolina to the invading forces of the
United States, under the command of General Sherman.
It was obvious to me, as I openly declared in my place
in Congress—at a time, too, when Mr. Davis and his sim-
ple-hearted admirers were predicting far different results
—that the city of Savannah would very soon fall into the
hands of General Sherman, and that the capture of Charleston, Branchville, Wilmington, and even Richmond itself,
could not long be delayed. Meanwhile, it was equally
evident that the Confederate government, in all its departments, was most rapidly losing the public confidence, and
becoming, indeed, positively odious. A series of legislative enactments had passed, under strong executive pressure, which left no hope of the preservation of popular
freedom in the states of the South, however successful we.
might be in the prosecution of the pending war. President Davis, in his regular annual message, had openly and
formally proposed a measure, apparently very much favored at the time by his supporters in the two houses of
Congress, as well as by the leading newspapers, known
to be specially affiliated with his administration, which
virtually relinquished the maintenance of what is known
as African slavery, and had deliberately asserted the power of the Confederate government to execute a sweeping
system of emancipation without even asking the consent
of the states within whose limits this system existed. The
Confederate financial system was clearly in a state border-
ing on *collapse*. A new Federal Congress was to come
into existence on the 4th of the coming March, which it
was known would be composed of *materiel* far less favorable to the granting of just and liberal terms of pacifica-

tion to the South even than the present Congress, though
it was also known that this body was proceeding with all
possible celerity to amend the Federal Constitution itself
(in the precise manner, though prescribed in that instrument) so as to bring about the immediate extinction of
African slavery throughout all the states constituting the
Federal Union. I saw, most plainly and painfully, that.
no time was to be lost if an honorable and advantageous
settlement with the North was desired, and I determined,
in pursuit of this object, not to stickle at mere *formalities*
of any sort; and, accordingly, under the deliberate advice, yea, at the earnest solicitation of some of the most
patriotic and statesmanlike personages that the Confederate States can boast, I entered upon the *experimental* expedient already referred to, a more particular account of
which will now be given. I set out from Richmond about
the 20th of December just passed, in company with my
wife, who had a passport from the Richmond authorities
empowering her to return to our residence in the city of
Nashville. On reaching the Potomac River, in the county
of Westmoreland, I addressed the following letter to the
Speaker of the House of Representatives, to which I now
ask your special attention:

    " ' *On the Bank of the Potomac, in sight of the Birthplace* }
         of Washington, December 24, 1864.   }

    " ' *Honorable Thomas S. Bococke, Speaker of the House*
         of Representatives:

    " 'SIR,—In an hour or two, if some unseen impedi-
ment shall not arise to defeat the execution of my present design, I shall cross the majestic river upon the banks
of which repose the ashes of my forefathers for many

generations past, and visit the city of Washington for
the purpose of ascertaining whether or not it is practicable to obtain for the people of the Confederate States an
early and an honorable peace, after the most bloody and
exhausting struggle of arms which has occurred in modern times, and in all respects the most deplorable that has
yet found record upon the page of history. No human
being save myself is responsible for this movement, nor
should I have undertaken it but for the notorious fact
that the two executive departments at Washington City
and at Richmond have relations with each other which
render it almost impossible that regular diplomatic intercourse should occur between them, and but for the additional fact that the two houses of the Confederate Congress seem to be altogether unwilling to do any thing
calculated to bring about a cessation of hostilities, and
the restoration of peace and amity between those who, in
my deliberate judgment, should never have allowed themselves to be drawn into a war so unnatural, and even
fratricidal in its character—so destructive of the best interests of civilization and Christianity—and which, if it
shall continue to be prosecuted for four years more, must
inevitably, from the natural operation of war itself, result
in the establishment of two of the most grinding despotisms that the world has yet known. Should I succeed
in my present undertaking, my country and the cause of
freedom will be materially benefited; should I fail, discredit, ridicule, and even contempt will be most surely-
visited upon me in full measure; even many sensible and
good men will recognize me as a mere visionary project-
or; while the envious, the illiberal, the malevolent—the

ignoble time-servers of the period—the slavish idolators
of power—will not scruple to denounce me as a traitor to
what is known as the Confederate Government. For all
this I am prepared, and I am likewise prepared to undergo trial for alleged treason to the government of the
United States, should those now occupying the seats of
authority in Washington City deem this the sort of treatment which should be awarded to a disinterested and
voluntary embassador of peace. I hope that it will not
appear either vainglorious or egotistical in me to declare
farther that, should it be my fate to die upon the scaffold
in consequence of undertaking to execute a mission so
fully approved by my own conscience, and so cordially
sanctioned by some of the wisest and most virtuous men
now upholding the Confederate cause, I feel, notwithstanding (though my sufferings will probably awaken but
little of commiserative sympathy in any quarter), that, in
passing from the stage of mortal existence, I shall be able
sincerely to exclaim in the language of classic poesy,

> " " "Dulce et decorum est pro patria mori."

I have the honor to ask that you will do me the justice
to lay this communication before the House over which
you preside, in order that such action may be taken in the
premises by the members thereof as they shall deem ad-
visable. Should it be decided by them that expulsion
from that body is necessary to the maintenance of its
corporate dignity, I beg you be assured that Aristides himself did not more serenely submit to the doom of *ostracism* than I shall to such punitory sentence, at the hands
of those with whom it has been my fortune to be associ-

R

ated for the last three years of unremitted toil and suffering, as they shall choose to inflict.   ·
     " 'I have the honor to be your obedient servant,
                                   " 'H. S. FOOTE.'

     "To this letter I subsequently appended a postscript,
in which, for reasons stated therein, I made known my
resignation of the seat in Congress then occupied by me.
Not succeeding in passing the Potomac River as I had expected, I proceeded to the neighborhood of Occoquan
Creek, in the county of Prince William, whence it was
my intention to proceed to the city of Washington, for
the purposes named in the above letter to Mr. Bococke,
when I was arrested by certain military persons acting
under Confederate authority, and was carried to the city
of Fredericksburg, where I remained in *military custody*
for nearly a week, and was finally reduced to the necessity of applying for a writ of *habeas corpus* with a view to
my enlargement. You have doubtless heard that I was
immediately released from prison by the *fiat* of the learned and eminent judicial functionary before whom I was
carried, and that I proceeded afterward, without delay,
to the hall of the House of Representatives in Congress,
and delivered a speech in vindication of my character
and motives before a large and evidently approving audience, with the exception only of those illiberal and heartless miscreants who, in my absence, had presumed to assail me, but who, when they found me once more in their
presence, and ready to hold them, face to face, to a just
responsibility, most disgracefully shrank from every thing
like manly contest with the individual whom they had,

at the bidding of their imperial master, so basely attacked with unjust and malignant charges which they well knew to be wholly unfounded. On concluding this, the *last* harangue certainly which I shall ever make in that *mob-bish* assemblage known as the Congress of the Confederate States, and after drawing up, at the request of numerous friends, the remarks which had fallen from me on this extraordinary occasion for publication, I proceeded, with-out delay, to execute my original scheme of seeking access to the Washington authorities. For this purpose, I traveled, under singularly uncomfortable circumstances, in the coldest weather that has occurred in Virginia for many years (being sometimes on rail-cars, sometimes on horseback, and sometimes even on foot), until finally I reached the head-quarters of Brigadier General Devens of the Federal Army, to whom I reported myself, unfolded frankly the objects of my journey to Lovettsville, where I had found him located, and asked for such facilities for corresponding with those in power in Washington City as he might feel justified in affording me. This courteous officer at once dispatched a telegram to General Sheridan, his superior in command, whose head-quarters were in the town of Winchester, which last-named officer, with-out delay, after communicating with the official author-ities in Washington, and acting under their instructions, directed one of his staff to call on me at Lovettsville and receive any communication which I might be inclined to address to official personages in Washington, and also to bear the same to its place of destination. I sat down im-mediately, and, in a hurried manner, drafted the following letter to Mr. Seward:

" ' *Lovettsville, January* 30, 1865.

" ' *Hon. Wm. H. Seward, Secretary of State of the United States:*

" ' Sir,—I have just received information that I shall be allowed to send a communication addressed to the authorities in Washington City touching the very delicate and important matters concerning which it is the purpose of the journey I am now making, to confer, if permitted to do so, with yourself and those officially associated with you in the administration of governmental affairs. I assure you that this mode of conferring with you is, in my judgment, far preferable, for various reasons, to any other that could have been adopted. My object in approaching Washington you will find very explicitly set forth in a letter addressed by me to the Hon. Thomas S. Bococke, Speaker of the House of Representatives of the Confederate Congress (of which body I have *voluntarily* ceased to be a member), a copy of which letter is herewith transmitted. On reading the communication to Mr. Bococke, you will see that I am alone actuated in making this effort to hold some interchange of views with the authorities at Washington in regard to the means of terminating this unhappy war, by an earnest and patriotic desire for peace and its attendant blessings, of which for four years past our dear native land has been so unhappily deprived.

" ' To you, sir, it is unnecessary for me to say that I had no hand whatever in the *origination* of that fierce and bloody contest now in progress. In 1850, in the Senate of the United States, of which august legislative body we were both members, I supported, with such moderate ability as I possessed, but with a zeal unsurpassed by none, the system of wise and equitable *adjustment* of the then outstanding *sectional* questions which had generated so much of unfraternal feeling between the North and the South. In 1851, upon the very issue of *Union or Disunion*, I had the honor of defeating for the office of Governor of the State of Mississippi the personage now known as President of the Confederate States. From that period up to the actual breaking out of hostilities between the states of the South and those of the North, though in a private station, I constantly exerted myself in every possible mode to suppress sectional irritation, and to prevent those fearful consequences we are all now so painfully realizing. To the *Kansas-Nebraska Bill*, the *Lecompton Constitution Bill*, and all kindred measures calculated to awaken sectional strife, I presented a steady and unyielding opposition. To the proposal to reopen the African slave-trade, agitated in certain localities of the South a year or two before the commencement of the war, I presented, as some doubtless yet remember, somewhat more than a calm and decided opposition. I had no hand whatever in 1860 in giving to the Democratic presidential platform a *sectional* and *aggressive* aspect, believing as I did that such a measure was likely to be productive of disunion and civil war, and that it was more certain, if possible, to uproot and to destroy the domestic institutions of the South, as Henry Clay (that august apostle of peace and union) had so emphatically predicted in your presence and mine in 1850. When Mr. Lincoln was elected to the presidency in 1860, I was *not* one of those who thought and said that this occurrence justified the attempt, immediately made by the secession *managers*, to break up the Federal Union. I was *not* a member of the celebrated Montgomery Convention, nor in the least degree a party to the counsels in which that ill-starred assemblage originated.

"'Until war was already raging, and until Virginia, the venerated mother of states, had resolved to enter into that war, Tennessee and Tennesseeans declined all connection with what they deemed and have ever deemed an unwise and dangerous enterprise; and when we did (either wisely or unwisely) finally resolve to take part in this fearful conflict, we did so with most painful reluctance, and *chiefly*, as we honestly avowed at the time, *in defense of our* brethren of the cotton-growing states, exposed, as we saw them most plainly to be, to the danger of being, in a few weeks or months at most, overrun and utterly ruined. As a member of the Confederate Congress for three years past, though doing all in my power, as I am not ashamed to confess, to place in the hands of President Davis all the means of defending the South against the large invading armies sent within her confines, yet never did I give a single vote calculated unduly to protract hostilities or to impart needless asperity to the pending conflict. I had no hand whatever in fixing a system of *forcible conscription* upon the people and states of the South, or in *confiscating* the estates of those who did not choose, for conscientious reasons (which I could not help appreciating), to bear arms against the government established by their venerated fathers. Not a session of the Confederate Congress has passed during which I have not done all in my power to bring about, if possible, a termination of the war alike honorable to both the parties to it.

"'About two months ago, when I became thoroughly satisfied that Mr. Davis and his associates were bent on establishing a despotism under *foreign* protection, and had determined never to consent to any peace except one founded on the overthrow of republican institutions, I resolved, in the most open manner too, to denounce the conspirators against the freedom of my fellow-citizens of the South and the heartless betrayers of the most sacred of earthly trusts, to resign my seat in the Confederate Congress, and seek refuge in some foreign land, where I might in quiet mourn over the ruin of my country and the desolation of a land once the abode of liberty, of prosperity, and of all earthly felicity. I thought it my duty, though, ere I should forever abandon a country and a people so dear to my affections, to make one more manly and earnest effort for an early and honorable peace. Hence my present attitude.

"'I now have the honor to say, for myself and for a large number of the most weighty and influential statesmen that the South contains, and, as I have good reason to believe, in accordance with the wishes also of a very large majority of the sovereign people of the Southern States, whether in or out of the Confederate armies, that we, the Conservatives of the South, are ready and anxious to enter once more into fraternal union with our fellow-citizens of the North; that we are resolved, if an opportunity of doing so *honorably* shall be afforded us, to withdraw at once from all political connection with the government now located in the city of Richmond, and to place ourselves and all we hold dear once more under the protection of the flag of our fathers.

"'No one knows better than I do that no such pacification as that which I now propose can ever come from Mr. Davis. His official position and his devotion to his own selfish schemes of individual aggrandizement alike forbid it. But let President Lincoln issue a formal *proclamation*, addressed *to the people of the Confederate States*, offering to them complete *amnesty* for the past, and a full restoration of the constitutional rights which they formerly enjoyed, and they will immediately hold Conventions in all of the said states and vote themselves back into the Federal Union, calling home their troops at once, and leaving Mr. Davis to enjoy, as he shall be able to do, the despotism which he has established, together with such *foreign protection* for himself and his ignoble projects as it may be in his power to secure.

"'There seems to me to be but one difficulty in the way of thus bringing this war to a close, and that stands connected with the *slavery* question—a question which has undoubtedly assumed, as was reasonable to have been expected, several new aspects during the present war. I should hope that, in consideration of the manifold advantages of such a peace as I have proposed (including, of course, the future enforcement of what is known as the *Monroe doctrine*), our brethren and fellow-citizens of the North would be inclined, through the action of the Federal government, to deal with us *liberally* and kindly. Consider, if you please, that the fate of slavery has been sealed by the operation of the war itself; that Maryland is now a free state, and Missouri likewise; that Kentucky, Virginia, Tennessee, North Carolina, and Arkansas are sure in a few years, *by their own voluntary action*, to adopt a system of emancipation; and that, in all probability, before the close of the present century, slavery will nowhere exist upon the continent. Can you not afford, then, to leave it where the Federal Constitution left it?

" ' If, though, circumstances exist which render such a plan of settlement *impossible*, then I am prepared to say, in behalf of those whom I represent, that we will agree to such a change of the Federal Constitution as will secure the entire extinction of slavery on the *first day of January*, 1900, and which will provide also for the freedom of all persons of African blood who shall be born after the *first day of January*, 1890.

" ' I shall not, in this very hasty letter, enlarge upon this scheme of settlement, or undertake to point out all the happy consequences which appear to me as likely to result from its adoption. Nor shall I undertake to depicture the *glory* which will be assuredly achieved by those who shall be prominently concerned in the consummation thereof—"*I speak unto wise men; judge ye what I say!*"

" ' In conclusion, I have to declare that if, as I have never heretofore believed, but as has been by certain persons diligently inculcated in the South, *subjugation*, instead of *fraternal pacification*, is intended by those who now bear rule in Washington City, I shall have to ask that (provided always you do not desire to try me as a criminal offender, an ordeal not altogether unanticipated by me, and from which assuredly I shall not shrink) you will be kind enough to send me such a *passport* as will

R 2

enable me to go to some foreign country without delay, being utterly unwilling to witness the unimaginable hor-rors of which the present year of this most unnatural and impolitic war can not but be productive.

"'If what I have here suggested (necessarily in a most hurried and imperfect manner) should have the good for-tune to command a favorable consideration, I stand ready to make such farther revelations, both as to *facts* and *per-sons*, as will leave no doubt upon the minds of President Lincoln and his constitutional advisers that ample facil-ities exist for the bringing about, in the short period of forty days too, such a *counter-revolution* as is above refer-red to. All that I desire is to receive *assurance* that the information which I deem it proper, for reasons alike of *prudence and of honor*, to hold for the present *in reserve*, if imparted, will conduce to the restoration of peace and the re-establishment of the Federal Union, in a manner and upon terms consistent with the present honor and future safety of the South, and I will at once proceed to make full disclosures.

"'Hoping soon to receive some response to this com-munication, I have the honor to be your obedient serv-ant,   H. S. FOOTE.'

"In about five days after the transmission of the above letter to Mr. Seward, I received, at the hands of the mili-tary officer through whom I had addressed him, the fol-lowing reply:

(*Memorandum.*)

"'*Department of State, Washington, January* 31, 1865.

"'A communication addressed to the Secretary of

State by Henry S. Foote, an insurgent who has voluntarily come within the military lines, and is held in custody
within Major General Sheridan's command, has been received and has been submitted to the President of the
United States. Any farther information which the prisoner may think it proper to impart to the government
may be communicated in the same manner as the communication which is now acknowledged.

" 'Major General Sheridan will, if Mr. Foote shall
choose, pass him back within the insurgent lines, or will
send him forward to Major General Dix at New York,
who will be instructed to allòw him to pass without unnecessary delay beyond the jurisdiction of the United
States, not to return during the continuance of the war
without leave from this Department.

(Signed),   " ' WILLIAM H. SEWARD.'

" On perusing this letter of Mr. Seward, I came at once
to the conclusion (I hope without sufficient ground) that
nothing that I could in addition say, either to himself or
President Lincoln, could, in the delicate and embarrassing situation in which they found themselves, at all avail
in stopping the deplorable effusion of precious American
blood—the terrible destruction of property and national
character, and the extinction of the once fondly-cherished
confraternal ties between those who ought yet to be
friends and brethren, both in feeling and in action, and I
therefore promptly announced my intention to proceed
at once to the city of New York and report myself to
General Dix, as Mr. Seward's letter directed. I 'set out
accordingly for the Empire City of the North, accompa-

nied by the gentlemanly young military officer already referred to. We arrived there on the evening of the 5th instant, and next morning called on General Dix at his head-quarters, who received me with marked respect and affability. I found him fully advised of the correspondence (if it could be really so called) which had been taking place between Mr. Seward and myself, and of the privilege which had been accorded me of going abroad, if I chose to do so. Intermediate reflection, though, had satisfied me that it was my duty, as a true friend to peace, and as a faithful agent of those at whose bidding I had taken it upon myself to become a *mediator* between the parties contestant, to make one more effort for the attainment of the desired end. I therefore requested General Dix to forward the following additional letter to Mr. Seward:

"'*New York, February* 6, 1865.

"' *Hon. Wm. H. Seward, Secretary of State:*

"'Sir,—Your communication of the 31st ultimo, headed "*Memorandum*," reached me at Lovettsville, in the State of Virginia, on the day before yesterday. There was something in the style and spirit of that document which I confess discouraged me not a little, and induced me almost to despair of being able to attain any beneficial end by communicating with you farther upon the very interesting subject to which I had previously called your attention. But, on farther reflection, in consideration of the vast public interests involved, and the fearful consequences which are, in my judgment, sure to result from the farther prosecution of the pending war, I have concluded, with your consent, to offer, in this form, a few

additional observations, which will, I trust, be at least received in the disinterested and patriotic spirit in which
they are presented.

" 'Though it is true that I am at this moment a "prisoner" (a *voluntary* one) in the hands of the government
with which you stand so honorably connected, and in the
establishment of which my own venerated ancestors participated, yet it is, as I conceive, neither just nor gracious
to refer to me as being *at present* "*an insurgent*," seeing
that, as I have heretofore endeavored to explain, I am no
longer, in any sense, a *participant* in the war now waging
against the government of the United States, and have,
some time ago, voluntarily and deliberately disconnected
myself, for the gravest and most satisfactory reasons (publicly assigned at the time), from the monstrous and intolerable despotism now existing in the city of Richmond
under the name of the government of "the Confederate
States of America." I beg you to be assured that no one
could be more fully advised than I am that Mr. Davis,
and those officially associated with him, have most shamelessly and criminally abandoned, and trampled under
foot, all the principles and objects for the maintenance
or furtherance of which they had heretofore avowed to
the world that it had become necessary to *secede* from the
Federal Union, and in the absence of which pretext for a
measure so insane and ruinous it is certain they would
never have been able to delude a generous and confiding
people into a conflict so palpably *unequal* in its character,
with a government, too, beneath the paternal shelter of
which all their rights and liberties had been so long and
so efficiently protected and guaranteed. I should not

now be addressing you did I not know of a verity that
state-rights and state sovereignty no longer exist south
of the Potomac River; that in that once happy but now
forlorn region freedom of speech, freedom of the press,
the right of jury trial, and, in fact, all the muniments of
civil liberty most highly prized in countries actually free,
are completely prostrated; that corruption and imbecil-
ity sit grimly enthroned where it was once fondly hoped
that virtue and ability would exercise supreme sway, and
that a selfish, hypocritical, and tyrannical executive chief,
unblushingly sanctioned and sustained by a servile and
incompetent Congress, has well-nigh deprived a high-spirited and eminently chivalrous people of all ground of
hope as to their own future safety and happiness.   The
egregious mismanagement of all the departments of government; the general spread of demoralization in all official circles; a series of the most appalling reverses, the
greater number of which it is evident might, with the
proper exercise of circumspection and energy, have been
easily avoided, and nearly every one of which is directly
traceable to the unpardonable intermeddling of a vain
and obstinate president, who, in some unaccountable way,
has become possessed of the unfounded notion that he is
himself a man of superior military capacity; the unsea-
sonable and injudicious displacement of military commanders of real ability and high merit in other respects,
to make way for others who had but little claim to respect, save such as may arise from their known devotion
to him whose smile is the sure guarantee of promotion,
and whose frown is the certain precursor of official degradation—these causes, conjoined with a multitude of

others quite easy to be specified, a detail of which on this occasion is not at all necessary, have at length compelled the people of the Confederate States, alike in the army and out of it, to relinquish all hope of separate independence under the management of Mr. Davis, who is, notwithstanding, fixed upon them irremovably for the next three years by the Constitution itself to which he owes his authority.

" ' Indeed, I am fully prepared to establish the fact, by testimony of the most reliable character, that a large majority of the more enlightened citizens of the South have at last come to the conclusion, in which I confess that I do for one most fully concur, that, should they be ever so successful in the prosecution of the war now in progress, they would find themselves at the end of it an enslaved and wretched people, and that *Southern independence*, at one time so thoughtlessly coveted and so zealously striven for, would be, if attained, precisely the most deplorable calamity which could possibly befall them; since they deem it now most clear that separate independence would of necessity imply continuous *border* wars; the keeping on foot of two antagonist standing armies for protection against territorial invasion, constantly in such a condition of things to be apprehended; and ultimately, perchance even very soon, the establishment of two of the most relentless despotisms that have ever existed. These melancholy views, I assure you, have become of late very general in the South, where even the very name of *secession* has recently grown odious, and where Davis and his wicked comrades in mischief are fast coming to be hated and distrusted; where, indeed, a complete *counter-revolution* would be inevitably seen to occur immediately, could it be in some way or other sat-' isfactorily ascertained that it was not really the intention of President Lincoln and his constitutional advisers to *subjugate* and *enslave* those with whom they are now contending in arms. Let me here repeat, that if, with the ostensible consent of the states and people of the North, President Lincoln should conclude to issue such a proclamation as I have heretofore described, tendering amnesty, gradual emancipation, etc., etc., the influential and efficient public men, in behalf of whom I am empowered to speak, and in accordance with whose earnest solicitation I am now acting, will undertake to bring about such counter-revolution at once, by conventional action, against the Davis despotism, and guarantee the restoration of Federal authority, thus putting an end to this most grievous and sanguinary struggle, and restoring once more cordial amity and good-fellowship among those from whose bosoms these sentiments have been long since banished.

"'I beseech you not to be persuaded to doubt the ef- fectual execution of the pledge here given by the fact that President Davis and his policy are at present appar- ently sustained by a majority in the two houses of the Confederate Congress, which bodies are not, and never have been, and never now can be, the reliable exponents of Southern public sentiment. I solemnly aver that in the declaration I am now making I am in unison with the judgments and wishes of the great mass of the South- ern people, who will cordially unite with me, upon the terms and conditions specified, in restoring at once the authority of the Federal government over all Southern territory.

" ' The late experiment at *pacification* reported to have
been essayed upon the soil of the "Ancient Dominion"
by Messrs. Stephens, Campbell, and Hunter, should, in my
judgment, by no means discourage the true friends of
peace. Could it, indeed, have been reasonably expected
that these worthy gentlemen, however abounding in qualifications of every sort, and however desirous to behold
an early termination of the war upon almost any honorable terms (as I chance to know that at least two of them
do), would be permitted by Mr. Davis to reach the designated place of *conference* except under such stringent *instructions* as would necessarily prevent them from either
proposing or acceding to any terms of pacification which
could by any possibility in the least degree compromise
the position and plans of their selfish and intriguing principal ? Could Mr. Davis himself be expected to consent,
through Messrs. Stephens, Campbell, and Hunter, to any
terms of settlement which would forever do away with
the *soi-disant* Confederate government, and thus bring to
naught his long-cherished notions of imperial greatness ?

" ' You will allow me to suggest farther, that it seems
to me that it would have been not less unreasonable to
expect that the *ultra pro-slavery men* of the South, Mr. Davis, Mr. Hunter, *et id omne genus*, who had so long and so
fiercely made the universal establishment and maintenance of African slavery throughout all the vacant territory of the old Union not only a test of party fidelity,
but a *sine qua non* also to the continued existence of that
very Union itself, and who had so recently, and with such
a fanciful ambition for scenic display, abdicated their
seats in the Federal Congress avowedly because they fear-

ed that Mr. Lincoln's election to the presidency, though in a perfectly constitutional mode, would in some way compromise their favorite institution, would now be found acquiescing with any thing like a graceful and becoming readiness in the overthrow of slavery in all the states of the South, under circumstances which will more than justify the future historian of this unhappy struggle in fixing upon themselves the responsibility of having initi-ated measures which have alone generated the sad neces-sity of submitting to a fate which but a limited amount of foresight and practical good sense would have so easily averted..

" ' The sovereign people of the South, in behalf of whom I am now addressing you, do, on the other hand, however painfully, recognize the existing condition of things as one from which, though they had no special agency in producing it, there are no present means of es-cape ; and being therefore prepared to acquiesce in it with something of a philosophic cheerfulness, and with that sober and practical intelligence for which they have been ever heretofore distinguished, are at this moment casting about for some means of alleviating the discom-forts and inconveniences which have been brought upon them by instrumentalities which, in their operation, seem more or less to resemble the mysterious dispensations of an overruling Providence. The *appeal for peace*, then, on the part of President Lincoln, as *Pater Patriœ*, should be to the people themselves, and in the most direct manner possible, whose response thereto I am certain would be such as I am persuaded you do really so anxiously de-sire.

"'I know that it is urged by certain persons in the North—in the same manner, by-the-by, as a similar view, *mutatis mutandis,* is presented by certain vaporing newspaper scribblers and half-witted legislative declaimers in the Confederate Congress—that Grant, and Sherman, and the valiant armies under their command are the best and only reliable *pacificators.* Indeed, I can not think so. These distinguished generals (and I am not one of those who have undervalued the capacity of either of them) may perchance be able to overrun and devastate the whole South; they may find it in their power to establish absolute military rule throughout the entire length and breadth of the Confederate States. But will this, I pray you, be the restoration of *the Union of our fathers?* Will this redintegrate amicable feelings between the people of the North and the people of the South? Will this secure permanent concord between the two sections? Will this, in short, secure such a hearty and perfect combination and commixture of all the energies and resources of the great Anglo-American family on that noble continent which God has so evidently allotted to them as their own destined *inheritance,* as will enable them to realize, in all its vividness and plenitude, the consummation of what our venerable friend, General Cass, in former days, was accustomed so solemnly and so significantly to indicate, when he spoke so inspiringly of what he called the "*manifest destiny*" of our noble and heroic race? Let me ask of you whether it would be quite politic—whether it would be altogether just—whether it would be generous needlessly and wantonly to mortify the lofty and manly pride, and cruelly extinguish or even enfeeble the noble *self-respect* of a high-minded and thrice-valorous people ? Indeed, indeed, sir, I can not at all conjecture how any man worthy to be recognized as a *statesman*, or who aspires to the honor of being classed among enlightened Christian philanthropists even, can possibly respond to all of these important interrogatories save with a most emphatic *negative*.

" ' You, sir, placed me under special and lasting obligations by your kind and gentlemanly civilities to my wife when, on a late occasion, it was her fortune to visit Washington City as a refugee from oppression, under circumstances not a little painful and embarrassing. For this accept my cordial thanks. Should a bounteous Providence inspire you with such liberal and manly views as, when fully acted out, shall rescue this once-happy republic from the multiplied horrors of civil war, you will earn, and will doubtless receive also, the grateful homage of countless generations yet unborn, and even those who now hate and revile you will be heard (if I can at all accurately descry the future) to bless and to honor your name.

" ' Before concluding, I hope you will pardon me for saying that while, for various reasons, it would be altogether repugnant to my sense of duty to do any thing injurious to my Southern countrymen, it is my fixed intention to remain altogether *passive* as to the future, being quite content, if my absence from the country shall be deemed desirable, to be a sojourner in foreign lands until my returning once more to a land that I so dearly love shall be deemed no longer objectionable.

" ' I have the honor to be your obedient servant,

" ' II. S. Foote.'

"Having handed this letter to General Dix and received his promise that it should be transmitted to Washington immediately, I remained in New York a day or two only, and, having engaged my passage to Liverpool, was almost in the act of setting out upon my destined voyage, when Colonel Ludlow, of General Dix's staff, came on board the steam-ship where I was, and handed me a note from Mr. Seward to the general, requesting him to advise me that my second communication had just been placed in the hands of President Lincoln for his consideration. Having no special reason for supposing that this second letter had been more favorably received than the former one had been, with great solicitude of mind I set sail. After the lapse of several days I determined to write to Mr. Lincoln as follows:

"'On board the Mail Steamer City of Cork,
February 21, 1865.

"'His Excellency Abraham Lincoln, President of the United States of America:

"'SIR,—It is with some hesitation that I venture to address you. We are personally strangers to each other, and I am quite conscious that I have no special claims to your kindly regard, and still less, if possible, to your political confidence. But the Hon. Wm. H. Seward having, in his official capacity, politely caused me to be informed, through the Military Commandant at New York, General John A. Dix (just as I was setting out for Liverpool, whither I am now voyaging), that my last epistolary communication to him had been placed in your hands for consideration, as a former one had been; being sensible likewise that, in the very hasty preparation of both these communications, I had left almost wholly untouched several topics which might possibly with advantage be somewhat more fully developed—at the hazard of being regarded by you as both obtrusive and pertinacious, and by others, perchance, as foolishly sanguine and fanciful, I shall now proceed to subjoin one or two additional suggestions upon the momentous subject of peace and the restoration of the Federal Union. I write to you from mid-ocean, while the stormy billows of the surrounding sea are every moment painfully reminding me of that fearful scene of commotion and turmoil which I have left behind me, in a land once so peaceful and happy, but now marked so woefully with ravage and the copious shedding of fraternal blood in civil strife. Sir, allow me to say, in all earnestness and sincerity, that in my opinion the ancient classic poets have not described Neptune himself as having more power, as the grand *composer* of the waves of the vexed and raging ocean, than you now possess, in your high official character, for calming the troubles which at present so deplorably convulse the enlightened and patriotic freemen who inhabit our own native America. You hold the *trident of pacification* in your hands; may it be wielded with true benevolence and wisdom, and in the genuine Washingtonian spirit!

" 'I have heretofore suggested for your consideration that the resolution now before the United States Congress, proposing an amendment of the Federal Constitution, should itself, if possible, be so modified, before its final incorporation into that instrument, as to provide for the *gradual* or *prospective* emancipation of the slaves of the South, in lieu of the plan, now propounded, of imme-

diate abolition. It seems to me that the examples which
have been heretofore supplied by several of the free states
of the North themselves (the anxiety of whose people to
rid themselves, as soon as conveniently practicable, of a
system which had grown exceedingly odious, and whose
admitted practical wisdom in regard to all matters appertaining to mere *economical* concerns fit them admirably
for the attainment of sound views upon such a question
as that under consideration) might well encourage the
hope that, if seasonable endeavors were essayed, it might
not yet be found impossible to obtain the consent of all
those states to such a change in the resolution of amendment above referred to as, for many reasons additional to
those heretofore stated, I regard as in the highest degree
desirable. The inevitable derangement of the complex
system of agricultural labor hitherto existing in the South,
which all must perceive will be the result of the immediate emancipation of the whole mass of slaves now engaged
in the cultivation of Southern plantations; the inconveniences and sufferings sure to result to all classes of Southern population from the putting in operation at once of a
new system of labor heretofore wholly untried in the cotton-growing states of the South, without allowing the least
time for preparing to meet such a prodigious shock to the
planting interests located therein, and for the providing of
comfortable arrangements in favor of the liberated slaves
themselves, it would really seem might well incline our
Northern fellow-citizens, if appealed to in time, to consent
to such an alteration in their plan of emancipation as
would be likely, while avoiding the fearful consequences
alluded to, to prevent also those feelings of heart-burning

and grave discontent—yea, even of resentment itself—
which would, even should the Federal Union be permanently restored, render the future relations of the two
sections hereafter any thing but mutually agreeable and
advantageous. If, as I shrewdly suspect will turn out to
be the case, a sufficient number of the states shall not be
found to have given their sanction to the proposed constitutional amendment to make it part of the organic law,
why, allow me to ask, shall not the form of amendment
heretofore so earnestly pressed by me upon your attention
be at once acquiesced in? Why should not you, Mr.
President, yourself propose it? Why should you not in
this way secure the peaceful extinction of slavery, by the
unanimous vote of all the states, both North and South?
Why, in other words, shall you not become the grand
reconciler of contending factions? Why should you not
aspire to become the second founder of the republic?

" ' Recollect, I beseech you, sir, that the Southern Extremists, unwise as has been their action, are not the only
offenders against the cause of the Federal Union; that
other factionists, influenced by strong sectional feeling,
by a strange and astounding *concordià discors*, co-operated
most fatally in the production of the present melancholy
state of affairs. Suppose we "*let by-gones be by-gones;*" let
us be friends and brethren once more upon principles
which will justify a reasonable hope that our *voluntary
reunion* may be *permanent.*

" ' I have, in the course of the present correspondence,
once or twice incidentally alluded to the celebrated Monroe doctrine as presenting, alike to the states of the North
and those of the South, a means of cordial reconcilement

and of future prosperity and strength. Let me say here, in addition, that I deem it one of the most fortunate circumstances which could be possibly imagined that such an opportunity of doing away forever with sectional distrust and animosity, and of *consolidating the national Union*, should have been thus seasonably afforded, as this same Monroe doctrine has so remarkably supplied. Just recollect, if you please, that the favorite idea of all the venerated fathers of American liberty, in the earlier days of the republic, was, that the moral ascendency as well as physical domination of the Anglo-American race, their peculiar institutions of government, and their social morals, were to be ultimately coextensive with the great continent itself where it is our fortune to be located. Bear in mind, also, that it is essential to the progress of liberal sentiment in this hemisphere, the healthful and beneficial advancement of science, and all the useful and elevating arts of civilized existence, that a cordial *consociation* and *co-operation* of energies of every kind should be in some way effectually secured, with a view to the attainment of the great end in contemplation; and I can not at all doubt that you will fully agree with me in the opinion that it is indeed the voice of true wisdom and of enlightened patriotism also, which invokes, which entreats you, with an earnestness not known to the selfish votaries of faction, to seize at once the golden opportunity which an all-bounteous Providence has so fortunately presented to you of becoming not only the restorer of your country's happiness, but the vindicator also of the principles of civil and religious freedom in our own favored hemisphere.

"'Doubt not, I pray you, that the chivalrous sons of the
S

South will, if justly and liberally treated in this the day of their sore travail and suffering, second you in all your exertions to maintain the Monroe doctrine in all its primeval scope and vigor. They know the history of that doctrine well, and it stands associated with many of their proudest and most inspiring recollections. They remember that though in *theory* originating in the generous bosom and expanded and far-reaching intellect of a renowned British statesman, the lamented George Canning* (sus-

* "Those who have made themselves familiar with the parliamentary life of Mr. Canning will not regard me as at all overstating his conduct on this important subject. Hansard's 'Parliamentary Debates' show that this truly upright and courageous British statesman not only acted the part attributed to him above, but that he, more than once, on very striking occasions, warmly felicitated himself upon having done so. His memorable declaration in Parliament, that he had called into existence new states in the Western Hemisphere 'in order to redress the balance of power disturbed in the East,' is of course remembered by all the admirers of this great master of speech. It is, perhaps, not known to all that, as early as the month of August, 1823, Mr. Canning, in an interview with Mr. Rush, the American minister near the court of St. James at that period, urged that the United States should unite with Great Britain in a formal declaration against any of the Continental powers of Europe being allowed to take possession of any portion of the territory of the American continent then recently rescued from Spain. Referring to the designs suspected at that time to be entertained by France in particular, he stated to Mr. Rush that he 'was satisfied that the knowledge that the United States would be opposed to it as well as England could not fail to have a decisive influence in checking it.' In a letter to Mr. Rush, written a few days after this noted interview, he said, referring to the apprehended transfer of Mexico to France, that Great Britain, while unwilling to interfere with any efforts on the part of Spain to repossess herself of her ancient colonial possessions, 'could not see the transfer of any portion to any other power with indifference.' In several other letters this view of the subject was earnestly presented by Mr. Canning to Mr. Rush, who was at last persuaded to concur with him, and to bring the subject, as he did in a very

tained, if my memory serve me faithfully, in this the most forcible manner, to the consideration of Mr. Monroe and his cabinet. The promulgation of what is known as '*The Monroe doctrine*' was the result. Mr. Monroe, in a message to Congress, expressed himself as follows: '*With the existing colonies or dependencies of any European power we have not interfered and shall not interfere; but with the governments who have declared their independence, and maintained it, and whose independence we have, on great consideration and on just principles, acknowledged, we could not view any interposition for the purpose of oppressing them or controlling their destiny, by any European power, in any other light than as a manifestation of an unfriendly disposition toward the United States.*' Referring to this very message, Lord Brougham, then a member of the House of Commons, said, 'The question with regard to South America now was, he believed, disposed of, or nearly so; for an event had recently happened, than which no event had ever dispersed greater joy, exultation, and gratitude over all the free men of Europe; that event, which was decisive on the subject, was the language held with respect to Spanish America in the speech or message of the President of the United States to Congress.' Sir James McIntosh, in one of his noblest speeches, alluding to the same message of Mr. Monroe, said, 'This wise government, in grave but determined language, and with that reasonable but deliberate tone that becomes true courage, proclaims the principles of her policy, and makes known the cases in which the care of her own safety will compel her to take up arms for the defense of other states. I have already observed its coincidence with the declarations of England, which, indeed, is perfect, if allowance be made for the deeper, or, at least, more immediate interest in the independence of South America, which near neighborhood gives to the United States. This coincidence of the two great *English commonwealths* (for so I delight to call them, and I heartily pray that they may be forever *united in the cause of justice and liberty*) can not be contemplated without the utmost pleasure by every enlightened citizen of the earth.' It is a very clear proposition that, if the Great Britain of to-day is the Great Britain of Mr. Canning's time (and who can doubt it?), that this same Monroe doctrine may yet become the nucleus of union and manly, efficient, co-operative energy among all who speak the English language in both hemispheres, and who cherish a true regard for the free institutions derived from a common ancestry. *So mote it be!—*H. S. F."

412 SCYLLA AND CHARYBDIS.

glorious movement of his public life, by such men as a Brougham and a McIntosh), yet that it is alike true that from the year 1823 up to the breaking out of the present unhappy war in 1861, every administration of the government of which you are now the chief executive functionary has uniformly asserted and maintained this *Magna Charta* of the Western Hemisphere with a steady firmness and with undiminished zeal. John Quincy Adams, Daniel Webster, Lewis Cass, Millard Fillmore, James Buchanan, President Pierce, and Edward Everett, of the North; James Monroe, John C. Calhoun, Henry Clay, William H. Crawford, Andrew Jackson, John Tyler, and James K. Polk, of the South, at different periods and in different modes, are well known to have signalized their devotion to the great American principle embodied in the far-famed Monroe doctrine; and it is a little too late now to expect any considerable portion of the descendants of those great men, some of whom have gone down to the grave with so much honor, to relinquish those muniments of national safety and freedom which have been thus far so nobly maintained.

" 'I venture to predict, Mr. President, that if such just and gracious treatment shall be now accorded to the South as her people have a clear right to demand in the adjustment of the terms upon which peace and union shall be once more restored, this same Monroe doctrine is destined shortly to become the effectual healer of *sectional distemperatures*—the sovereign uniter of hearts which should never have been divided — the veritable Macedonian sword itself, which, skillfully wielded, will yet be seen to cut asunder that Gordian knot of discord which has heretofore so fearfully puzzled and perplexed even the most gifted of our statesmen. I shall not venture· to specify all the noble results, whether present or prospective, which are now so obviously placed within reach of a lofty magnanimity and a wise statesmanship. There are certain delicate considerations connected with this deeply-interesting subject upon which I. do not deem it at all expedient to enlarge. I have already, I fear, occupied more of your attention than you will consider altogether justifiable, and will therefore now conclude with assuring you that I am your obedient servant,

" 'H. S. FOOTE.'

"On arriving in the city of London, I sat down to draw up this address to my valued neighbors and friends of Tennessee. It is not now my fortunate lot to see you face to face; I may possibly never again have that satisfaction; but I intreat you, my countrymen and fellow-citizens, whatever may be the action of President Lincoln and the politicians now in power in Washington City, upon the propositions submitted to them in this correspondence, that you will yourselves lose no time in returning to the bosom of the Federal Union. It is far better, in my deliberate opinion, that you should do so, and do so at once, than to take the chances of future military success under Jefferson Davis and his present official associates, and rely upon them for the future restoration of your liberties, after they shall have been once completely surrendered to the most unfeeling and degrading despotism that has existed in the world since the days of Dionysius of Syracuse."

When I left the port of New York, in the month of February last, I expected to be absent only eight weeks. The *passport* which I had received did not in express terms allow of my coming back to the United States unless with the consent of the government; but I did not in the least degree doubt that when President Lincoln should learn that I was again on American soil, and had come back *alone for the purpose of adding my personal persuasions to those which I had already addressed to my Southern friends in behalf of a ready and cheerful submission to Federal authority*, he would not fail to perceive that my *motives* and intentions were at least good, even if he should deem it prudent to reject my assistance in the work of pacification. Anticipating, as I did (which anticipation I had publicly avowed in the Confederate Congress previous to the vacation of my seat in that body), that long before the month of April should expire General Lee would be compelled to surrender both Richmond and the gallant army which he commanded, and with the purposes just named in view, I did not deem it safe to remain across the ocean more than two months; so, after issuing the pamphlet referred to, I took a rapid tour through England, France, and Italy, and returned to New York only a day or two previous to the making known of the act of surrender in that city. In relation to the obstacles which were so painfully and unexpectedly interposed to the full execution of this scheme I have nothing now to say in the way of complaint.

I will now conclude this chapter by expressing the fervent hope which I feel that the day may not be far distant when *sectionalism* and all its evil concomitants shall cease to exist in our noble republic, and when union, concord, and confraternity may every where prevail in the land of Washington, of Jackson, of Webster, and of Clay.*

* Last summer, while in Canada, having an opportunity, as I thought, of ascertaining what was likely to be the tone and temper of the present Congress, I took the liberty of admonishing my Southern fellow-countrymen in regard to their own future course upon this all-important subject. I warned them that, in order to secure their own restoration to the civic rights of which the war had deprived them, it was indispensable that they should promptly, and without any appearance of *unwillingness*, grant all those reasonable concessions to those who had been liberated by the war as the government of the United States had undertaken to guarantee. I labored to show them that the granting of these concessions could alone so strengthen the arm of the President as would enable him to shield them against the attempts making in certain quarters for their own permanent enslavement. I endeavored to make manifest to them the undoubted fact that Mr. Davis and the satellites by whom he was surrounded in Richmond, by obstinately refusing to allow any negotiations for peace to be set on foot at a time when large Confederate armies were yet in the field, had placed them absolutely at the mercy of their conquering foes, who had it in their power now to deal out to them, in all their harshness, the disabilities and discomforts which it is so often in war the fate of the conquered to suffer. I brought to their view the fact that those with whom they had been contending in arms stood solemnly pledged to the recently liberated blacks of the South that they should henceforth enjoy *freedom, with all the means of preserving it;* and I besought them, promptly and with as great an appearance of *cheerfulness* as possible, that they would themselves formally grant liberty to those who had been in fact already virtually emancipated by the war, in such a form as to preserve the newly-enfranchised race from all possibility of being thereafter resubjugated. I even went so far as to suggest that this course was alike necessary to be taken, in order to rescue the white millions of the South from a state of permanent degradation, as it was to the future concord and safety of the *whole population* dwelling in what had been so long recognized as the slaveholding region, among whom feelings of mu-

tual trust and kindness could not be reasonably expected ever to arise unless all serious *inequalities in civic rights should be effectually done away*. I
regret to say that the course pursued in several of the states of the South
in regard to this matter has not been such as might have been reasonably
anticipated. By tardy and apparently reluctant action in the granting
of those things which it is really not in their power ultimately to withhold, several of the states referred to have, it is to be feared, greatly weakened their own position, and enfeebled the President, their only protector
now, in his efforts to serve them.   How long they will, under the counsels of shallow and senseless demagogues, persevere in their present course,
remains to be seen.   For their own sake, and for the repose and happiness of the whole republic, I hope that in a week or two we shall learn
that wiser and more considerate action has been finally adopted; that, in
consequence thereof, the Southern representatives and senators have been
received in Congress; that military organizations in the bosom of the
states of the South have been dispensed with; that the *habeas corpus* has
been every where restored;. that all need for the Freedmen's Bureau has
ceased; and that *perfect federative equality* may be thus secured among
all the states of this grand and glorious republic.

While I now write, it is painful to learn that the Legislature of the
State of Tennessee, a body elected by less than a *third* of the qualified
voters of the state, the members of which have been heretofore claiming
to be far more devoted to the cause of the Union than the hundreds of
thousands of their fellow-citizens whom they obstinately hold in a state
of cruel *disfranchisement*, and whom they are day by day driving, by intolerable oppression, into *exile*, has deliberately refused to grant to persons
of African descent the right to testify in courts of justice.   This, I repeat,
has been done by the Union men of Tennessee, *par excellence* the persons
who are boasting every day that they are the zealous .and faithful supporters of the President!   Now I undertake to say that such action as this
is really more *hostile*, practically, to the avowed reconstruction policy of
President Johnson than any thing besides which these individuals could
possibly have done.

Outside of the state, I do not doubt that the whole people of Tennessee-
will be held responsible for the insane and illiberal conduct on this subject, which I feel assured that a very large majority of those not now allowed by a despotic faction even to exercise the right of suffrage, were it
in their power, would emphatically *repudiate*.

It is really astonishing to hear that men in this enlightened age should for a moment hesitate in regard to the propriety of allowing persons of African descent to testify in courts of justice, especially in cases where their own life, liberty, or property is involved. It is the most cruel *mockery* to call them *free*, and yet deny this essential right; it is, moreover, the most palpable and unblushing *hypocrisy*. In the name of Heaven, who could possibly be injured by such an act of simple justice in behalf of an unhappy race who have long submitted cheerfully to bondage, and who have only *accepted* liberty when it has been tendered to them? Every lawyer of philosophic mind would say at once, that to allow freedmen to testify, *in any case*, would be attended with no evil consequence whatever to those who were free from nativity. Each witness brought into court to give evidence would be necessarily subjected to examination and cross-examination, and an astute and unprejudiced jury would then determine how far such evidence was entitled to credence. I can well imagine a thousand cases in which this same right to testify might, in its exercise, be eminently beneficial to white citizens—yea, lives might be saved from the scaffold, character be rescued from undeserved discredit, and the most valuable property rights be secured from destruction, by the veracious, manly, and unprejudiced testimony of one who had himself been born a slave. It is heartlessly unjust to the black man to assert that he is less a respecter of truth and less inclined to the exercise of justice than the white man. I have lived among this race all my life, and what I now say on this subject is the fruit of more than half a century's experience and observation.

At any rate, I now feel authorized again to declare to that portion of my fellow-countrymen of the South who are still perilously tampering with this delicate and important matter, that there is no possible ground for hoping that the white men of the South will themselves be restored to their suspended civic rights until they consent themselves to do justice to others.

☞ By-the-by, I see that the Freedmen's Bureau has been given (and rightfully too) increased powers in the State of Tennessee, in consequence of this strange conduct on the part of the Legislature.

S 2

CHAPTER XVIII.

Observations mainly upon the Facts recited in the preceding Chapters.

I PROPOSE now to bring this volume to a conclusion with the presentation of a few additional *observations*, hav-ing reference, either direct or indirect, to facts already brought to notice, or to others too obvious and familiar to have required an earlier specification.

1. No clearer proposition could, in my judgment, be possibly stated than the one insisted on so emphatically in all that I have heretofore written, that the war, from the devastation and suffering of which the country is now slowly emerging, did not *necessarily* grow out of the fact that African slavery existed in the South, and did not exist in the North, and that there was not really any thing worthy the notice of a philosophic mind in the fact that, while white men and white women in the North per-formed the greater part of all the rougher physical labor, and *voluntarily*, this was done in the South chiefly by persons of a *black* or *brown* complexion, and after the manner that has been called *involuntary*. The truth is, that the opposition to the continuance of African slavery in the region wherein it has just become extinct, as the inevitable result of the war that has been for four years raging, was confined in the North to, comparatively speaking, a very small number of persons, and still few-er of these were, until very recently at least, possessed of

any large amount of influence over the general public mind of the country. Outside of small fanatical and political cliques, there was not, even as late as five years ago, any strong *antagonism* of *sentiment* between the slaveholding and the non-slaveholding sections of the republic. As for any antagonism of *pecuniary interest* in connection with Southern slaveholding, the *ascertained* existence of which, as a source of large pecuniary gain, if believed also to be permanent, might, in an age so mercenary as ours, prove, perhaps, to some extent, productive of a sort of reciprocal *rivalry* of feeling, this is the merest phantom that ever vexed the over-fevered brain of a fanciful visionary. The pecuniary interests of the North and South, in connection with slaveholding, it is true, were not *identical*, but so far were they also from being *conflicting* and *irreconcilable*, that they were positively in perfect accord with each other, and were, anterior to the war, constantly multiplying and intensifying ties of sympathetic kindness between the two sections. There is no necessary antagonism between the blacksmith and the miller, the fisherman and the hunter of game, the culti-_vator of the land and the mariner who plows the fields of ocean. On the contrary, all of them, and a thousand *diverse* but not necessarily hostile classes besides, may not only subsist in quiet as members of the same community, but their very differences of employment, leading them naturally into the interested *reciprocation* of the respective products of their labor, must necessarily generate *amity* instead of *hostility*. It is quite safe to affirm that, anterior to the war, there was more capital in the North than in the South dependent for its profitable employment upon the African slaveholding system. The growers of cotton, sugar, tobacco, and other slave-raised products in the South, though their multiplied responsibilities, moral as well as physical, were indeed most burdensome, derived far less of *clear profit* from the outlay of their capital than did the merchants and manufacturers of the North, and the other numerous classes dependent upon them. The truth of this statement was alike manifest in innumerable instances of individual fortune in the North, arising, directly or indirectly, from the slaveholding system—in the rapid and unprecedented growth of large commercial marts, and in the innumerous ramifications of manufacturing industry. It is said in Holy Writ that "where a man's treasure is, there will his heart be also," and thus it undoubtedly was in the case under consideration. It was not in nature for those who were, daily and hourly, over the whole North, becoming richer and richer from the cultivation of Southern soil by the sons and daughters of Africa, to cherish feelings of illiberal hatred for those whose skillful and vigilant administration of a system to them so productive of gain was constantly increasing the aggregate quantity of their wealth, and with it the means of luxurious accommodation, of extended influence, and of magnificent liberality. There are many who write and speak on this subject, and who speak and write, too, most flippantly and plausibly, who really imagine because *they*, before the war, hated the slaveholding system of the South, the whole people of the North did the same thing. There never was a greater mistake committed. I have had in my time much interest in looking into the truth of this matter, and have enjoyed good opportunities too of finding out actual facts, and I aver now that it is my solemn and fixed conviction that there were not, five years ago, two twentieths of the whole Northern population who would not have greatly preferred slavery to continue in the South for an indefinite period, to participating, in the least degree, in its sudden extinction. It is, indeed, not at all important to discuss this matter at present with a view to the possible revival of African slavery in the South at any future time. The man any where who calculates upon such a revival is not far from being a fit subject for some insane asylum. African slavery in the South is indeed gone forever, and I am confident that there are not one thousand intelligent persons in that region, of all the former slaveholding class, who would now resuscitate this defunct system if they had it ever so much in their power to do so. But it is important that the large and influential class in the South who were former owners of slaves, and who for many years to come will undoubtedly exercise a most potential influence there, should be assured, in an authentic and satisfactory manner, that *the destruction of their property* was not deliberately sought by a majority of their Northern fellow-citizens, but that their present condition—so far, at least, as any one in the North is responsible for it—is the result of influences originally very feeble and limited in their scope of operation, and whose capacity for mischief has been supplied in a great degree by the indiscretion and overweening ambition of individuals holding high official position among themselves. *Secession is chiefly accountable for the destruction of African slavery.* The combined action of extremists of the North

and of the South brought on the war, which a few feeble
abolitionists could never have created; and, in a moment of unparalleled folly, the only solid *guarantee* that
it was possible in the nature of things that this anomalous and world-hated system could possess, viz., the Constitution of the United States, with the consent of the
slaveholding class themselves, was cast aside, and is now
lost to it forever! This result though, should not now,
and I am well assured it will not be hereafter, a source
of permanent regret to the white population of the South.
They will, indeed, be far better off in time to come *without slavery* than *with it.* They. will be relieved from a
most painful and perplexing responsibility. If the new
system of agricultural labor shall succeed (and all good
citizens must earnestly desire that it should), the whole
Southern people will be far more prosperous hereafter
than they have been heretofore. Labor in the South will
be more diversified, and be likely to yield more solid benefits of every kind. Manufacturing and mineral industry
too will be now seen.to flourish, for the first time, in that
great and prolific region, and even Southern commerce
may hereafter attain a more healthful and *self-supporting*
existence. But no man need expect less antagonisms of
interest hereafter to be manifested between the North and
the South than have heretofore prevailed; and if certain
people who are now making a great noise in particular
Northern vicinages can have their own way, in spite of
all that the beneficent wisdom of government can do, it
is to be feared that antagonisms of feeling, "imbedded"
in the moral constitutions of bigoted and narrow-minded
zealots, may breed new and fatal discords and conten-

tions where peace and happiness might be restored, and continue permanently to abide.

2. There surely never was a time when mutual forbearance and moderation were more necessary to be exercised on the part of good and patriotic men, both North and South, than at present, when certain editors of the South are urging that none of the reasonable concessions demanded by the President at the hands of his fellow-citizens of that section shall be yielded by them, without which the only being on earth who can restore them to their forfeited rights and privileges will be utterly powerless for their relief; and when one or two editors in the North, whose newspapers are stated to have a very wide circulation, are vehemently insisting that the constitutional amendment now proposed, if adopted, would give to the Federal government *absolute control* over all the domestic concerns of the states, and thus inevitably organize an imperial despotism in Washington City. The fight between the two bands of sectional extremists, which is still lingering, is the only circumstance at present existing which would seem calculated to renew the dangers to which the liberties of the country have been for four years subjected by an unnecessary and impolitic war. All truly reasonable and patriotic men in either section will be inclined to say to the President (as the leader of those now so happily co-operating with him in the putting down of extremists both North and South),

"IN MEDIO TUTISSIMUS IBIS."

3. Cicero, in several of his incomparable epistles, expresses his conviction that if Cæsar, after the termination of the great civil war in which Pompey had perished,

should be allowed an opportunity of putting in exercise his own generous wishes, he would gradually, and by such means as were open to him, restore the *ancient Constitution of Rome, with its curious and complex system of checks and balances.* Julius Cæsar himself was far too profound and discerning a statesman to suppose that any man could accomplish a work so difficult *in an instant,* especially when there were still a few men every where to be found in whose bosoms the spirit of revolt was ever ready to rekindle, and while the mercenary and selfish members of his own faction were constantly crying out for *new confiscations and executions.* Improvident and short-sighted politicians destroyed Cæsar's life by assassination before *his* beneficent plan of *restoration* could be accomplished; civil war was renewed, and, lo! Augustus, Tiberius, Caligula, and a host of bloody tyrants beside, succeeded. History is constantly repeating itself; unfortunately, though, her oracles are either not listened to or are received in unwilling ears. *Oh, my country!*

4. A little more than twelve months ago, I introduced in the Confederate Congress at Richmond resolutions assertive of the *Monroe doctrine,* as embodying the true policy of all the friends of freedom in this hemisphere. Several newspapers of the South took me very pointedly to task on account of these same resolutions, charging me, in fact, with having made a movement toward *reconstruction.* Who could then have believed that, within a few months from that time, men high in Confederate confidence, and ultra advocates of state-rights and state sovereignty, would voluntarily fly beyond the limits of the only reliable republic on earth to seek protection at the

hands of a *confessed despot*, and give such aid as it might be in their power to supply in the propping up of the tottering imperial throne of an Austrian usurper—thus consigning to the most degrading servitude the upright, gallant, and persecuted supporters of republican institutions in unfortunate, down-trodden Mexico!

O tempora! O mores!

5. Since the question whether the existence of African slavery shall or shall not continue on this continent is now *forever settled;* since there are but few among those who were formerly interested therein who would now, after all that has been occurring for a twelve-month past, be willing to have it restored, it may be permitted to me to say, that I shall always be of opinion that the adoption of a plan of *gradual emancipation,* instead of the one now in operation, would have been far better for all concerned. For then the great shock to the planting operations of the South—which all now admit to be very serious indeed, the whole effect of which, too, is yet to be ascertained—would have been avoided; those who are now freedmen might have been kindly and skillfully prepared for the great change which was ultimately to occur in their condition, and most of the difficulties with which President Johnson has had to contend, but which he has met with such manly energy and resolution, would have been happily avoided; and the Southern people, coming back *voluntarily* into the Union by a peaceful *counter-revolution* most easy to have been effected at the time, and taking it upon themselves the restoration of domestic concord and the dominion of law, reconstruction would have occurred in a manner to have left no heart-burnings be-

hind, and *secession*, overcome as it would infallibly have
been by the cheerfully-exerted energies of the deluded
masses themselves, would have been as thoroughly *derac-
inated* and *destroyed* as the most devoted Unionist could
possibly have desired. Hereafter the whole world will
learn how easy of execution this counter-revolutionary
project would have been.

6. It is curious to observe that some of the champions
of abolition are claiming all the credit of overthrowing
slavery in the South. Now the destruction of this system was undoubtedly the *fruit of the war* which has just
terminated; so that, in attempting to deprive the Southern secession leaders of their portion of the honor of uprooting slavery, these *monopolizing* gentlemen must inevitably take upon themselves the *exclusive responsibility* of
bringing on one of the bloodiest and most exhausting contests of arms that was ever prosecuted. In thus violating
the truth of history, instead of securing to themselves an
honorable fame, they really place themselves in a most
odious and discreditable condition. Let the real fact be
confessed: secession and abolition *united* brought on the
war, and the ruin of the slaveholding system of the South
is their *joint work*. The striking poetic picture presented
by Milton in his "Paradise Lost," wherein we learn that
the cohabitation of *Satan* and *Sin* brought *Death* into existence, would really almost seem to have been again ex-
emplified.

7. If there be any either so stupid or so illiberal as to
have heretofore taken it for granted that all in the Northern States concerned in the emancipation efforts were deficient in the high moral attributes of *justice* and *humanity*,

how much must they have been surprised of late to discover that some of the most earnest and strenuous advocates of *universal amnesty*, as applied to those lately in
rebellion, are persons who for twenty years or more have
labored unceasingly for the destruction of African slavery! The noble and enlightened efforts of the Hon. Ger-
rit Smith and others of the class mentioned, to counteract
the unwise and wicked policy of subjecting to capital punishment large numbers of those called rebels, have established in their favor claims to the general respect of their
countrymen and of the world, which ought, for the good
of mankind, to prove far more enduring than the fame of
the most renowned conqueror that has ever led soldiers
to battle.   Mr. Smith's discourse on this subject last summer, at Cooper Institute, is instinct with the most generous
sentiments of kindness and true Christian charity, while
his argument supplying demonstrative proof that it was
not even possible for *treason*, as that great offense has been
heretofore understood, to have been perpetrated by Jefferson Davis and his associates, under the peculiar circumstances existing (sustained as that argument was by numerous authorities the force of which it is impossible to
counteract), ought to bring the deep blush of shame to the
cheek of that class of *hireling advocates* and upstart demagogues who had *before that* been contending that nothing
could be more easy than, in accordance with British and
American judicial precedents, to work conviction in the
cases referred to.   This view of the subject by no means
negatives the position that the levying of war upon the
Federal government is *treason*, but simply that the right
to treat such conduct as treason may be *waived*, or *volun-*

tarily yielded up by a government of unlimited power to do all things in war convenient and needful to its own successful prosecution of measures of defense.

8. True wisdom requires that, while all appropriate means should be employed by those who are intrusted with the administration of a government professing to be *free* for enforcing the authority of the laws and the established principles of order, due care should also be exercised, in order to avoid the extinction of the spirit of popular liberty, with the idea of which is always necessarily coupled that of prompt and *manly resistance* to all palpably unconstitutional and oppressive governmental acts. It may be well said that this principle of resistance to unjust and deeply injurious measures of government is the very *main-spring* of all that we know of republican freedom. The Constitution of Tennessee contains language, in reference to this matter, of most emphatic import, and the celebrated proclamation of Andrew Jackson, as well as the able and eloquent speech of President Johnson, delivered four years ago in the American Senate, may be severally regarded as containing a most sound and practical exposition of this principle of *legitimate resistance.*

9. It is admitted by all who are in the least degree worthy to be called *statesmen*, that, in our complex system of government, the *reserved* and *correlative* powers of the states are indispensable to the prevention of *centralism*, and, *consequently*, essential also to the preservation of liberty. Those, therefore, who are now urging that, in opposition to the manly and reasonable exposition of the true meaning of the lately adopted constitutional amend-

ment, the Federal government, under that very amendment, should exercise *unlimited control* over all·the most essential domestic concerns of all the states, would seem to be willing, in order to execute a favorite theory for the amelioration of the condition of a comparatively small number of our people recently enfranchised, to consign all the remainder of our thirty millions to bondage the most degrading, and, at the same time, *interminable.* This would be, indeed, a good deal more absurd than the conduct of the man who is represented by Æsop as *cutting up the precious goose that laid the golden egg!*

10. Since those who were lately slaves in the South are now *freemen*, it is obviously necessary to the welfare and happiness of all classes of our population that the people who have been thus *enfranchised* should, in every legitimate and proper mode, be fitted for the judicious exercise of their newly-acquired civil rights, and that they should be likewise supplied with the most convenient means of maintaining these rights also against future assailment. How far it may be politic, in particular states, for the attainment of the purpose mentioned, to extend the right of suffrage to persons of the African race, is a point well worthy of mature consideration; but President Johnson would seem very wisely·to have decided that this must be left to be regulated *exclusively* by each of the states interested. That these states might, all of them, in the condition in which they now find themselves, provide at once for the extension of the privilege of voting to all possessed of the requisite amount of intelligence, and who are, by ties of property, substantially connected with the body politic, there appears to be but little reason to doubt.

The proposition now so freely discussed in various quarters, *to put all the classes of the population in all the states upon precisely the same footing in regard to suffrage, requiring uniformly the duplicate qualification specified,* if found practicable, may possibly yet turn out to be the true solution of a difficulty which might well puzzle the wisest men that the world has yet produced. As already stated, though, this is most clearly a matter for *local cognizance* alone, and any impertinent or dictatorial intermeddling with it from exterior quarters must inevitably be productive of the greatest mischief. It will be far "better to bear those ills we have, than fly to others that we know not of." Calm, courteous, and *brotherly* interchange of views, and temperate, unprejudiced discussion of the question under dispute, would probably, in a short time, dissipate all existing difficulties. If we can manage to keep out the bane of *sectionalism*, all will probably be well.

11. Since penning the above, President Johnson's first annual message has reached my hands, and I gladly extract therefrom the following emphatic declaration of principle, the importance of which declaration by the executive chief of the republic, *at such a moment,* can not be too highly appreciated:

" Without states, one great branch of the legislative government would be wanting; and, if we look beyond the letter of the Constitution to the character of our country, its capacity for comprehending within its jurisdiction a vast continental empire is due to the system of states. The best security for the perpetual existence of the states is the "supreme authority" of the Constitution of the United States. The perpetuity of the Constitution brings with it the perpetuity of the states; their mutual relation makes us what we are, and in our political system their connection is indissoluble. The whole can not exist without the parts, nor the parts without the whole. So long as the Constitution of the United States endures, the states will endure; the destruction of the one is the destruction of the other; the preservation of the one is the preservation of the other.

"I have thus explained my views of the mutual relations of the Constitution and the states, because they unfold the principles on which I have sought to solve the momentous question and overcome the appalling difficulties that met me at the very commencement of my administration. It has been my steadfast object to escape from the sway of momentary passions, and to derive a healing policy from the fundamental and unchanging principles of the Constitution."

It is not in my nature to be the adulator of men in power; besides, I have lived too long, and have experienced too many of the changes to which the fortunes of men are subjected in this state of being, to expect much or to *fear much* from those who any where wield the sceptre of authority. But I can not, in justice to myself, refrain from declaring that, if President Johnson shall persevere to the end, as I do not doubt that he will, in the execution of his admirable scheme of reconstruction, it is evident that the most signal success will crown his patriotic efforts. Ninety-nine hundredths of his country-men every where will, I am satisfied, accord to him their warmest support; and when the good work of pacification shall have been once accomplished, he will be justly

recognized by all truly virtuous and enlightened men as
the restorer of his country's liberties and the renovator
of its glories. In view of the great object, now apparently almost attained—the renewal of that noble federative
system devised by our fathers, but which the earthquake
shock of civil war has so seriously disordered—how contemptible appear the puny sophisticators of the hour,
who are painfully taxing their overheated brains with
the utterly unprofitable question whether or not the
states lately in rebellion did or did not succeed in getting
out of the pale of the Union by the now exploded expedient of *secession!* One thing seems to be sufficiently
certain : these lately seceding states are at present sufficiently in the Union to co-operate most promptly and effectively in the great constitutional amendment which
has forever extinguished slavery on this continent, and
deprived a vaporing and restless fanaticism of that food
upon which it has heretofore banqueted and grown fearfully potential for mischief. The special message of the
President, which is placed in my hand while I now write,
sustained as it is by the manly and magnanimous report
of General Grant, supplies full assurance as to the state
of public feeling in the South in regard to the condition
of things brought about inevitably by the war, and renders it manifest that, so far as the great body of our voting population both North and South is concerned, a cordial and general reconcilement has been already consummated. We are now fully justified in expecting for our
country the realization of all that national prosperity and
happiness which the most sanguine of our statesmen formerly anticipated for her, before either abolition or seces-

sion had yet attempted to disturb the public repose, or, by their *conflicting* yet *conjoint* operation, had involved in peril our own hopes of civil and religious freedom, and those of the whole world besides.

CONCLUSION.

IN the present volume facts have been presented and reasonings stated which, it seems to me, leave no reasonable doubt as to what should be the present action of the government if it be desired to resuscitate the happy condition of things existing before the commencement of the war, the effect of which has been so deleteriously to discompose the wise and salutary system of *checks and balances*, without the existence of which a state of pure republican liberty would have been impossible. It is probable that in a second volume, drawn up under more favorable circumstances, and admitting greater freedom of exposition, many additional facts may be exhibited, somewhat bolder arguments be adduced, and numerous additional sketches of individual character and illustrative personal anecdotes be supplied, should the plan of this work seem to have secured a fair portion of the public favor. I shall close now, for the present, by an emphatic affirmation of a great truth, which I can not but hope has been already made sufficiently apparent, that the peculiar civic institutions framed by our fathers can not be made preservative of permanent freedom except by restoring as soon as possible the original *coequality* of

T

the states, upon the essentiality of which Mr. Pinckney
so cogently and eloquently insisted in the memorable
Missouri struggle of 1819. Extinguish this coequality
in any way, and, instead of a republic, we will necessarily bring into existence an *imperial despotism*, by whatever name called. Subject to *enslavement* the numerous distinct communities formerly enjoying liberty, and
vest the power of controlling all the domestic concerns
of each of them in a central government, whether that
central government shall consist of a Roman Senate,
with an *Imperator* or military commander in chief at
its head, or of an American Congress, with a similar
commander-in-chief called *President*, empowered to counsel it in regard to all public questions, and it will not
be possible to prevent the rapid concentration of all
civil power in the legislative and executive department
of the system first, and very soon thereafter the consol-
idation of all power in the hands of a single individual,
which individual will, of course, be the executive officer
who wields the *war power*. The experience of nations
is uniform on this subject; and even had no such fatal
example of the ruin of freedom heretofore occurred, it
would really seem that a mere statement of this proposition, as a yet *unproven theorem*, ought to be sufficient to
enforce the important truth referred to upon the most
opaque intellect. I do not desire to be understood on
this occasion as denying, nor is it indeed at all necessary
for any purpose the attainment of which is at this moment desirable, that the government existing in Washington City was not, in order to preserve its own existence, fully justified in wielding all the powers which it

is known, upon the ground of *military necessity*, to have
employed; nor is it necessary either to dispute the proposition so earnestly insisted upon in certain quarters at
present, that these vast powers, once seized upon, may
continue to be wielded by that government permanently, if it shall choose to do so, over those unfortunate
eleven millions of American people whom the terrible
exigencies of war and the unwise perseverance in hostilities up to the moment when, as has been seen, they
were compelled to submit unconditionally to the will of
the conqueror.   But the still graver and more vital question now is, Shall this sweeping enslavement be enforced,
when such enforcement must inevitably result in the ultimate enslavement also of the additional nineteen millions of our whole federal population?   In other words,
would those in the two houses of Congress at this moment act wisely in pursuing such a course as all far-seeing and considerate statesmen would unite in assuring
them must necessarily subject to despotic rule the very
people who have selected them as THE defenders of their
own liberties?   I am afraid that unprejudiced men in
future generations will be inclined to recognize the struggle now progressing in Washington City, in connection
with President Johnson's reconstruction policy, as a struggle between philosophic and discriminating statesmen on
the one side, and factionists and demagogues on the other.   For, after all, what is the distinction between these
two classes of individuals?   I understand that a statesman is one who understands the concerns of his *whole
country*, and who exercises also a kindly and providing
care over *all* of these concerns for the general good of

the whole nation, and not only for its *temporary* good, but for its *lasting* welfare; while a factionist is *purblind* in his very nature and moral constitution, delights in indulging one-sided and *narrow* views, acts alone in furtherance of what he supposes to be the interest of his own particular class or faction, or, what is worse still, in order to obtain for himself and his immediate associates a little momentary eclat, or the contemptible and unprofitable gratification of his and their ungenerous prejudices, or unphilosophic and unamiable lust of power. The conduct of the patriot statesman is ever regulated by *principle;* for the maintenance of principles he will dare to despise *faction*, and all its seductive rewards and fiendish menaces. Party, as we all know, is far superior in dignity to faction; and yet the patriot statesman will not hesitate to disjoin himself from party itself, in order to preserve his country's freedom and happiness. Who now blames Edmund Burke for openly abandoning the Whig party in England, with which he had been so long and so honorably allied, in order to aid in rescuing the British isles from Jacobinical influences, at that moment being imported from the school of Marat, of Dantòn, and Robespierre? Who now rails at Sir Robert Peel for dissolving his political affiliation with the opponents of Catholic Emancipation, of Free Trade, and of Parliamentary Reform? Who, save a few absurd bigots, now denounces Mr. Clay for declaring, in 1850, that if the Whig party, of which he had been once the acknowledged *embodiment*, should become *abolitionized*, he would no longer hold connection with it? Who does not admire even Washington still more highly when he learns from Mr.

Jefferson's posthumous writings, that the Father of his Country was never seen even for a moment to sink into a mere party devotee? It is even asserted, on high authority, that circumstances may exist in which a great statesman might feel justified, amid the fierce and ever-shifting currents of party conflict, to act, on *principle*, sometimes with one of two antagonizing factions, sometimes with the opposing one, in order, by casting the weight of his influence now into one scale, now into another, to preserve the contending civic forces in a state of harmless *equipoise*. It was just such conduct as this which posterity has so much admired in the incorruptible and enlightened Halifax, in the latter part of the seventeenth century, and on account of which the illiberal zealots of party denounced him as a "*trimmer;*" and it is gratifying to learn from the page of authentic history that this gréat and good man,* "instead of quarreling with his nickname, assumed it as a title of honor, and vindicated, with great vivacity, the dignity of the appellation. Every thing good, he said, *trimmed between extremes*. The temperate zone trims between the climate in which men are roasted and the climate in which they are frozen. The English Church trims between the Anabaptist madness and the Papist lethargy. The English Constitution trims between Turkish despotism and Polish anarchy; *virtue* is nothing but a just temper between propensities, any one of which, if indulged to excess, becomes *vice;* nay, the perfection of the Supreme Being himself consists in the exact equilibrium of attributes none of which could preponderate without

* Macaulay.

disturbing the whole moral and physical order of the world."*

* Those familiar with the public career of Cicero, who was unquestionably the ablest and most politic statesman of ancient times, and if not the
first of orators ancient or modern, certainly only inferior to Demosthenes,
will remember that there was much in his conduct at different periods
which indicated that he too had learned that it was neither wise nor safe
for a public man of great eminence and of extended influence to suffer
any political faction, struggling fiercely for ascendency, to appropriate to
itself exclusively his whole weight and influence. Accordingly, we find
him now the champion of the knights, now the vindicator of the Senate,
and now the professed advocate of popular rights. While it seemed possible to effect reconcilement between Pompey and Cæsar he joined the
faction of neither, professing friendship for both, and striving to prevent
that collision between them which he feared might result in civil war.
When, in spite of his efforts to prevent it, war between these celebrated
chieftains commenced, it is known that he hesitated long whether to join
the one or the other, or to remain neutral; and when, finally, he withdrew
from Rome and took refuge in Pompey's camp, it was so impossible that
he could play the ignoble part of a mere partisan, that he more than once
found his life in danger from the violence of those who, forgetful of the
cause of freedom, had become the willing slaves of him whose ruin was
soon to be consummated at Pharsalia. Even Cato condemned him for
not remaining upon *neutral* ground, so as to interpose effectively, if possible, for the restoration of peace; and, long after Pompey had perished,
Cicero more than once expressed doubt whether it had not been better for
Rome and the general interests of freedom for Cæsar to have been triumphant, than to have been compelled to succumb to the power of his less
magnanimous rival. Such a man as this could hardly be expected to
"give up to *party* what was meant for *mankind*."

Additional Note.

I am far from assuming that I have read more of history than other
men, but yet I feel justified in declaring that, to the extent of my historic
knowledge, there is no instance which can be cited wherein distinguished
public men have more signally blundered than have several gentlemen of
no little renown in the two houses of Congress in regard to the manner in

In view of the cheering signs of national redintegration
now disclosing themselves in Washington City, I am sure

which it is now proper to deal with the Southern people, in order to insure
permanent domestic quiet and the general happiness of the republic. The
people of the South have been conquered in war; they feel and know this
fact, and in general they submit to their fate with a calm and unmurmuring acquiescence which might well awaken the sympathy and admiration
of the world. They know that slavery is dead, and they would not revive
it even if they could. The former slaveholding class are especially inclined to acquiesce in all the results which the war has produced; and it
is an undoubted fact, of which I could adduce innumerable evidences, that
any hostile feeling now existing in the South toward the enfranchised
blacks is almost exclusively confined to the poor laboring whites, who,
very naturally perhaps, are unwilling that the field of industry shall be
occupied by the sons and daughters of Africa to their own exclusion. I
speak of what I personally know when I assert that there is a widespread
and almost universal feeling of good-will and sincere amity prevalent
among the people of the South at this moment toward those with whom
they were lately conflicting in arms, so far as the treatment they are receiving will allow of it. They are full of respect and gratitude toward
President Johnson and those now so nobly aiding him in the endeavor
to restore them to the free and independent condition which they occupied
before the war; and they are, above all things, anxious to have an opportunity of showing how sincere they are in their desire to perform all the
duties of free citizenship, and co-operate with good men every where in
all that can promote the national honor and happiness. Independent of
the information which the President has recently caused to be laid before
Congress on this important subject, I may be permitted here to state, that
the senators and representatives who have been recently sent from the
South are, almost to a man, persons heretofore pre-eminently distinguished as imbued with conservative feeling. If admitted promptly to their
seats, I am confident that their conduct will be such, in all respects, as will
best conduce to the restoration of general amity and concord. The moral
effect in the South of such early admission can not be well estimated, save
by those who, from a long Southern residence, are familiar with their eminent standing, both in social life and upon the general popular mind. If
admitted, the voice of faction will be immediately quieted, sectional dema-

that I shall rouse no feeling of painful self-consciousness in a certain high official quarter, if I assert that a President of the United States, to be truly worthy of his high position, amid such dangers and difficulties as now exist, must, to a certain extent, hold himself aloof from party and faction, and be able to survey, with a calm composure of spirit, all the strivings and blustrous agitations of those who seek to make him the mere slave and instrument of party malevolence and prejudice, while a *nation* is demanding at his hands the performance of the most exalted duties which man has it in his power to perform on this side of the grave.

gogues will have at once to go into retirement, and such a burst of gratitude will resound as this republic has not heretofore known. *Coercion* has now done all that it was capable of effecting toward the work of national pacification. *Conciliation* and kindness are at present alone needed to consummate this work, and sagacious statesmen will not fail to perceive the truth that Milton has so strikingly enforced, when he says,

> " Who overcomes
> By *force* hath overcome but half his foe."

THE END.